Specialty Retail Report's

Ultimate Guide *to* Specialty Retail

How to Start a Cart, Kiosk or Store

PATRICIA NORINS

PINNACLE
PUBLISHING GROUP, INC.

Printed and bound in the USA.

ISBN 0-9678237-5-7

10 9 8 7 6 5 4 3 2 1

How to Order

Single copies may be ordered from Pinnacle Publishing Group, Inc.
293 Washington Street, Norwell, MA 02061; 800.936.6297
Quantity discounts are also available.

Visit us online at www.specialtyretail.com

Acknowledgments

This book would not have been possible without the inspiration of the many retailers throughout the country who encouraged us to put it together. And it wouldn't be complete without the industry experts who graciously took the time to review portions of the manuscript and contribute their invaluable insights:
Frank Blumer, Alberto Cabilan III, Fred Delibero, Cindy Kern, Kevin Kern, Virgil Klunder, Heidi Maybruck, Robert Norins, Glenn Rosengard, Tim Runner and Ron Yoder.

Many thanks to *SRR*'s associate publisher, editors and designers, who were instrumental in bringing the book into being:
Maria Scarfone, Linda Saracino, Jim Mills, Nancy Tanker, David Stirling, Joanna Drew and Betsy Gold.
From initial concepts to final page proofs, their spirited ideas and countless hours made invaluable contributions to every page.

From the heart: My thanks to my parents, Evie and Robert Norins, who are not only pioneers in specialty retail but also industry publishers. They started me on the path, encouraged me to find my own road, and continue to cheer me along. In addition, thanks to my aunt and uncle, Rainey and Leslie Norins, who are also publishers and have given me invaluable tips and advice.
My thanks also go to Cari Meister Kust, children's book author and my dear friend, whose creativity inspires me to follow my dreams.

And lastly, special thanks to my husband, Adrian Clapp, who believed in me every step of the way.

contents

Not Your Average Introduction

If I had only known, I would have been a locksmith.
                                        –Albert Einstein

Great achievements take extraordinary effort, effort that sometimes leaves even the most successful entrepreneurs wondering why they started in the first place.

Launching and managing your own retail business is no different from any other major undertaking: It won't be easy. You'll have dozens of obstacles to hurdle. You'll make a few mistakes along the way. And there will be many, many long days and sleepless nights. Some days, you'll wish *you* decided to be a locksmith or a butcher, baker or candlestick-maker instead, where you learn clearly defined, hands-on skills from someone else. When you do have those days, know you're in good company—every entrepreneur has doubts from time to time. But perseverance, organization and a good plan will get you where you want to go.

About this book

Where *do* you want to go? Unlike most start-up business books, this one doesn't start with pages of self-tests designed to answer the question, "Should I go into business for myself?" Nor does it have "goals worksheets" for determining what you want to achieve. Here's why:

- You probably wouldn't have bought this book if you weren't already seriously considering starting your own business. Perhaps you've even made the decision to (even if you haven't said so out loud yet).

1

- Chances are, your goals are to create a thriving specialty retail business, enjoy your work, be your own boss, and make money.

Doesn't that pretty much size things up? You want to get into the $10 billion specialty retail industry, and you need dependable, detailed, expert information on how to turn ideas into reality. Maybe you need to know how to build a solid business plan. Or maybe you don't have a fully formed retail concept yet, so you need suggestions to get you started. Either way, you need to know the steps to take—and the pitfalls to avoid—to take your business from concept to cash-maker. Right?

Then you bought the right book. Here's a quick look at what it includes, so that you can get your specialty retail venture off the ground and into the black as fast and as smart as possible:

1. You need a plan.

Strategy without tactics is the slowest route to victory.
Tactics without strategy is the noise before defeat.
–Sun Tzu

Information overload Picture juggling all of this with just two hands: Creating your retail concept, finding the right product and getting the best cost, choosing the right location, negotiating the best rent deal, landing start-up capital, getting permits and licenses, buying insurance for the business, moving in, hiring and managing employees, pricing products, bookkeeping, tracking inventory, advertising, ringing up sales, being profitable, paying taxes, increasing sales and growing the business. And these are just part of the start-up process. You need solid information, and a plan. That's what makes the difference between keeping it all going, or it all crashing down around you.

All you really need to know The best start-up plan is one that's realistic. Rosy financial estimates or optimistic schedules will get you in trouble every time. Chapter 5, "Creating a Solid Business Plan," walks you through writing a complete, solid plan you can take to the bank to apply for a loan, take to the mall or other retail venue to secure space, and use as your guide to building a successful business.

2. You need a product.

> *I cannot give the formula for success, but I can give you the*
> *formula of failure—which is try to please everybody.*
> –Herbert B. Swope

Information overload Every year, consumers buy more than $1.5 trillion in goods and services. These are a few of their favorite things: Apparel, aromatherapy, artwork, automotive, books, cameras, candles, collectibles, computer products, crafts, electronics, fashion accessories, flags, food, furnishings, garden, gifts, handbags, hardware, herbal/natural, health and beauty, holiday, housewares and kitchen, incense, Infants' and children's, jewelry, kitchenware, leather, luggage, music, novelties, office supplies, party, perfume, pet supplies, phones and accessories, regional/ethnic, religious and spiritual, security, services (all kinds), sporting goods, sunglasses, tobacco, toys, videos, watches. Every day, retailers scan five million barcodes as they ring up sales.

All you really need to know The "best" product for you to sell is the one that appeals to your target customers. (It helps if you like it, too.) Who are your target customers? And what motivates them to shell out hard-earned money? For answers to these and other key questions, start with Chapter 1, "Choosing the Right Product." To find out how to buy those products from your suppliers—and at the best price—see Chapters 2 and 3, "Finding Suppliers" and "Buying from Suppliers." For a pricing strategy that works best in your market, see p. 36, "Pricing Products for Profit."

3. You need a location.

> *Put yourself in your customer's place.*
> –Orison Swett Marden

Information overload Malls, strip shopping centers, outlet centers, beach areas, boardwalks, theme parks, convention centers, festivals/fairs, arenas, casinos, office buildings, hospitals, bus/train stations, vacation/seaside/ski/spa resorts, entertainment venues, downtown, airports, riverfronts, hotels, colleges. With more than 1,800 regional and thousands of other shopping venues in the US, the trick isn't finding a location, it's finding *the right* location. Your goal: to be where your customers already shop, not make them come to you (which is a *lot* harder).

All you really need to know If you already have a product in mind, you need a location that attracts the right shopper for that product. If you don't have a product in mind, you need one that shoppers in your (proposed) location want or need. So which type of retail venue is best for you? Check out Chapter 4, "Finding the Right Location."

4. You need approvals.

We can lick gravity, but sometimes the paperwork is overwhelming.
–Wernher von Braun

Information overload Red tape equals green light: business license, certificate of occupancy, employer ID number, state sales tax number, fictitious name application, sign permit, health permit, employment verification, Workers' Comp, unemployment insurance—the paperwork you'll need to complete and the approvals you'll have to get from local, state and federal government agencies may leave you wondering if you'll ever see opening day.

All you really need to know You *will* get to opening day, and with everything in good order. Getting approvals and permits isn't hard, but it can be time-consuming. Chapter 7, "Forming Your Company," details the approvals you need, and where and when to get them. You'll also find guidance on naming your company and protecting your copyrights, patents and trademarks and service marks (and not on infringing on others').

5. You need money.

A bank is a place where they lend you an umbrella in fair weather, and ask for it back when it begins to rain.
–Robert Frost

Information overload Money, money, money: for start-up inventory, fees, deposits, overhead, payroll, advertising, taxes, growth, and more. Launching and running your business takes money, a lot of money. Where are you going to get it? Will you use your own? Other people's? Some of each? If you borrow it from a bank or anyone, you have to pay it back. More than a hundred books and videos, thousands of Web sites and countless consultants can tell you how to raise start-up capital.

All you really need to know The money's out there: you just need to know which sources to tap. From liquidating personal assets to charging your credit cards to raising "love money" and maybe even bringing in a partner or two, Chapter 6, "Finding Start-Up Capital," details the options.

6. You need a team.

The nice thing about teamwork is that you always have others on your side.
—Margaret Carty

Information overload Countless books, magazines, videos and Web sites, dozens of consultants; all your friends, family, neighbors and fellow retailers—all sources of more advice than you can possibly handle.

All you really need to know You need to build your team: hand-picked, experienced professionals who can give you solid, expert guidance. Accountant, lawyer and insurance agent SBA or SBDC counselor. Your banker. Your leasing manager. Your employees. These are the valued members of your team who can help you make intelligent, fact-based decisions. You'll find advice on how to tap these resources--and get the most and best information you can—throughout this book.

7. You need to go for it!

There will come a time when you believe everything is finished.
That will be the beginning.
—Louis L'Amour

Information overload The opening day checklist: Hot new product? (check.) Well-stocked shelves? (check.) Great retail look? (check.) Employees on board and ready to work? Permits, licenses and ID numbers all taken care of? Operating cash in the bank? Cash register/POS set up? Accounting system? Advertising plan? Strategy for growth? (check check check . . .)

All you really need to know Once you have all of your ducks in a row, the only thing left to do is open your doors and treat your customers like gold. Because that's what they are.

Of course, you don't have to read this book in order. You can skip around. It might even be more useful to you that way. And you'll probably return to a few key chapters several times later on, to fine-tune your approach.

Every chapter has useful start-up tips and helpful advice for first-time retailers. If you have questions about those tips or any other information in this book, feel free to e-mail me at norins@specialtyretail.com.

Web notes

■ The Web site addresses in this book don't include www. because most browsers fill in the www. automatically. But if yours doesn't, all of the addresses here do start with www., so just type it in.

■ There's a good deal of outdated information on the Web. Be sure you're getting up-to-date (and even up-to-the-moment) information from credible sources—government sites, media sites (e.g., the New York Times, the Wall Street Journal, CNN), bank and trade-association sites (e.g., the International Council of Shopping Centers), and the like. Then confirm the information you find (for example, tax regulations) with your lawyer or accountant before you act on it.

□ □ □

Choosing the Right Product

C hoosing the product you want to sell is the most important decision you'll make. It will affect many other decisions along the way, from the location you choose to the pricing strategy you adopt.

Whether deciding on specific products is easy or difficult depends on two factors: your ultimate business goals, and your current circumstances. Perhaps your ultimate business goal is one or several of these:

- Make a killing selling a trendy or "hot" product with a high-profit margin, so you can retire in a few years.

- Make extra money during the peak holiday season selling a product you like and think shoppers will like, too.

- Build a thriving, long-term business you'll be passionate about running for decades to come.

- A combination of these.

And perhaps in your current circumstances, these factors may influence your product decision:

- Your start-up budget. Maybe you have visions of selling dozens of themed products in a wide-open mall store . . . but the budget forces you to focus (at least initially) on selling a selection of the best of those products, and in a more compact location like a cart or kiosk.

- Your potential location. If you're already set on a location in a nearby mall, theme park, airport or other high-traffic venue, you need a product that appeals to the types of shoppers that venue attracts. And that means doing some market research (see "Finding the Right Location" on p. 59). If your research tells you that the mall attracts mainly older shoppers, for example, your products have to appeal to that market segment. No matter where you choose to start—with a hot product in search of a location, or a location in search of the right product—the two must be a good match in the end.

- Your own passion, interests or talent. Collectors, crafters and hobbyists often have an easier time of deciding on a product to sell because they want to share their passion with others. Even so, if you're one of them, you still have to consider the budget and find locations that attract the right buyers. And with handcrafted products, you have to consider whether you can reorder and get restocked quickly if sales skyrocket: handmade items aren't always available when you want them.

Right product in the right place

Before taking a look at the kinds of products to consider, consider this: Experienced specialty retailers know that a great product in one location isn't necessarily a great product in another location. The only real winning combination is a great physical location that brings the right demographic— the most likely buyers—for the product being sold. Many retailers started out in attractive malls with high traffic but didn't have buyers until moving to another location, one that drew shoppers better suited to that retailer's product line. No matter where you're starting—with your product or your location—the two have to be well matched. (See chapters on "Finding a Location" and "Market Research" for more on these issues.)

Sell products you love

Are you a collector? An artist? A carpenter? A golfer? Thousands of specialty retailers have started successful businesses based on their own hobbies or interests. And when asked, they'll tell you that their passion for the products they sell makes all the difference. If you sell a product you believe in and love, your enthusiasm will be contagious: it spreads to customers who can tell how you feel about your product by your salesmanship and your body language.

Do you have a hobby, interest or product you love that could be a successful business in hiding? For example, if you're an avid golfer or NBA fan, you might enjoy selling related products. Or if you're a collector—dolls, movie memorabilia, Harley-Davidson merchandise, whatever—you might enjoy running a business that caters to others who have been bitten by the collecting bug. Or maybe you like to cook and always thought of opening a kitchen ware or gourmet store. The list goes on. The point is, if you're in the collector category, your goal is to determine the types of products you might want to offer shoppers based on your own interest. Then once you decide on one or several product categories, you can decide how wide a selection you want to carry.

If an idea hasn't immediately jumped out at you, do a little internal inventory. On a sheet of paper (better yet, start a notebook you can use throughout your start-up process), answer these questions:

- What do I really enjoy doing in my leisure time?

- What hobbies and interests do my relatives, friends, co-workers and neighbors pursue? (and spend money on?)

- What skills or areas of expertise do I have that I could share with others if they were my customers?

- Where do I enjoy shopping, and why? Where do my friends and neighbors enjoy shopping, and why?

- What products do I enjoy using? Do I know enough about it to sell to others? If not, could I learn enough to sell it effectively?

- What product solved a problem for me? Is it something I can or want to sell? Do many other people have that same problem?

Brainstorming

If you need help or a kick-start brainstorming an idea, see "Brainstorming Tips" on p. 134. The principles are the same, even though the focus is different.

If after answering those questions you have a good idea of the products you can sell, the next step is to start on some market research (see "Identifying Your Target Customer," p. 64) and shop for suppliers (see "Finding Suppliers," p. 39). Then you can crunch numbers and analyze your profit potential.

But if you can't come up with a business concept based on your interests, consider a product that's already popular in specialty retail. Visit the local mall for ideas. What are those specialty retailers selling? Here's the scoop on the products that account for majority of specialty retail sales year after year.

Sell established, popular products

Generally speaking, specialty retailers sell unusual products with high curb appeal. That is, they sell merchandise designed to catch the shopper's attention, reel them in and give them a reason to buy. More often than not, the most popular products in the specialty retail industry fall into the following categories:

- Impulse items

- Personalized items

- Trend products

- Collectibles

- Licensed merchandise

- Seasonal or holiday

- Experience products

- Demonstration products

- Handcrafted items

- Themed merchandise

Sometimes the categories overlap. For example, many impulse items are personalized. The ever-popular personalized Christmas ornaments, for example, combine elements from three categories: impulse-buy pricing, personalization, and demonstration (the item is personalized while customers watch). In fact, the more categories you can incorporate into your business, the better—as long as you don't lose your focus. Here are details about the products that are perennial favorites, plus start-up tips specific to each type.

Impulse items

Impulse items are designed to spark a spontaneous purchase, and for that reason they tend to be low-cost products, $20 or less—generally. But because context is everything and customers' perceptions of value are key, experienced retailers know that terms like "low cost" or "impulse price" are relative. It depends on the income levels and buying habits of shoppers in a particular location. For example, retailers in upscale malls have found tremendous success with impulse products retailing at $50 or more; and some of those shoppers don't think twice about spending $80 on a purse or cashmere sweater attractively displayed on a cart or kiosk. (For more on customer value perceptions, see "Pricing Products for Profit" starting on p. 33.)

Income levels aside, because of the considerable flow of customers around carts, kiosks and other *RMUs* (retail merchandising units; see p. 62), impulse items sell particularly well in malls and other high-traffic venues with common-area retailers. Whether year-round or seasonal, impulse products include cosmetics, figurines, candles, flowers, T-shirts, bath-and-body, jewelry,

.dy/foods, hats, books, calendars, key chains, ties, mugs, sunglasses, ports-related merchandise, incense, toys, watches, apparel and accessories (belts, scarves, etc.), aromatherapy, picture frames, and a seemingly endless variety of home-décor items. Add to all of that the myriad holiday products for Valentine's Day, Christmas, and everything in between (see "Seasonal products" in this chapter for details).

Because so many products fall into the impulse category, it's impossible to calculate the total market for them, but suffice to say that it's a multi-billion-dollar market. Two examples: jewelry sales totaled more than $39.8 billion in 2000, and candle sales topped $2 billion in 2001. New impulse items are introduced every year, which adds a dynamic element to selling this category. In fact, some retailers sell nothing else. They specialize in impulse products, rotating or switching their merchandise lines as new products replace or complement the older ones.

Another benefit of selling impulse products: since there are so many types of products available, you shouldn't have a difficult time finding suppliers (for tips on how to find suppliers, see p. 39, "Finding Suppliers") and setting your retail prices.

Personalized products

Personalized products appeal to shoppers of all ages, cultures and income brackets for two main reasons: people like seeing their names on things, and personalization is a special service shoppers don't typically get from larger retailers. Products that are personalized on the spot sell particularly well because shoppers are drawn to the activity taking place in the common area, and buyers enjoy watching the item become indelibly theirs.

Personalization products come in two formats: already pre-personalized (usually with common first names, occupations, etc.); and ready-to-person-alize on site, by hand or computer. You can find suppliers online or through a number of retail trade resources (see p. 39).

Some product lines require computer systems to create the personalization (you can either create your own system or buy one of several already on the market). Others just require a steady hand and a permanent marker. Here's a look at some of the products that draw shoppers year after year, and the methods specialty retailers use to personalize them:

Personalization by hand

Holiday merchandise A traditional favorite is personalized holiday merchandise, including two of the top sellers: Christmas stockings and ornaments. These can be great businesses to own because retailers who personalize these items usually need only the most basic tools. For example, Christmas stockings can be personalized with glue and glitter to spell out a name. Ornaments can be personalized with a permanent marker. Some retailers use paints or adhesive letters and graphics (e.g., boats, balls, bears) that are popular with their target customers. Each method requires minimal artistic talent. And products aren't limited to Christmas: some specialty retailers sell personalized products for Hanukkah and Kwanzaa, Valentine's Day, and more. (See "Seasonal and holiday products" in this chapter.)

Non-holiday merchandise If there's room for a name, you can personalize anything. Shoppers are drawn to personalized products during the holiday season, but that's not the only time they buy them. Parents (and grandparents!) continue to be drawn to hundreds of products displaying the names of their children: picture frames, kitchen magnets, wall hangings, calendars, growth charts, doorknob hang-tags, to name just a few. For the grown-ups, a host of products based on occupation or interest, especially sports—from caricatures and cartoons to intricate drawings to mini figurines—are also widely available either pre-personalized or ready-to-personalize.

Personalization by computer

The equipment you'll need depends on the finished products you plan to sell. For example, personalized T-shirts and personalized mugs both require computer set-ups, but each needs different equipment. If you have the know-how, you can create your own personalization system. Otherwise, check into one of the systems on the market. Some companies sell each component of personalization equipment separately: computer, personalization software, thermal printer for image transfers, blank products, etc. Other companies sell complete business "turnkey" packages that include everything from the computer to the blank merchandise that's ready for customizing. Laser engravers have hit the specialty retail market recently, which let retailers engrave just about anything with laser precision. Personalization concepts that draw shoppers year after year include:

Photo-image merchandise Countless specialty retailers have successfully used computer technology to transfer personal photos onto merchandise for that one-of-a-kind T-shirt, mug, calendar, wall hanging, mouse pad, greeting card, clock, and novelty items (even cakes) that have space for a photo. Depending on the computer system, photo-transfer equipment and the merchandise to be personalized, the entire process can take just a few minutes. Of course, start-up costs for a quality photo-personalization system will be higher than a Christmas-stocking cart for example; but photo personalization offers a year-round market for customers, and not just those celebrating certain holidays. And you don't have to be an artist or a computer whiz to start a photo-image business: today's software makes the process easy.

Genealogy merchandise Using an online connection or genealogy software, some entrepreneurs have created thriving businesses using computers to research family trees, coats of arms, surname histories or first-name meanings—and selling products that show the results of that research. The final product your customers want can be just about anything: framed family trees . . . plaques and mugs with family crests . . . name histories enhanced with graphics and printed on specialty paper . . . and anything else you might come up with.

Children's books With the help of a special software package and printer, many specialty retailers have become "custom publishers," printing books on-site that integrate a child's name and other details into a choice of pre-printed storybooks. Personalized books are fun for adults to buy, and a thrill for the child who is the "star" of the story. At first only available via mail order, these books have been on the specialty-retail market for more than a decade, and continue to generate strong sales because of their unique nature and an ever-renewing market of young kids and the adults who love them.

No tech? No problem

Thanks to advancements in software design, you don't have to be a techie to use a computer personalization system. It helps to have some computer experience, but today's software is highly "intuitive," which means with common sense and little training, most people will find it easy to use. For those who need some help, many of those companies offer online or on-site training programs to get you started.

Celebration merchandise Birthday cards, mugs bearing birth-year trivia, a *New York Times* front page (headline: "Jack Turns 40!"), and much more—the personal touch sells. There are endless ways to turn an ordinary product into a personalized memento that celebrates a birthday, wedding, new baby, anniversary, graduation, retirement—any event in a person's life. Numerous software packages allow retailers to research a date such as a birth date for a variety of details of the day—who was president, how much a gallon of gas cost, the number-one pop song, etc.—and reproduce them on all kinds of products like mugs, T-shirts, greeting cards, newspaper pages, plaques and certificates, to name just a few. Some software packages can also generate custom poetry or art based on information the customer provides.

Embroidered merchandise As is true of most technology, on-site embroidery equipment has become more compact in the past several years, and today there are embroidery systems that are small enough for retailers to use on carts and kiosks. These systems require computer and software, an embroidering machine and supplies (threads, needles, etc.) and, of course, the items to be personalized—T-shirts, caps, sweatshirts and more. Embroidery software is sophisticated but not too complicated for the average retailer or employee to use quickly and easily. Most embroidery equipment manufacturers also offer training. Many embroidery software packages also come with graphics libraries with thousands of ready-to-go images the customer can choose from. These include images depicting hobbies, sports, occupations, interests and the like.

Starting an on-site embroidery retail business will cost more than some other personalization businesses that use lower-tech methods. But the value perception gained from seeing quality embroidery done according to customer specs—and while they wait—can mean high sales and considerable repeat business. In fact, some on-site embroidery retailers say it wasn't long after they opened that local sports teams and business owners started ordering embroidered merchandise by the dozens.

When it comes to personalization, the options are nearly endless. But whichever products you choose, make sure it can be customized *easily* and *quickly*. Customers want fast results and instant gratification, and why not. The longer they have to wait for an item to be personalized (and they'll ask—or just observe), the less likely they'll stick around long enough to buy.

 Start-up Tip

To keep your customers satisfied and coming back, make the personalized effect as permanent as possible. If it won't stand up to machine washing, for example, say so, both when you sell the item and in a note that goes with the product. The last thing you want is for your customer to inadvertently damage the product, ask you for a refund, and never return.

Trend products

Trend products can be highly lucrative, but the trend market is subject to the whims of ever-changing fashion dictates and customer taste. Trends are either short-term (which most people think of as fads) or long-term; and trends can be localized geographically, demographically (age, gender, etc.), or a combination thereof. To sell trend merchandise, you have to become a trend monitor. You have to pay constant attention first to what your friends, family and colleagues say about the products they use, where they shop and how they spend their leisure time and dollars . . . and what pop culture is up to at any given moment. Which means you have to read the newspaper and keep your finger on the latest movies, TV, fashion, décor, sports and more—because a hat or earrings a rock star wears can be the next fashion craze.

Long-term Some products capitalize on long-term societal trends. One good example: baby boomers (people born between 1946 and 1964) buy products that make them look good (e.g., skin care products), feel vital if not downright young (e.g., yoga tapes, mats, clothes), and improve their health—experts say boomers were a major factor in making nutrition products a nearly $50 billion industry. In recent years, a variety of weight-loss products and herbal supplements have done extremely well in the specialty retail marketplace, thanks in large part to this market segment. And this trend continues to be strong, as more people than ever reach 50, 55 and 60.

If you're interested in selling merchandise that capitalizes on long-term or societal trends, subscribe to *American Demographics* magazine (available on newsstands or through demographics.com). For an information-packed, in-depth analysis of generational buying patterns, check out *Rocking the Ages: The Yankelovich Report on Generational Marketing* by J. Walker Smith and Ann S. Clurman (1998, Harper Business). From Gen-X to seniors, this outstanding book compiles decades of market research to give readers an in-depth profile of each generation's attitudes and buying behaviors. The book is also available in digital-download format (audible.com).

Short-term Some products are designed for a quick in-and-out, capitalizing on short-term consumer interests—for example, movie merchandise. Big-budget pictures churn out merchandising opportunities (to the tune of $44 billion a year), and many specialty retailers have taken advantage of movie marketing and merchandising to start carts or kiosks. In fact, some specialty retailers ring up record sales operating a short-term a cart or kiosk that's strategically located just outside a mall's movie theater.

Trend: small spaces

Because of the transient nature of trends, an in-line store is much trickier to manage and stock. Plus, trend merchandise is often an impulse buy. So setting up shop in a cart or kiosk is ideal for those reasons and more.

Games and toys can also fall into the trend category (think Pokémon and scooters). One trend product that had an outstanding run is Beanie Babies, thanks first to kids and then collectors. A number of specialty retailers have had record-breaking sales with these little plush products.

Popular trend products at the moment (remember, trends are always changing) that specialty retailers sell (especially on carts and kiosks) include remote-control and interactive toys, aromatherapy products, fleece apparel and products, denim apparel and accessories, funky slippers, tie-dyed items, hemp apparel and products, nostalgia merchandise, garden items, weight-loss supplements, New Age products of all kinds, and just about anything for the home, from music and electronics to décor. Over the past decade, spiritual products have sold exceptionally well—especially all things angels, and anything that simplifies life, strengthens values or clarifies meaning. Among religious (as distinguished from generic spiritual) products, non-denominational Christian merchandise alone (from cross pendants to "WWJD" items) represents a $3 billion segment of the retail market.

 ## Start-up Tip

> *If you plan to sell quick-hit, short-term trend merchandise, your products must come to market quickly so you can take advantage of surging and fast-peaking demand. But be ever aware of equally fast cooling: Keep a sharp eye on your sales figures for any hint of a downturn, and have your next quick-hit product already lined up, so if sales flag and demand sags, you'll know it right away and can change product lines quickly. That way, you won't be stuck with thousands of dollars' worth of merchandise that doesn't sell.*

Collectibles

Nearly everyone collects something these days, which is why collectibles generate sales of almost $8 billion a year. Popular collectibles lines include action figures, die-cast models (cars, airplanes and other to-scale minia-tures), memorabilia (including nostalgia/vintage), plush, toys, art, posters, trading cards, handcrafted items, figurines, dolls, Christmas, coins and stamps, and logo products (e.g., Harley-Davidson, Coca-Cola), to name only a few. Collectibles offer virtually unlimited product lines, but they require the retailer to have in-depth product knowledge to sell them successfully. The retailer must be on top of the specific product lines' supply and demand, and must always be in tune with fluctuations in the market. A col-lectibles business can be highly rewarding, but retailers have to stay on top of the market—some say *ahead* of the market—in order to make a profit.

To become and then stay familiar with your collectibles market, subscribe to consumer magazines on the topic, as well as trade publications for col-lectibles retailers. To find these magazines, newsletters and other publica-tions that focus on your product line, check with your local library or go to ecola.com for an online directory of print media. The Collector's Information Bureau in Chicago (312.379.2940; collectorsinfo.com) publishes the annual reference guide, *Collectibles Market Guide and Price Index,* and their Web site lists the major collectibles manufacturers by state.

Licensed merchandise

Insiders who follow the licensed-merchandise market say the industry really took off in the mid-'70s, when consumers scooped up a reported $2.5 billion worth of *Star Wars* merchandise. If ever there were questions about the high profit potential for licensed merchandise, the exceptional sales of Star Wars merchandise answered it, and served as something of a model ever since. Today, specialty retailers can choose from thousands of products licensed by entertainment companies, corporations, sports teams, non-profit organ-izations, museums, fashion designers and even specialty retail entrepre-neurs who have created their own brands.

According to the International Licensing Industry Merchandisers' Association (New York, NY), which estimates the total market at $95 billion in retail sales annually, entertainment products—movie, TV and game merchandise—make up the largest share of the market. One of the biggest and well-known sources of licensed entertainment-related merchandise is Disney. Corporate or brand-name products, like Coca-Cola, are the second best-selling category. Sports merchandise is third, which includes clothing, accessories, and novelty and gift items like mugs, picture frames, paperweights, posters—the list goes on. Just about any product can be imprinted with a licensed logo, saying or image, provided there's room.

Of course, not every licensed product is a blockbuster (Disney's *Pocahontas* merchandise reportedly didn't do much, for example). And not all licensed products come from nationally known companies. Many specialty retailers have started businesses selling licensed products such as T-shirts that feature the art of up-and-coming artists. Others sell licensed apparel and accessories created by retail entrepreneurs years ago, which still strike a chord with customers coast to coast. In some cases the *licensor*—the company issuing the license for the right to sell the merchandise—may be willing to help new retailers with matters like visual merchandising, pricing suggestions, and selling tips. Some companies have complete business packages, too. To find companies that offer licensed merchandise either piece by piece or as a specialty retail start-up package, you can search online or contact the sources suggested in "Finding Suppliers" (see p. 39).

How licensing works

Retailers can sign a license agreement directly with manufacturers/distributors for the right to sell these products under certain terms and conditions (e.g., at a certain price point, in a certain location, for a certain period of time). In return for the right to sell the products, retailers pay in one of two ways: a royalty based on a percentage of the cost of goods or on gross sales; or a flat licensing fee paid either once or annually, depending on the agreement.

Licensing can also work on the wholesale side. The wholesaler becomes the licensee, and the cost is then built into the wholesale cost of the merchandise and passed on to retailers.

✔ *Start-up Tip*

License agreements vary among companies and can include complicated terms and conditions. These agreements are quite different from the legal paperwork you may be familiar with. So it's crucial to have your attorney and accountant review any license agreement before you sign it, so they can explain its specific benefits and drawbacks.

Seasonal and holiday products

Seasonal products generally fall into two categories: holiday merchandise, and products that relate to weather or the seasons of the year.

Holiday merchandise isn't limited to the religious or cultural holidays at the end of the year. Thanks in large part to the benefits offered by short-term license agreements, specialty retailers everywhere have created successful businesses that cater to just about every holiday on the calendar.

Sweet deal
Candy sales for Valentine's Day have reached more than $1 billion a year.

Some specialty retailers have created thriving holiday-only businesses, switching product lines as holidays come and go, and sometimes even switching locations to reach certain shopper segments. Holiday retailing can be highly lucrative because retailers are able to get in and get out quickly, taking advantage of peak buying periods without the burden of the periodic downtimes that year-round retailers have to grapple with. Plus, holiday retailers often realize higher profit margins because they're operating when customers are "squeezed to buy" before the holiday's over. Christmas-only retailers are perhaps the biggest group of seasonal retailers and generally open November 1st and close December 31st. Approximately 10 percent of those who operate during Christmas sell only Christmas merchandise; the other 90 percent sell general gift or stocking-stuffer merchandise that doesn't necessarily have a Christmas theme but is in peak demand during the biggest gift-buying season of the year.

Other seasonal retailers don't focus on holidays per se as much as on the seasons of the year. Some operate year-round, others only during the seasons that relate to their product lines (e.g., sunglasses and beach accessories in the summer). Year-round retailers selling seasonal products rotate or switch products as the seasons change. In spring, for example, product lines might include T-shirts and other apparel; in summer, those lines are switched to beach merchandise; in the fall, sweatshirts might take center stage; and in winter, fleece jackets and hats. Other retailers sell only summer or winter items and operate only at those times of the year. In short, the term "seasonal retailer" may say more about the products the retailer sells than how long the retailer is signed on as a mall tenant.

 ### Start-up Tip

> If you're going to sell seasonal merchandise, order it from your suppliers at least six months *before the consumer buying season. That way, you're likely to get the best price and delivery options, and you'll have the merchandise on hand when customers start shopping for it.*

Experience products

In recent years, specialty retailers have come up with some exciting ways to add entertainment and customer interaction to the retail experience. Dubbed "shopper-tainment" (The Mills Corporation coined and trademarked the word) and "retail-tainment," one example is a children's photo-studio kiosk where high-energy, costumed staffers act zany to draw a crowd and to put the photo subject in great spirits—and make happy pictures. One of the more innovative retail concepts to hit the market in the last few years is "stuff-it-yourself" stuffed animals. At these stores, carts or kiosks, shoppers choose their animal's "skin" and the type of stuffing (soft, hard, or in between), and one or several outfits (sold separately) to dress their new stuffed buddy. This concept is popular because the process is fun, engaging and rewarding: customers get more than a stuffed toy—they get an "experience." An experience of a different kind comes from "water massage" stores and kiosks, where tired shoppers get into a whirlpool-like device that pulses away their stress and fatigue while they stay fully clothed and dry (they pay a per-minute rate). Retailers say shoppers are drawn to businesses like this when they watch someone else experience the effects. The "product" is sold on a per-minute or per-session basis, with retailers charging whatever they think the market will bear.

Practice, practice, practice

Hone your "retail-tainment" skills and delivery before opening day. Established retailers who sell entertainment products say they've benefited from having a script they and their employees follow. Rehearse in front of a mirror till you have it down. Then practice on friends, family and anyone else you can find to see exactly how to engage the customer's attention for maximum effect. Note their reactions, and make adjustments as necessary.

Themed merchandise

Every business has a theme. But savvy entrepreneurs know that the theme has to be carried and reinforced throughout—from the name of the business to the product itself to the visual display to the—if you want shoppers to stop in their tracks (and you do).

A theme can be anything you want it to be. Some retailers' themes are based on something as simple as a color (all purple products, for example). Others have more complicated themes, such as antique-y home décor products. For businesses built around a single product line (tie-dye, for example), that's the theme. Or if they feature multiple product lines with a unifying common denominator (sci-fi merchandise, for example), that unifying element is the theme. In fact, with imagination, brainstorming and creative merchandising, you can turn any product or group of products into a theme—even items that don't seem to "go together," like ice cream and magnets. There's more than one old-fashioned ice cream parlor/magnet store these days, where shoppers buy a cone and an "I Love Ice Cream!" fridge magnet at the same time. The concept's a hit with shoppers, especially in resort/tourism areas.

✔ *Start-up Tip*

Once you've picked your theme, expand it throughout your visual displays. Brainstorm for an hour, writing down every word and every item you think of that relates to that theme (no matter how far-fetched or goofy it seems). Then review your list to see which items or concepts are affordable and easy to integrate into your visual presentation. If you need help, consider hiring a visual merchandiser to pull the theme together.

Demonstration products

Some of the highest-grossing specialty retail concepts are based on demonstration. Products that are demonstrated in front of customers engage their interest and invite them to interact with the product. And the more they're invited to interact, the greater the chance of making a sale.

Popular demonstration products include food-prep equipment (choppers, grills, juicers), cosmetics, hair accessories, nail care merchandise, toys and games, stress-relief products and herbal products and magic tricks, to name a few. And as discussed earlier, personalization products can also be demonstration products.

Some products *require* demonstration because of their unique features. For example, mugs that change color or design when hot water is poured into them don't sell as well when they're just sitting on a shelf with a before/after picture as they do when they're demonstrated face-to-face with the customer. Customers want to see the "magic" happen for themselves. Because demonstration is such an effective selling tool, even retailers who can't fully demonstrate products on site find ways to illustrate their product's features by other means. Some use video presentations. For example, with the help of a TV and a VCR, some retailers who sell apparel that changes color in sunlight run a video loop—a tape that automatically rewinds and replays—showing how the colors change.

✔ *Start-up Tip*

Keep the demonstration as simple as possible. The more complicated it is, the more confused shoppers may be, and that can cut into sales. To fine-tune your demonstration, practice on friends and family (they may suggest helpful techniques!), and watch your sales carefully to identify exactly what techniques work best.

Handcrafted merchandise

Each year, thousands of talented artisans spend nine or ten months creating unique hand-made products . . . and make big money in November and December with a holiday cart, kiosk or store. Your hobby or talent may be a successful business venture just waiting to make some money. Do your friends marvel at what you make? Have you sold your crafts at festivals or fairs or even the church bazaar? If the answer is yes, you have buyers but not a business—and it may be time to put that craft to work.

Handcrafted merchandise is great to sell because it's one of a kind. There's no downward pressure on prices due to competition! Plus, unique items bring impulse buyers: shoppers know they won't see that merchandise anywhere else. The tricky part is being able to buy or produce enough merchandise to keep your retail location stocked . . . and then to price your handcrafted merchandise based on your customers' value perceptions. Ask too much and they'll go elsewhere; ask too little and you rob yourself of profits. So if you plan to sell handcrafted merchandise, it's crucial to know your target customers.

✔ *Start-up Tip*

Before you sign a lease, make sure you have enough inventory to carry you to the end of the buying season or year if sales are strong or exceptional. Few things are worse than being open for the Christmas buying season and selling out of merchandise by December 5th.

Estimating start-up inventory

How much actual product you'll need for opening day depends largely on the type of location you have in mind—cart, kiosk, in-line store, etc. In some cases, the nature of your product may suggest or even dictate the type of location you need. For a demonstration product, for example—where attention to the product means sales—a cart in the path of shopper traffic in a large mall might be the best choice for attracting attention, rather than a spacious in-line store. Or the size of your product might define the type of location. Selling oversized teddy bears from a cart can be problematic (no matter how cute they are) because of space and the display limitations.

How much to order

Unfortunately, no magic formula exists to help you pinpoint how many items you need to stock for opening day. That's because there are so many variables—type of product, dimensions of the product, retail price, the space you're filling, how you're going to merchandise your location (i.e., displays, fixtures, etc.), and more. But for starters, the available selling space usually dictates how much you need to start with. And it's often in terms of a dollar figure rather than number of items.

Carts require the least amount of start-up inventory because at 40-80 s/f, they're the smallest and most compact. On average, cart-based retailers spend $2,000-$8,000 (wholesale cost) for start-up inventory. Because kiosks are larger (120-160 s/f), start-up inventory typically costs $3,000-$10,000 (wholesale) to fill the bigger space. And an in-line store, whether 500 s/f or 5,000 s/f, takes a significantly larger investment. Even merchandise that retails at modest prices can cost $50,000 or more for stocking a larger in-line.

With so many variables, the trick is to get comfortable with educated guessing. Your goal is simply to determine a *reasonable* level of inventory, not an exact number products you need, down to the last unit. To start to estimate how much start-up inventory you need, answer a question like this: "How many widgets can I attractively display on a 2'x 4' shelf?" That answer multiplied by how many 2'x 4' shelves you have, gives you as good an estimate as any.

No need to make yourself crazy with exact calculations—rest assured, they're going to change later, when your visual-display plan takes shape and your suppliers tell you the quantity of their minimum order. And suppliers may be able to help you determine your first order. (See p. 47 for more about suppliers' terms and conditions). Visual merchandisers often have valuable suggestions for how much inventory you'll need. So if you plan to work with one, ask.

If you've already decided on a location or have one in mind, ask the leasing manager for the specific measurements of its selling area. If you haven't decided on a location yet, you can still make educated estimates for a cart, kiosk or in-line. To get a starting point, call several leasing managers to get typical measurements for the type of RMU you're considering.

Using these measurements, either make a sketch of the location to scale on graph paper (one square equals one square foot, for example), or create it on your computer with inexpensive space-planning software. Include and indicate the areas that won't be used for merchandising, such as cash-wrap and storage. Then calculate the space that's available for product display.

Blueprint
Many malls already have sketches or blueprints for carts, kiosks and stores. Before you spend time creating your own from scratch, it's worth a call to the leasing manager to see if you can get one.

Taking the size and nature of your product(s) into account, plus any fixtures you'll have, will help you estimate how much product you need to attractively stock your location for the grand opening. For in-line stores, block off areas of the store according to product category. This way, you can calculate the space needed for various lines one at a time, rather than being overwhelmed by the prospect of trying to fit 15 product categories into one big empty space.

Cart and kiosk-based retailers sometimes use inexpensive materials like foam blocks or cardboard to simulate products and set up a mock display. Some leasing managers even allow you to come in and "borrow" a cart or kiosk for a day to test how products might fit, especially if you're considering a location in that mall.

Once you sign on, most leasing managers are happy to help first-timers get a handle on inventory from the start—if you just ask them. Some leasing managers have ten or more years of experience to draw from when they analyze a start-up, and all of them want to make sure their tenants are fully stocked and well merchandised from the outset. Leasing managers can also help you avoid overbuying by giving you information on historical norms for that venue, such as start-up inventory averages and sales figures. And remember, some malls have visual merchandising pros (at low rates or sometimes even free) who can help you determine your start-up inventory.

Finding more help

Don't overlook existing specialty retailers for help. Successful specialty retailers are also often willing to help newcomers. They've been through the same start-up difficulties, know what it takes, and often do it as a "payback" for the network of people who helped them get started. Some take a more public route by speaking at business events or trade shows about getting started; others prefer to mentor first-time retailers one-on-one. So track down a few retailers you admire in your area (or beyond) and make contact. Many of them will help you solidify your start-up plans and give you invaluable advice from first-hand experience.

And remember to ask your suppliers to help you figure how much start-up inventory you need. Some companies offer set start-up packages, and many include display props. Suppliers without start-up packages will also often take time to help you devise a start-up inventory strategy. One caution, though: when you work with suppliers on matters of inventory, remember that their goal is to sell as much product possible. So when you speak with them, keep your location grid handy and stick to your space allocations (and your budget!) as much as you can.

Buying a turnkey package

Sometimes the best way find the right product for your new business is to buy into a fully formed retail concept, a "turnkey package" (such as a franchise) that's based on a product that has already racked up a string of successes. Entrepreneurs buy turnkey packages for one reason: they want to get into business without having to start a business from scratch.

Most specialty retail turnkey packages are structured as ***owner-operator*** or ***independent reseller*** programs, not franchises or "business opportunities." The Federal Trade Commission (FTC) defines and heavily regulates those types of businesses, but not owner-operator, independent-reseller or certain other retail business structures whose terms and conditions are left to the parties involved to determine as they see fit (within the confines of federal, state and local laws, of course).

Owner-operator or independent-reseller programs are usually arms-length relationships where the entrepreneur who buys the business "package" is fully responsible for all retail operations, and purchases inventory at wholesale from the company offering the turnkey package. Franchises and business opportunities, on the other hand, usually require the retailer to operate under stringent terms and conditions, such as setting specific retail prices and displaying merchandise as the company dictates and, with some, buying inventory only from them. Whether this is an advantage to the buyer often depends on how much entrepreneurial independence that retailer wants. Some turnkeys offer exclusive territories. That can be a plus if it's a good territory and you have no plans to expand, but a minus if it's a lousy territory or you want to expand into regions that are already taken.

Targeted to specialty retail Dozens of turnkey packages are available specifically for the specialty retail market. The vast majority are offered by companies started by individual retailers with a single location in a high-traffic retail venue. Many of these successful entrepreneurs continue to operate their own company-owned locations while offering others a chance to start their own enterprises through a turnkey package. By combining the two types of retail operations—owner-operator locations (which would include your location) and company-owned locations—the offering company expands both its retail visibility and wholesale sales base. In return—and this is the payoff for start-up retailers—a novice can get into the specialty retail market with the help of an experienced retail "mentor" who has a product and concept that are ready to go.

Because of their experience in the specialty retail marketplace, most offering companies know exactly the type of customer to target with their product. They can help new entrepreneurs find retail locations that match the product, establish sales goals based on sales history and visually merchandise the product for maximum impact. In addition to training materials for entrepreneurs and occasionally on-site training, many companies have extensive training programs at their corporate location, which are usually worth the investment in time and money it might take to attend.

Start-up costs   Start-up costs for cart or kiosk turnkey packages (including inventory, but not rent, permits, insurance, etc.) vary from around $500 to more than $45,000. With most of them falling between $3,000 and $10,000. For in-line store turnkeys, start-up costs can go from as little as $1,500 to more than $150,000; most of them fall between $10,000 and $50,000. For additional ideas and a chance to get some first-hand information and answers, attend one of the franchise or business-opportunity trade shows that appear throughout the country. They're usually listed in the local paper's business section and advertised on TV. You can also check the resources listed in "Finding Suppliers" (p. 39).

When you find a turnkey package that interests you and you begin to analyze it, review the offering company's sales record and ask key questions like these:

- Does this product sell well at owner-operator locations? You want a product that succeeds with turnkey operators, not just company-owned locations.

- How long has the offering company been in the specialty retail market? Because specialty retail is different from other types of retail, and has some of its own issues and challenges, experienced specialty retailers really know how to help you navigate these obstacles quickly and efficiently.

- Has the product succeeded in some locations but not others? While it's exciting to hear about top locations with record sales, don't be so dazzled that you forget to ask about locations that didn't do as well as expected, and the factors that caused or contributed to it. Companies run by experienced specialty retailers will have answers that will help you zero in on factors that help ensure success—such as identifying the best demographic market for that product.

■ Does the offering company/product have name recognition? If that company is well established and its product is well respected, mall managers may be more willing to rent space to entrepreneurs with little or no experience. Investigate the offering company's reputation, and ask some of their independent retailers about their experiences with the company.

■ Can the offering company deliver? Do they guarantee product availability and delivery? There's nothing more painful than facing a Christmas season or other peak time without enough product. Ask about the company's turn-around time on product orders, especially during peak ordering periods. If you can, visit company headquarters and while you're there, ask about their order-fulfillment processes. And again, ask some of their owner operators about their experiences with the company's ordering and delivery systems.

✔ Start-up Tip

Before you buy into a turnkey package, whether a franchise or owner-operator program or other business structure, have your attorney and accountant review all of the documents related to that business. They can point out any downsides you haven't considered or even suggest a better deal that may give you greater profit potential or be a better fit.

For more product ideas

If the product categories discussed here haven't sparked some exciting or at least reasonable ideas for your new venture, there are a host of resources that can give you more ideas, from retail trade magazines and directories to a huge range of online resources. Trade shows and merchandise marts are great places to get ideas, too. You can find the details on these and other resources in "Finding Suppliers" (p. 39).

And finally, as you look for the product that's right for you, remember that good ideas can come from just about anywhere. Keep your mind open to the possibilities and, who knows, you may end up with more good ideas than you'll know what to do with.

Making the decision

Before you make a final decision on which product(s) to sell, check to see how well the product category (e.g. watches, candles, silver jewelry) is selling, so you know you're not starting with a product that's already lost or beginning to lose its consumer appeal. You can find a great deal of product-specific sales information by contacting retail-trade associations and magazines (online or in print), or by visiting one of the many Web sites that track product sales by category (some sites are free; others charge a subscription or membership fee). Go online to search for companies or organizations that track the type of product you want to carry. Type in a short string of relevant keywords—for example, if you plan to sell apparel, you can use the key words "apparel sales" and "industry." Adding the "industry" will narrow the search to sites that deal with the entire retail industry, rather than the ones that want to sell you apparel.

If possible, also talk to specialty retailers who are selling the products you're considering. Find out where they're buying their products and how satisfied they are with their suppliers. Take a look at the retail-pricing strategies they're using and observe their sales approach. And of course, find out all you can about how much product they are selling. You may not get concrete sales figures, but many retailers will tell you if their sales are increasing (or decreasing!) year-over-year.

Pricing products for profit

How will you know what to charge? How will you know if the prices you set will appeal to customers and at the same time generate enough profit? And that, after all, is the dual goal of a successful pricing strategy. The retail prices you set need to more than cover your expenses—everything from cost of goods and inventory restocking to rent, salaries and commissions, and advertising—if you expect a profit at year-end.

Sure you'll crunch numbers to come up with those prices. But before you do, it's helpful to realize that pricing is often a trial-and-error process. And over time, most likely during your first year, you'll probably change those opening-day prices as you gain experience and become more familiar with your customers, your competition and the retail market in general.

Pricing strategies

Most retailers use one or more of these four pricing most common methods: markup pricing, manufacturer's suggested retail pricing (MSRP), competitive pricing, and value pricing. Based on your products, location, market demographics and other factors, you may decide to use just one pricing strategy across the board, or a combination: for example, markup pricing for some products, MSRP for others, and then price still other products according to competitive pressures or value perceptions. Also keep in mind that no matter which of these methods you use, you have to stay aware of the ever-evolving factors that can affect your pricing, and be ready to adjust as necessary.

Markup pricing Add a fixed percentage to the cost of goods to come up with a markup-based retail price. Many retailers use *keystone* markup pricing, which is simply a doubling of the cost of goods to arrive at a retail price with a 100 percent markup. (For more on markup and margin, see p. 35.) If the cost of goods is $3, for example, a quick calculation is all you need to set the retail price at $6. Partly because the keystone method is so easy, it's widely used in the industry. But depending on your own operating and other expenses, you may find that keystone markup *isn't enough* to ensure your profitability. For this reason, you may want to consider a markup of 200 percent or even 300 percent, which is typical for temporary retailers. Of course, if you do consider a higher markup percentage, do your competitive-pricing homework to make sure you haven't priced yourself out of the market. Customers don't care that your overhead is higher than your competitor's; they care that they can get the product from your nearby competitor for less.

MSRP pricing If you're thinking of using manufacturers' suggested retail pricing (MSRP) because it requires nothing from you (the prices might even be pre-printed on the packaging), be careful. MSRP might be the simplest pricing strategy but, in effect, someone else is setting your prices for you— someone who knows nothing about your overhead, loan-repayment deadlines, profit goals and other fundamentals of your business. Not only that: MSRPs that are set at a national level may not reflect what the market will bear in *your* area. So you may be overpriced—or underpriced—without even realizing it, and with no flexibility to change the price.

Competitive pricing With this strategy, you set retail prices according to what you know consumers expect to pay based on competitive comparisons. Competitive pricing is more difficult to implement than markup or MSRP pricing because it requires you to first identify competitors within your target market, and then continually adjust your prices in relation to ever-changing competitive pressure. If your customers are aware of your competitors' prices and you aren't, your sales could suffer. So before setting prices by using this strategy, visit ("shop") the stores in your target market that sell the same or similar items. Take note of each retailer's prices on individual items and on their overall pricing strategy (e.g., high prices, average prices, discount prices). While you're at it, investigate product prices online, since millions of consumers are now "multi-channel shoppers" buying online, through direct mail catalogs, and at brick-and-mortar stores. (For more on competitive analysis, see "Determining the Impact of Proximate Retailers" on p. 69.)

Value pricing With this strategy, you set retail prices after doing an in-depth analysis of your target customers' perceptions of value in relation to your products and your overall "selling environment." In other words, your store's image, marketing messages and product packaging will affect your customers' perceptions just as much as your prices, product quality and customer service will. Since your customers probably won't absolutely "need" your products (the way they need products like food), it's up to you to give them a reason to buy based on value perceptions rather than basic needs. Granted, this isn't a nuts-and-bolts approach to setting prices; it's a great deal more intuitive. But there is information you can base your decisions on. You can learn a great deal about your target market's value perceptions by talking with other retailers and professionals who are familiar with shoppers in and around your location. And demographic data will give you great insight into your target customers. (For more on finding demographics, see "Sources of Market Data" starting on p. 71.)

Calculating markup and margin

Markup refers to gains *anticipated* prior to sale. Margin refers to gains *realized* at the time of sale. When you negotiate prices with suppliers (or customers), you need to be able to calculate markup quickly and accurately. Miscalculations made on the fly will mean lost profits—a direct hit, dollar for dollar, to your bottom line.

To follow the examples using the formulas to calculate markup and margin, assume the following details:

> Price paid to supplier for goods . . . . $ 4.75
>
> Shipping costs (from supplier to retailer) . . . . . . $ 1.50
>
> Purchase price paid by customer for goods $10.00
>
> Cost of goods . . . . $ 6.25

"Cost of goods" (or "cost of merchandise") is the total amount the retailer pays the supplier for product, including shipping.

Wholesale price paid for product + shipping = cost of goods:

$4.75 + $1.50 = $6.25

Markup The difference between the cost of goods and the retail price, expressed as dollars or percentages. (Sometimes called "markon.")

> **To calculate dollar markup:**
>
> *retail price – cost of goods = dollar markup*
>
> *$10.00 – $6.25 = $3.75*

> **To calculate percentage markup:**
>
> *Divide the dollar markup by the cost of goods:*
>
> *$3.75 ÷ $6.25 = 60%*

Margin The difference between the cost of goods and the retail price the customer pays at the time of purchase. Margin (also called "gross margin") is expressed as either dollars or percentage.

> **To calculate dollar margin:**
>
> *purchase price – cost of goods = dollar margin*
>
> *$10.00 – $6.25 = $3.75*

> **To calculate percentage margin:**
>
> *Divide the dollar margin by the purchase price:*
>
> *$3.75 ÷ $10 = 37.5%*

What if there's not enough profit?

After you calculate your cost of goods, taking into account market pressures and your business expenses, you may find that your profit margin isn't enough to warrant selling the product you're considering. If this happens, you'll need to:

- Reduce your cost of goods by negotiating with your suppliers or finding other suppliers with lower costs.

or

- Raise the price to raise the profit margin. Then give shoppers additional reasons to buy from you other than price:

for example, highlight product-quality features or customer services or other features and benefits that offset the
higher price.

or

■ Sell a different product.

If you can't reduce your cost of goods or justify a higher retail price in the
consumer's mind, then consider selling a different product. After all, it
doesn't make sense to be married to a product that isn't profitable enough.
Even if you have the best location, the coolest visual display and the hottest
product on the market, if you can't make the profit you need, you won't be
in business for long.

□ □ □

Finding Suppliers

inding suppliers, or vendors, is not as difficult as it might first appear. Most manufacturers and wholesalers are eager to land new retail accounts, and one or two suppliers might be all you need to get your business off the ground. In most cases, manufacturers offer retailers the lowest cost of goods, but because many manufacturers don't have sales forces to handle retail accounts, small retailers usually order product through a wholesaler or distributor (which are basically the same) or a manufacturer representative (who may represent more than one manufacturer). No matter which route you choose, the ultimate challenge is to locate suppliers who can deliver the product you need, when you need it, at the right price.

Trade magazines

Retail trade magazines are an excellent source of information on suppliers, and provide editorial coverage and vendor advertisements well in advance of consumer buying seasons. In some cases, ads indicate if the supplier is a manufacturer or wholesaler.

Specialty Retail Report (specialtyretail.com or 800.936.6297) is the only magazine specifically targeted to retailers who operate from carts, kiosks and in-lines, but there are also many good general retail magazines in circulation today. *Gifts & Decorative Accessories* (800.309.3332; giftsanddec.com) *Giftware News* (888.545.3676; giftwarenews.com) and *Giftware Business* (847.647.7987; giftline.com) are packed with supplier ads and lists of various product lines.

Dozens of specialized publications are available, too, like *Specialty Coffee Retailer* (314.487.6568; specialty-coffee.com), *Pet Age* (312.663.4040; petage.com), and *New Age Retailer* (800.463.9243; newageretailer.com). There's even a quarterly magazine for smoothie retailers called *Juiced!* (480.990.1101; juiced-mag.com). To find trade magazines that pertain to your business, look into resources like the *Wilson Business Periodicals Index* in your library or online (hwwilson.com).

Trade directories and buyer's guides

Trade directories, sometimes called buyer's guides, are also good sources of information. Some are available only in print, but each year more become available online (see "Online resources" on p. 43). Online directories are sometimes more current than print directories (since an online database can be updated more easily). Search them by company name, product name or any other key words that seem logical to you. On the downside, using some online directories isn't free; in fact, some of them can be downright pricey, and may not be worth it to you. Only you can decide. And when it comes to the Internet, what's free today might not be free tomorrow, so if you find good information online without having to pay for it, nail it while you can.

Of course, there are also directories and buyer's guides you can buy at bookstores, from an online bookseller, or from the publisher. You can find some of the larger directories in the reference section of your library. But if you're going to use a particular directory frequently, it may be worth buying a copy or paying for online access.

The most comprehensive manufacturers' directory by far is the *Thomas Register of Manufacturers* (800.699.9822; thomasregister.com), a multi-volume publication that gives detailed information on more than 170,000 manufacturers. Companies are listed by name, product brand names, and product categories. Most libraries have the *Thomas Register*, or you can buy it directly from the publisher in print, on CD or DVD (currently $129 each), or access it online for free.

A state directory of manufacturers is also available in most libraries, and your local Chamber of Commerce likely prints a directory of its members, many of whom are manufacturers. But remember, many manufacturers don't sell directly to retailers, so don't be surprised if some of the ones you contact send you to their wholesale representatives.

To locate wholesalers/distributors directly, check out the *American Wholesalers & Distributors Directory,* published in print each year (The Gale Group, 800.877.4253; galegroup.com/gale/). This directory ($240, or available in most libraries) lists more than 27,000 companies by name, product categories, and geography. Other wholesale directories might also be on the library's shelves. Some cover both manufacturers and wholesalers, such as the *American Manufacturers & Wholesalers Blue Book* & CD-ROM (Data Direct International, 800.977.7959; directintl.com). The book, which includes a companion database on CD ($139), contains detailed listings of more than 175,000 US manufacturers and wholesalers, including more than 5,000 e-mail and Web addresses. This directory is most likely in your library, or you can purchase it online (however, the database itself isn't online).

SRR's annual *Retail Resource Guide* (Specialty Retail Report, 800.936.6297; specialtyretail.com) is a directory of products, locations and services specifically targeted to specialty retailers. Updated yearly, the *Guide* ($199) lists hundreds of manufacturers and wholesalers in the US and Canada by company name and by product category.

There are other buyer's guides that cover specific product categories, such as toys or apparel. To find guides for your business, head to the library or search online.

Trade shows

Trade shows come in two formats—wholesale shows, "to the trade only"; and retail or "public" shows. To attend a wholesale show, you need proof that you're a retailer—primarily your tax ID number. Even if you don't have an ID number yet, don't rule out trade shows. Just go to the retail shows that are open to the public. Although you won't be able to buy product at wholesale costs, you'll get plenty of ideas from dozens of retailers, and observe consumer buying patterns. The easiest way to find a trade show near you is online by visiting a trade-show database web site such as tsnn.com. They have show information sometimes as early as a year in advance.

Thousands of trade shows take place each year in the United States, but only one is just for specialty retailers: the International Council of Shopping Centers' *Short-term Specialty Retail Conference & Expo.* This annual trade show, which takes place in the first quarter in a different major city each year, attracts more than 1,000 attendees. It features dozens of companies offering products specifically targeted to the specialty retail market. Over several days, mall managers, retailers, wholesalers, RMU manufacturers and professional-services firms interact with and learn from each other. And here's more good news: the show's registration fee is *free* for first-time attendees, who benefit greatly from the seminars on topics that range from accounting to lease negotiation to visual merchandising. (Call the ICSC at 646.728.3800 or visit icsc.org for more information.)

Merchandise marts

Few places offer retailers more wholesale product selection than merchandise marts, the large (sometimes huge) buying centers where dozens (sometimes hundreds) of wholesalers display their products for retailers to see, touch and buy. The largest marts are in cities such as New York, Los Angeles, Chicago, Atlanta, Miami and Dallas. The Dallas Market Center's Web site (dallasmarketcenter.com) says that, according to the *Guinness Book of World Records,* it's "the largest wholesale merchandise resource in the world." The Miami International Merchandise Mart (mimm.com) boasts more than 6,000 product lines, including home furnishings, gifts, apparel, jewelry, novelties and collectibles.

The key to getting the most from a merchandise mart is doing some homework. Find out when a mart is open. Not all wholesale showrooms are open every day, and most marts host special events (or "market days") when many wholesalers offer special discounts. Find out if you have to preregister. Many marts require advance registration for market days and other special events, including trade shows. Some marts have recently added online shopping services to their Web sites, and most sites offer wholesale product details online. Searching a mart's site before you go can help you plan your buying strategies without pressure from a salesperson. Doing that homework will also help you make better use of your time once you get there.

Few marts are open to the public, so again, to get in you'll need documentation—usually your tax ID number and a canceled business check. Some marts require retailers to show wholesale invoices totaling more than $5,000 within the last year. To find out more about where merchandise marts are located as well what their admission policies and operating hours are, check your local telephone directory, or look in *SRR's Retail Resource Guide*, which lists more than 20 U.S. marts. You can also search online. To find the closest merchandise mart, search for "merchandise mart" plus the name of the largest nearby metropolitan area.

Online resources

Many retailers prefer to use the Internet to find suppliers. Unlike the library, the Internet is always open, you don't have to get in your car, and you can search for suppliers in your skivvies if the mood suits you. Plus, a lot of what's available in the library is also available online.

As mentioned, the *Thomas Register of Manufacturers* online (thomasregister.com) is free, but registration is required. Then you can search the database by company name, product name or keyword. For example, "jewelry" as a keyword brought up more than 500 manufacturers under 93 product categories. You can narrow and refine your results by adding words such as trademark, brand name, product description, and even city or state. One more feature of the online version: thousands of company catalogs that you can download. These are in .pdf format, so if you haven't already, you'll need to download a free copy of Adobe Acrobat Software (adobe.com) to read them.

In recent years, a host of wholesale Web sites have cropped up, and some of them feature product from dozens of manufacturers. Some sites specialize

—for example, farcountries.com focuses on international products. But before you can search a site for products, you'll most likely have to register first. A few sites ask for a sales tax ID number; others let you look for products and then ask for your tax number later if you ultimately decide to buy something. Purchases are usually completed right on the Web site, but in some instances you may be linked directly to the manufacturer to complete the transaction.

Here are a few more wholesale Web sites you may want to visit. As of this writing, they're all free:

BuyLink	**buylink.com**
Farcountries.com	**farcountries.com**
Gifts Wholesale	**giftswholesale.com**
GreatRep	**greatrep.com**
MITECH Trading	**mitechtrading.com**
One Nest	**onenest.com**
Toy Directory	**toydirectory.com**
Where O Ware	**whereoware.com**
Wholesale Buyer's Guide	**wholesalebuyersguide.com**
Wholesale Central	**wholesalecentral.com**
Wholesale Crafts	**wholesalecrafts.com**
World Gift	**worldgift.com**

Online search engines (or "portals") can be extremely handy in the search for suppliers. Key in the words "buyer's guides" or "wholesalers" and a word or two describing your product and get a wealth of information. A recent search on Google.com with the keywords "wholesale" and "plush" (retail jargon for stuffed animals) yielded 22,900 results. By adding "pigs" to those two keywords, the results narrowed to 280 possible suppliers. Out of those, chances are that at least a half-dozen sell plush pigs.

As you use the Net to find suppliers, keep in mind that while you can come up with a vast amount of information in a short time, that benefit sometimes comes at the cost of up-to-date information. Stale information is not uncommon on the Web. Sometimes even the better search engines can take months to register new sites, and the sites themselves may not be updated. It's a good idea to print out the info you find online, and keep those print-outs. (But keep in mind that prices posted on those sites are subject to change without notice.)

□ □ □

Buying from Suppliers

Now that you've found at least one potential supplier, it's time to get to the nitty-gritty of what buying from them will really cost you, so that you can close the best possible deal. Unlike some other aspects of retail, you have a great deal of control over your inventory and purchasing strategies. The hours, days, perhaps even weeks you spend now analyzing your purchasing options will pay off substantially after opening day. Suppliers' prices, delivery methods and terms will directly impact your bottom line, for better or worse. As you contact potential suppliers, keep in mind that more than just price matters. Undependable vendors, even those with the lowest prices, can leave you with bare shelves and slow sales. Reliable suppliers with competitive prices translate into a well-merchan dised location and maximum sales potential for you.

Common terms and conditions

During the start-up phase of any business, it's vital that you know and understand the terms and conditions of all the agreements you enter into, *especially* those that concern your biggest investment—your inventory. Terms vary among suppliers, but here are details on some of the most common vendor practices.

Payment During the start-up phase, some manufacturers and wholesalers are reluctant to extend trade credit terms. That means they give you a certain period of time to pay for the goods after you receive them (usually 30 days). Terms give you, the retailer, time to sell the merchandise before having to pay for it—in theory, anyway. Generally speaking, most suppliers will consider extending terms only after the retailer has successfully placed, received and paid for several orders. In short, you've established a good credit track record with them.

For new retail accounts, most suppliers want the first few orders to be paid in advance by cash, check from a US bank, or credit card (VISA, MasterCard, Discover and American Express are commonly accepted). Some suppliers prefer the first few orders be shipped COD, which isn't ideal for you: it means you not only have to have the cash on hand at delivery time, but you also incur a COD fee of $5 to $10 on each shipment.

If you do get terms, suppliers commonly charge interest at 1.5 percent per month on invoice balances that aren't paid within the agreed-upon time period. If a retailer becomes delinquent or other major problems occur, suppliers may take that retailer's future orders COD only . . . or stop delivering altogether. By the way, if you pay by check—whether on time or late—know that every supplier charges for returned checks, though the fees vary.

Minimums orders The majority of suppliers have minimum-order requirements, stated in either product-units (a dozen, a case, and so forth) or dollar amounts, usually $50 to $500. First orders often have higher minimums, so ask. That way you're not caught off guard or forced to order more product than you need, or budgeted for. Sometimes vendors will waive the minimum requirement, but only if they can tack on a handling charge of $5 to $10. It may be more cost-effective for you to order the minimum rather than pay the handling charge. Review each supplier's ordering terms to see what your best options are. Remember, most suppliers will want to work with you to get your business. But be smart: when you talk with suppliers, resist the temptation (and it will come!) to complain about other suppliers' terms or conditions. Instead, let suppliers know that as a start-up retailer, you consider it crucial to maximize every buying dollar if you're to be around to buy from them year after year. They're business people, too: they'll appreciate your professional approach. Make it clear that you see them as "partners," not adversaries, and that you're not going to haggle over every dime. The payoff? Good relationships with them (they may even suggest innovative ways you can save money!), and an improved profit potential for you.

Shipping   Most suppliers ship via UPS, FedEx, DHL or other well-known carriers, and many companies have contracts with a single carrier that gives a discount based on volume. So use the supplier's preferred carrier to keep your costs low. And don't forget to ask about U.S. Postal Service options that might be even cheaper. By the way, you should know that many shipping companies won't deliver to post office boxes; and as mentioned, nearly all of them tack on a $5 to $10 charge for packages shipped COD.

Manufacturers and wholesalers frequently state shipping costs in terms of "FOB," or freight-on-board, from a particular location, usually a factory or warehouse to your store. "FOB-origin" (the factory or warehouse) means the retailer will pay the shipping charges from that origin point. "FOB-destination" means the shipper is picking up the freight costs to the product's destination (your warehouse or store).

Returns   If you receive the wrong merchandise or defective or damaged products, notify the supplier as soon as possible. Most suppliers won't accept merchandise returns unless you get prior approval for the return within a reasonable period of time. When you call, they'll give you a return-authorization code number that you must include with the returned merchandise. And most won't even accept returns if the request is made more than 30 days after delivery — in other words, they won't give you a return-authorization code or take the merchandise back. Suppliers usually issue credit for returned merchandise. But you may be charged a re-stocking fee (typically 10 percent of the product cost) if the merchandise is being returned for reasons that aren't the supplier's fault (for example, if you ordered more than you need). You will pay to ship it back due to any reason (unless other arrangements are agreed to in advance). It's a good idea to insure the package you're returning, in case it's lost en route.

Backorders   Sometimes a manufacturer or wholesaler can't fill an order (or part of an order) when it comes in, because the product isn't available. In that case, the missing products are put on "backorder," to be shipped to the retailer as soon as available. According to trade laws, suppliers *must* send you precisely what you order (the exact size, color, etc.), unless they have a "reasonable substitution" clause regarding orders and backorders. Some suppliers' backorder policies do allow for "reasonable substitutions," which you agree to accept when you put in your order. For example, if the supplier is out of red bracelets, they can substitute the same ones in green, and you have to take them. Obviously, with a policy like this, you'll be "stuck" with whatever substitutes the supplier makes. But some suppliers have policies that let you decide to keep or return the substitutes once you see them; then if you don't want them, you can send them back according to that supplier's rules for returns.

Suppliers often *guarantee* backorders above a certain dollar amount (typically $50 or $100), and automatically *cancel* orders below that amount. Some manufacturers will deliver backordered products within 60 or 90 days of the order, after which, if the product is still unavailable, the order is canceled.

 Start-up Tip

> *If you're notified that a product is on backorder, check with your supplier on the backorder's status frequently. Otherwise you may be waiting for a product that's not coming because the order has been canceled.*

Key questions to ask suppliers

Several factors influence the cost of goods other than the price per unit. In some cases, once shipping costs and payment terms are taken into consideration, it may be more cost-effective to buy three different products from one supplier—even if the supplier's per-unit cost is slightly higher on one or more of the items. Some manufacturers also provide free or inexpensive display props and/or merchandising fixtures with first orders and subsequent orders of a pre-determined amount. The more you can take advantage of these deals, the less you end up spending for visual merchandising. Even freebie displays that don't quite work because they're too big or too red, etc., can be altered to fit, or saved for later use.

As you contact potential suppliers, keep in mind that your buying patterns and goals will likely change over the course of your first year, so ask questions even if they don't seem to apply at this time. For example, a volume discount may not be the right option for you at start-up, but what about later? It may be your most-cost effective option six months down the line. And jot down the answers you get. Your life as a retail entrepreneur will be a lot easier if you keep detailed notes for future reference.

Here are the questions to ask suppliers. Feel free to photocopy them to use as a worksheet for each of your vendor files.

- Is the supplier the manufacturer? If not, is it possible to buydirectly from the manufacturer at a better price?

- Does the supplier have a print or on-line catalog with a price list?

- Does the supplier have a toll-free number for orders and customer service? (Is there a Web site, and can you order through it?)

- What are the minimum-order requirements? Do first orders have higher minimums? If so, what are they?

- What are the shipping options and costs?

- How quickly does the supplier ship reorders? And what is the turnaround time during peak buying seasons?

- Does the supplier guarantee delivery of reorders? Is delivery guaranteed only on advance orders?

- What are the terms for first orders and reorders?

- Will the supplier offer credit for 30 or 60 days? What are the conditions?

- What discount packages does the supplier offer? According to what criterion (e.g., number of units or dollar amount)? Are there scheduled seasonal discounts? If so, how far in advance of the consumer buying season (such as Christmas) does the supplier schedule them?

- Will the supplier provide display props and/or merchandising fixtures for a grand opening? Are they free? If not free, what are the costs?

- Are the products under warranty? What are the warranty provisions?

- What's the return policy?

- Is the supplier offering exclusive rights to sell the product in a particular area?

- Will the supplier give you current retail accounts as references?

That last one is as important as all the others. Make sure to check those references. Ask them about the supplier's record for delivery and customer support during peak buying periods. Was the supplier able to deliver Christmas orders on time? If not, what caused the delay? The answer might give you insight into whether they can deliver your biggest order when you need it. (In some instances, you may want to follow up with the supplier to make sure past problems have been resolved.) Also ask the references if there were any disputes, what kind (orders? money?) and how the company resolved them. Purchasing problems do occur, but you want vendors who focus on solving the problem, not denying responsibility for it.

Key questions suppliers might ask you

Some suppliers will want to know more about you and your new retail business, depending on the size of the supplier and the terms you're looking for. If you're looking for 30-day terms from a large wholesaler, for example, be prepared to answer a lot of questions about your business concept and your finances (both business and personal). On the other hand, if you're paying cash in advance for an order from a small company, that supplier may only be interested in getting the money.

In addition, the questions your suppliers ask may depend on where you are in your start-up cycle. If you tell them you're in the research phase, they may ask you general questions about your planned location, product lines, etc. But when it's time to order, the same supplier may want in-depth financial information as well as your sales tax ID number (p. 143 has more on how and when to apply for your tax number). Generally speaking, most vendors will ask questions to determine if you are or soon will be:

- Actively engaged in the business of reselling the supplier's merchandise.

- Maintaining a brick-and-mortar retail location with regular hours.

- Financially able to meet the minimum order and reorder requirements.

- Willing to complete and sign an account application, and provide financial information and credit references.

First, a credit check

Don't be surprised if suppliers ask your permission to get your credit report from one or more of the credit reporting companies. A credit check is standard procedure before most manufacturers and distributors will sell to a new retail account. (For more about your credit report, see p. 113.)

Credit references are written confirmations from companies or financial institutions that have extended credit to you in the past. These reports include information about your payment history—i.e., whether you made payments according to the terms of the agreement. Suppliers like credit references. They provide a sense of security because they indicate that you honor agreements and pay your bills on time.

But for first-timers, providing credit references during start-up may be difficult—which is why many of them finance their initial inventory from personal savings, credit cards, short-term loans from friends and family, or other sources that don't require references. (For more on financing options, see "Finding Start-up Capital" on p. 103.) The good news is that once you have established terms with one supplier, you can use them as a credit reference for other suppliers.

Discounts and deals

Make the most of your buying dollars by asking suppliers about the discounts and deals they offer at various times. Even if you don't qualify now, or if a supplier offers a seasonal discount later in the year, you want to build those "buying incentives" into your purchasing strategy. Most suppliers also run periodic sales on certain products or lines during the year. Being poised to taking advantage of all of the available incentives can save you money—and raise the profit level of your product. Here are a few typical incentives.

Discounts Manufacturers and wholesalers typically offer a variety of discounts, including volume discounts, seasonal discounts, cash discounts and advance-order discounts. They can be in the form of a percentage off or free shipping or other savings. Some suppliers give volume discounts *and* allow split shipments (e.g., sending half of the order now and the other half later), and sometimes even split payments, in return for your commitment to buy.

Ask your suppliers to explain their requirements for giving a discount (the rules vary from company to company). Make it a point to ask about discounts several times during the year, so that you can plan your buying to take advantage of them as much as possible. You may not be able to get a volume discount on your first order, but as your business grows, that and other discounts may kick in.

When you contact suppliers, stress that you want them to notify you of all their sales and discounts as they become available. While you're at it, confirm that your suppliers have up-to-date contact information on you, including your fax number and e-mail address. Then when you get announcements of seasonal incentives and other buying incentives, note the dates on your calendar. Some retailers keep a separate "buying calendar" for recording those dates so they can stay on top of and take advantage of the discounts.

Trade show discounts The vast majority of manufacturers and wholesalers also offer discounts on products at trade shows, often in advance of product availability. Discounts usually apply only to orders placed during the show. By carefully planning your show budget, you can save from 5 to 20 percent on new orders, depending on the size. (Reorders of the same product may not be discounted.) With so many trade shows and marts across the country, chances are you can find an event close enough to home that won't require airfare. In any case, thanks to trade-show discounts, a well-planned buying trip near or far can pay for itself.

Reducing shipping costs

Shipping costs often catch retailers off guard. Not only do retailers sometimes neglect to factor shipping into their cost of goods, they also simply neglect to ask their suppliers about less-expensive options that may be available.

Many suppliers have standard ("default") shipping carriers. Using the vendor's preferred shipping company and method (overnight, express, ground) can save you money. That said, ask them about the options they offer for decreasing the shipping expenses. For example, receiving a shipment a day or two later can sometimes mean major savings for you. So it pays to be as flexible as you can in order to get the best deal. And don't forget, COD-shipping fees are a direct hit to your bottom line. Avoid them completely by paying in advance, or by getting credit terms as soon as you can.

Getting credit terms

Credit terms are the lifeblood of any business that wants to succeed in the long run. By getting credit terms from your suppliers, you keep your money working longer for you, rather than going into suppliers' pockets right away. The first step is to ask for credit terms. The supplier will tell you their rules and requirements—complete financial information on you and your business, and good credit references. (If they have an application form, ask them to fax it to you.) The second step is actually a process: establish good credit history with the supplier by paying your product invoices in full and on time over a set period of time. Once you have a good history with your suppliers, they'll review your account and make a decision.

One caution: once you have terms, don't let that 30-day window tempt you into overbuying. Before your next order, pay close attention to which products are selling well, and buy only what you can reasonably expect to sell.

(You should be doing this routinely anyway.) Rosy, inflated estimates that translate to overbuying will likely mean overdue invoices later. And that means messing up your good credit history, losing your credit terms, and thereby decreasing your profit margins.

Confirm the terms! Most suppliers' quotes have a "shelf-life," a time frame (typically 30 or 60 days) during which the prices are "good." The time frame is stated right on the quote. (If it isn't, ask.) After that time period, those prices can go up or down. That's why it's important to confirm product availability, prices and terms as you get closer to putting in your first orders for opening day product. You want to be sure nothing major has changed since you first contacted the supplier.

To confirm the availability of the product and the terms under which the product will be purchased, you can ask the suppliers to send you a final quote in writing, or you can send the suppliers a confirmation or Request for Quote (RFQ). A complete confirmation or RFQ should include:

- A detailed description of the goods, with the supplier's product codes if available

- Quantities: by unit, dozen, case (including number of units per case), gross (stated as either "12 dozen" or "144 units"), as applicable

- Price of goods

- Display props/merchandising fixtures included, with prices as applicable

- Required delivery date and place

- Shipping methods and costs

- Terms and method of payment

- The shelf-life of the quote

During the harried days of start-up, it's tempting to skim suppliers' quotes for the "big" items like price per unit—and then miss something smaller but just as crucial, like a change in the delivery date. Don't count on the supplier to point out any changes that were made. Read your suppliers' quotes carefully, every word and any fine print. (That goes for correspondence, too.)

□ □ □

Finding the Right Location

Every retail entrepreneur dreams of finding the "perfect" location—the one with dirt-cheap rent that attracts hordes of customers with fat, open wallets. This rarely happens. You can bet that if there are hordes of customers with fat, open wallets, the rent won't be cheap. It's also a fair bet that locations with the cheapest rent won't have the foot traffic you need.

Foot traffic and fat wallets aside, even if you happen to land a great deal on rent in the busiest mall, tourist venue or retail district of any kind, there's no guarantee that the *type* of customers it attracts are customers who will buy *your* products. Even the "best" malls (the highest traffic counts, premier tenant mix, superior demographics and dynamic marketing) can't guarantee that your retail concept will strike a chord with *their* shoppers. Retail is challenging enough—no need to make your life harder by trying to sell to the wrong customer population.

Selecting potential locations

First thing to know about finding a location: *don't rush*. It can take weeks, even months, to find the right spot for your business. Rushing the process and settling for a so-so location just to meet a loan-approval date or keep to a (changeable) start-up schedule can end up costing you dearly. If you're in the wrong location, it can be extremely difficult to survive, and impossible to grow.

Here's the good news: Unlike 30 years ago, when there were no established specialty retail programs, today's entrepreneurs have a wealth of choices for finding the best location. Where to look? Anywhere large numbers of consumers visit, gather, or walk past. If you're in the U.S., you probably live within an hour of at least two malls and dozens of other places where specialty retailers operate and thrive. These places include:

Shopping venues: Malls of all sizes, strip shopping centers, outlet centers, outdoor shopping centers and "markets," grocery stores

Tourist venues: Beaches and beach resorts, boardwalks, theme parks, casinos, mountain and ski resorts, spa resorts, hotels, convention centers, national and state parks, historic sites, recreation locales

Visitor venues: Entertainment events and locations, festivals and fairs, national and regional sports events

Hometown venues: Office buildings, hospitals, downtown areas, city sidewalks, colleges/campus villages

Sports venues: arenas, stadiums, skating rinks, skateboard parks

With so many location possibilities, you have an excellent chance of finding one that's perfect for you (more about specific factors to consider in a moment). From this list alone, you can probably identify at least three potential high-traffic locations for your business within easy commuting distance. As you think about your options, keep in mind that each location you investigate will have a certain pre-existing customer base. For example, the typical outlet-center shopper tends to buy different products at different price points than the typical airport shopper buys.

Malls and their retail spaces

Most specialty retailers open their first location in some type of mall. So here's the lowdown on the different kinds of malls and the types of spaces they offer specialty retailers. The International Council of Shopping Centers (ICSC), a trade organization, defines shopping centers according to size.

There are about 1,800 enclosed malls in the U.S. today. More than two dozen have been built in the last two years, adding more than 30 million s/f of retail real estate to the collective portfolio. According to the ICSC, the average mall being built today has more than 1,000,000 s/f of *gross leasable area* (GLA)—the total square-footage that retail tenants can occupy. Here's how the ICSC defines the different types of centers, including GLA and a brief mention of the type of retail tenants each type houses:

Super-regional malls: Typically more than 800,000 s/f. These centers often have several entertainment-oriented retail tenants.

Regional malls: 400,000-800,000 s/f. These centers have the usual complement of retailers: several department stores as anchors, and several dozen in-line stores ranging from national chains to independent specialty retailers.

Community centers: 100,000-350,000 s/f. **Neighborhood centers:** Less than 150,000 s/f. Both types are designed to serve needs of the local community, and many of them have chain grocery and/or drugstore tenants for that reason.

Power centers: 250,000-600,000 s/f. These usually have anchor tenants that are "category-dominant" or "big box," such as chain office suppliers and off-price department stores.

Outlet centers: 50,000-400,000 s/f. At least half the retail tenants here offer discounted merchandise (often factory-direct, and often seconds).

Fashion or specialty centers: 80,000-250,000 s/f. Higher-end, tenants with fashion-oriented merchandise.

Themed or festival centers: 80,000-250,000 s/f. Retailers here focus on leisure- and/or tourist-oriented merchandise.

Lifestyle centers: 150,000-500,000 s/f. These open-air centers are usually near upscale neighborhoods; the retailers here focus on lifestyle-based products such as fitness gear, books, music and home décor.

Size matters

A mall's size is the biggest factor when it comes to the number of specialty retail tenants the center can effectively manage. The average regional mall, for example, might have 15 to 30 specialty retailers operating in the common area year-round, and twice that for the Christmas season. Many centers have two leasing managers, one for short-term tenants and one for long-term tenants.

Most common-area tenants operate on freestanding carts or kiosks, referred to as *RMUs* (retail merchandise units). The average *cart* is 40-80 s/f; the average *kiosk* is larger, at 100-160 s/f. In recent years, additional RMUs have been introduced to the market, including *wall units* and *bump-back stores.* Both are retail spaces that are created from unused space in a mall or other retail venue. Wall units, as the name implies, are usually pre-built merchandising units that are installed against a blank wall, providing retailers with display space, lighting, cash-register space, and locks for overnight security. Bump-back stores, similar to wall units (in that they provide shelving, etc., for the retailer), are created by "bumping back" a vacant store's front entrance 6'-8' to give a "temporary" retailer space to display goods (until the in-line is occupied, that is).

A retailer by any name

Specialty retailers who operate in the common areas are sometimes called "common area tenants," for obvious reasons. Because of the short tenancy terms, they're also sometimes called "temporary tenants" to differentiate them from the "permanent tenants."

And then there are traditional mall storefronts, referred to as *in-line* stores. They average about 2,500 s/f, although they can range from 500 to 10,000 s/f, and some are significantly larger. Some specialty retailers start in in-line stores, but most start on RMUs, and some later expand into in-lines as their businesses grow. In some cases, in-lines are so well designed, stocked and merchandised that the only way to tell the difference between "temporary tenants" and "permanent tenants" like Gap or Bombay Company is to look at the lease terms. Large national retailers typically sign leases of 10 years or more. Specialty retailers, on the other hand, usually sign license agreements that last anywhere from one day to one year (for more about leases vs. license agreements, see p. 80).

Key site-selection factors

Whether you want to sell in just one mall year-round or at a variety of seasonal festivals across the country, you want maximum sales and the best chance to turn your hard work into a thriving business with long-term potential. To help ensure that's what happens, you need a location that offers the following:

- access to a large base of target customers

- a healthy retail environment

- the physical space necessary to showcase merchandise effectively, achieve the retail image you want, and generate the most sales possible

- minimum competition and maximum synergy—good fit and interaction— between your store and other retailers in the area

- all at a cost you can afford

To come to an informed decision about location, you have to weigh the strengths and weaknesses of each these key site-selection factors. How? It's easier than you think: simply ask yourself certain questions (they're in this chapter) that pertain to your business, and then find the answers in the data you'll gather from a variety of sources—in other words, do *market research* (resources start on p. 71). Some of the data will be easy to find, and some won't. But you can find even the most obscure information if you're focused and persistent.

First, a few words about types of data—the statistics that categorize groups of people ("populations") in different ways:

- **Demographics** categorize according to "hard" data: factors like age, gender, income, ethnicity, occupation, marital status, number of children, home ownership, education, employment status and (more recently) Internet access.

- **Psychographics** categorize according to "soft" data such as personal interests, leisure activities, hobbies, reading and music preferences, political beliefs, religion, cultural habits and the like.

- **Technographics**, the newest type of collected data, categorize according to use of technology, such as number of hours spent online, dollars spent online, primary reason for Internet use, motivation for shopping online, payment preferences, and use of other electronic devices (e.g., PDAs, digital cameras)

> ### Don't be shy!
> Go after the answer to every one of your questions, and don't let go until you have an answer that satisfies you (even if you don't like the answer) . . . because the information you collect—and the conclusions you come to based on that information—will be the foundation of your retail concept, your business plan, and your success.

Identifying your target customers

Who's going to buy the product you're selling? You need to identify and define who your target customers are. Then you need to find where they shop, so you can evaluate a particular location for the degree of access it provides to those target customers.

Being able to describe your target customers is like building the foundation of a house: without it, you can't build at all. If you don't know who you're target customers are, start by answering a few questions about your product(s), since what you plan to sell will point you toward the type of customers you're likely to attract. Write your answers to the following questions.

About the product

- What specific products am I planning to sell?

- What are these products' anticipated price points? (See "Pricing Products for Profit" on p. 33.)

- What image do the products project based on quality, price and other factors unique to the merchandise?

- Are the products already available in the marketplace?

- Are they new to the market, or have they been available for some time?

- If currently available, where are they sold?

- In either case, where are shoppers most likely to look for the products?

Who is most likely to buy most of your products? What's the profile of the shopper who accounts for the majority of those sales? By answering these questions, you'll get a snapshot of your target customers. Check or answer as many of these demographics as apply:

About the target customers

Age _____ M _____ F _____ Married _____ Single _____

Children? _____ Younger _____ Older _____ Single parent? _____

Occupation _____

Income level _____ Education level _____

Owns ___ Rents ___ Lives with parents ___ Lives at school/college ____

Personal interests _____

Ethnic/cultural interests _____

Why they'll buy: Impulse/Fun __ Need __ Luxury __ Entertainment __

If you have trouble profiling your target customers, don't worry—there's a lot of consumer and market information out there—tap the resources listed later in this chapter. If you can't find information on your specific product, pick one that's similar to what you're planning to sell, and search for buying patterns, reports or articles that will give you an indication of who is buying those products.

Evaluating access to your target customers

Now that you know who your target customers are, how do you know if they shop in the location you're considering? Your goal is to identify a location that attracts them in droves, or make sure the location you're considering already does. To do that, take a close look at the consumers in the center's *trade area*—the geographic region from which a mall or center's "resident" retail tenants draw the majority of their customers.

The size of the trade area depends on factors such as the venue's size and tenant mix. A typical mall, for example, with a several department-store "anchors" and a few dozen in-line retailers, might draw most of its shoppers from within a 20- or 30-mile radius, or a 20-30 minute drive time, and have a "trade area population" of 80,000 or more consumers.

Now that's *a trade area!*
Fifty percent of the visitors to the Mall of America, the 4.2 million-s/f shopping/entertainment complex in Bloomington, Minnesota, travel more than 150 miles to get there, according to the Mall's research.

Specialty retailers can and do lure new and repeat shoppers by means of advertising and marketing. But the fact is, every retailer who operates as part of a larger shopping district from the mall to downtown Main Street relies on *the venue's ability to draw shoppers.* You can get this information on a district's shopper traffic—and the types of shoppers the venue draws—from a variety of sources like mall management, government agencies, and companies that specialize in demographic research (see the resources on p. 71). But no matter which sources you use, you want to find data that answer these questions:

- Does the location's trade area contain a large number of my target customers?

- Has the population of target customers in the area grown, shrunk, or stayed the same in the past five years?

- Is that population likely to grow or shrink in the next two years?

If you plan to sell skateboard accessories but the number of households with children has dropped steadily in the last few years, you may want to consider another locale, or choose a different product that targets "empty nesters."

Analyzing the retail environment

Being in a mall or any retail venue that's struggling to bring in customers can be disastrous, no matter how eye-catching your product display or how desirable your products may be. The more you know about a mall and its shoppers' buying patterns before you move in, the better. Ask these questions about each location you're considering:

- How is this mall classified? For example, regional mall, outlet center, lifestyle center, etc.

- Is this the appropriate type of place for shoppers who are looking for my products?

- What are the mall's sales per s/f for the year to date? For the past five years?

- What sales-per-s/f ratio is typical for my type of business in this location?

- What are the total annual sales for this mall? What's the dollar amount of the average transaction?

- What's the average weekly shopper traffic? monthly? annually?

- What percentage of visitors make purchases?

- Are specialty retailers in the mall realizing increased sales year after year? At what rate of increase?

- What is the mall's occupancy history? Has it been gaining, retaining, or losing retail tenants?

- What happened to the business that last occupied the location I am considering?

- What factors influenced the failure of retailers in this mall? Is the mall becoming run-down, or is it growing and changing with the times?

- What is the economic climate in the trade area and the larger region? Are surrounding businesses doing well? Or are they struggling? Closing their doors?

- Are there pressures on the economy, such as declining industries that local consumers rely on for their livelihoods? Is the local unemployment rate high?

- Does mall management seem prepared to help me get my enterprise off the ground?

- What is management's reputation or track record for helping entrepreneurial ventures grow?

As you collect and review all of this information, you'll be able to spot weak numbers and the factors that may be working against you. If you find that the space you're considering was occupied by someone selling the same merchandise you want to sell, proceed with caution. You may not have to bail just yet, though. First find out what caused the retailer to leave: it may have no bearing. For all you know, the owner just wanted to retire.

Sizing up the space

You need the right space to showcase your merchandise, create the retail image you want, and ring up the most sales possible. Ask these questions to size up each location you're considering.

- Is there too little space to effectively merchandise my products? Too much space?

- What's the physical condition of the space? What work ("build-out") does it need?

- How much will I have to spend to turn it into an attractive, well-equipped retail space?

- Can I achieve the retail image I want by operating in this location?

- Does the location put me in a high-traffic area?

- Are there adequate signs and lighting to announce my store's presence? If not, what are my options?

- Are there adequate electrical outlets and phone lines? If not, what are my options?

- Is there enough customer parking? Is customer access convenient, safe, well-lit?

- What long-term inventory-storage capacity does the location offer? If none, what are my options?

- Will my inventory/equipment be secure in this location?

- For RMUs, if you need to move inventory/equipment on a daily basis, is there a secure place to move it to? And how convenient is the overnight-storage location?

As always, watch for red flags. If you anticipate problems with inventory security, either resolve those issues or consider another location. And if you're considering an in-line space, be particularly cautious about estimating build-out costs. It's easy to spend at least $5,000 turning what used to be someone else's store into *your* store.

Determining the impact of nearby retailers

Who are your retail neighbors? Does their presence help you or hurt you? Gauging how nearby ("proximate") retailers would impact your business is critical. To do this, you'll look at the same two factors that mall and other retail-venue managers use: First, what pressures will the competition put on your ability to succeed in the long run? And second, which retailers can benefit your business by drawing shoppers toward you, or by creating synergy between your store and those around you? Ask these questions to evaluate the nearby retailers at each location you're considering.

- Who will my retail neighbors be?

- Which businesses will complement mine and bring traffic to my location?

- Are there strong retail anchors and other tenants who bring customer traffic to the center?

- Does my product mix fit in with the center?

- Which businesses will compete with mine?

- Are there any "first-tier competitors" nearby—retailers who sell the same or similar products? Who are they? What are their price points? What are the strengths and weaknesses of each one?

- What products or services could I offer that would differentiate my store from these competitors?

During the Christmas selling season, specialty retailers swear by "the Santa effect": The closer you are to the mall's Santa's Workshop, the better. That's why you see so many seasonal retailer's carts right there, smack dab in the middle of the Santa action. Of course, it's not just during the holidays that the location of a retail space within a mall or other retail center matters. Some cart- and kiosk-based retailers say being near the food court is a must. Others say it's critical to be near synergistic neighbors no matter where they are. For example, the owner of a floral kiosk may find that sales are higher when the kiosk is near a bridal shop. On the other hand, if you want to launch an upscale women's accessories store, you may not want to be sandwiched between two value-priced retailers.

Sources of market data

The U.S. Census Bureau is the largest collector and publisher of demographic data that will give you insight into the population in your potential trade area. But if wading through government data to find the information that's relevant to your business isn't your idea of a good time, you can go to a secondary source that's likely to have the same data compiled in a format that's easier to understand. Secondary sources include the Small Business Administration (SBA), the Service Corps of Retired Executives (SCORE), and your local chamber of commerce or merchants association. (See p.113 for contact information for the SBA.)

Retail center management

If you're considering a location in retail venue like a mall or airport, your first stop for market data is the venue's management. Most specialty leasing managers are more than willing to help new retailers find the information they need, so don't hesitate to ask them for assistance or referrals to other resources. These managers want to see your business succeed and expand—they want to be the ones who helped you get started and "knew you when." You can expand your research efforts outward from there.

Contact the center's leasing manager or marketing director for all available market information. In addition to sales figures, ask for the results of any in-house research, such as customer surveys and foot/auto traffic counts. Also ask for the leasing manager's opinion about the specific areas within the center that have the most and least traffic. At a minimum, you need to know how many visitors the center gets, what percentage of them make purchases, and the average purchase dollar amount. (See the questions on p. 65.) Armed with this information, you can start to gauge your ability to generate sales. Also, because of their near-constant contact with center shoppers, management can provide you with a wealth of "anecdotal information"—not statistics but in-the-trenches accounts that can sometimes be even more valuable. If you're willing to make an appointment (and maybe pick up a lunch tab), you can learn a great deal about your potential operating environment and its retail customers.

Government agencies

The U.S. Census Bureau A large portion of the Bureau's best-known project—the 10-year census—can be found on its Web site (uscensus.gov). There you can browse, search and map Census 2000 data; access population reports, rankings and comparisons; and get help accessing and interpreting the data. The Bureau also publishes the Census of Retail Trade, the Census of Manufacturers, City and County Business Patterns reports, the Sourcebook of County Demographics, and the Sourcebook of ZIP Code Demographics. These and other reports are available through the same Web site, or you can review Census reports at more than 1,800 state and local organizations and 1,400 public and university libraries that are designated Federal Depository Libraries. In addition, reports in print and on CD are available for public use and review at 12 regional offices around the country. To find a location with the latest data, call the Bureau (301.457.4608) or visit its "Access Page" (census.gov/mso/www/npr/access).

Census Bureau State Data Centers Known as SDCs, these are the official Census Bureau-supported offices in every state and Washington, D.C. Here you can find demographic, economic and social statistics from the Census Bureau. SDCs make data accessible to governments and to private citizens "at no charge or on a cost-recovery or reimbursable basis as appropriate." To find the nearest SDC, call the Bureau or go online (census.gov/ftp/pub/sdc/www) and click on the map.

Small Business Administration The SBA has a wealth of data for small-business entrepreneurs, including business-survival statistics and national and state economic reports—far too many reports and statistical analyses to list here. To find SBA data and reports that are relevant to your business and location, call the SBA (800.8.ASK.SBA) or go online to their "publication room" (sba.gov/library/pubs.html) and the informative "reports room" (sba.gov/library/reportsroom.html).

Some SBA reports are published by SBA subdivisions. **The Office of Advocacy,** for example, publishes two valuable reports for any retailer: the state-by-state "Small Business Profiles" (which give baseline statistics on small business income, employment, financing data, business-failure rates and other factors), and the "Small Business Economic Indicators" report, which provides even more economic and historical analysis than the "Profiles" report. For a copy of these and other reports, contact the Office of Advocacy (202.205.5533; sba.gov/ADVO/stats/profiles).

State and local organizations affiliated with (or financially supported by) the SBA also provide site-selection research data and advice. **The Service Corps of Retired Executives (SCORE)** has chapters in every state staffed by successful retired business people who volunteer to assist aspiring entrepreneurs find information to make informed decisions. SCORE can be an *excellent* source of data and business savvy (800.534.0245; score.org).

The SBA also backs **Small Business Development Centers (SBDCs)** in every state and Washington, D.C., whose mission it is to counsel and train small-business owners. SBDCs are usually located on college campuses, thereby providing an added bonus: access to that college's vast library resources. Many SBDCs also have their own Web sites. To find an SBDC or its Web address, call the SBA or visit the SBDC page (sba.gov/sbdc).

SBA-funded **Business Information Centers (BICs)** are usually located in a city's Empowerment Zones and specialize in helping entrepreneurs who want to operate in economically challenged areas. BIC locations across the country are listed on the SBA's Web site, or call the SBA.

The U.S. Bureau of Labor Statistics, the principal fact-finding agency for the federal government for labor economics and statistics, publishes reports on wages, salaries and employee benefits; inflation rates; consumer attitudes; business investment and spending; and industry-specific growth/decline rates. The Bureau's "Consumer Expenditure Survey" provides in-depth information on the buying habits of American consumers, including income, specific expenditures by product category, and "consumer unit characteristics" (e.g., families vs. singles). It's available online and in print. To get a copy or to find out about other Bureau reports, go to the Web site (bls.gov) or call the Bureau (202.691.5200).

Location directories

Location directories are a great resource, especially for comparing locations. Each of these three directories, published annually, has a different focus. Together, they provide details on tens of thousands of centers.

The **Directory of Major Malls** (Nyack, NY; 800.898.MALL; directoryofmajor malls.com) covers more than 3,500 U.S. and Canadian malls of 250,000 s/f or more. Details include: center location, metro area, size, design, number of stores, tenant lists by category, date opened, latest renovations or improvements, sales per square foot, general market demographics, space availability and key contact information. A helpful time-saver: each entry indicates whether that center has an established common-area specialty retail program. The *Directory* is available in print ($499), on CD ($599-$1,499, depending on the geographical scope) and online (a subscription for full access is $799).

Retail Resource Guide (Specialty Retail Report, Norwell, MA; 800.936.6297; specialtyretail.com) covers more than 2,000 U.S. and Canadian retail locations that have established specialty retail programs (including malls, airports, outlet centers, festival marketplaces and more). Details include: center location, size, design, latest renovations or improvements, general demographics, RMU amenities (electric, phone, storage, etc.), space available, percentage-rent rates, monthly rent rates, seasonal rent rates, average sales per square foot, size of the specialty retail program (available carts, kiosks and in-line space), and key contact information. Available in print ($199).

The Shopping Center Directory (National Research Bureau, Wilton, CT, 203.563.3000; nrbonline.com) covers nearly 39,000 shopping centers of various types (neighborhood strip centers, super-regional malls, outlet centers, festival centers and more). Details include: center location, metro area, size, design, number of stores, tenant mix, date opened, date of latest renovations or improvements, sales per square foot, general market demographics, space availability, and key contact information. The directory is available in print, on CD, and online. Prices start at several hundred dollars and go up to several thousand, depending on format and the scope of information you want (national, regional, etc.).

Locations online

Some mall developers' Web sites have information on available space, leasing terms and other data for potential tenants. The General Growth Properties site has details on nearly 150 mall locations on its site (generalgrowth.com)—click on "Our Malls" and then on "Mall Directory" for details about the center, demographic data, current retail tenants, and more.

Market research firms

Market research firms come in many shapes and sizes, and can be excellent resources of highly targeted data, if that's what you need. Some firms specialize in retail analysis, tracking consumer segments or product categories each year. Market reports are often available in both print and digital formats, with prices ranging from $100 to more than $5,000, depending on the nature and scope of the research. Custom research (while potentially invaluable to some start-up enterprises) can be very expensive. For that reason, it's usually not worth it for most specialty retail start-ups. And as you now know, there's plenty of information out there for free or next to nothing.

In fact, some of these firms provide limited data for free on their Web sites. Check the "Press" or "Media" section, where hidden data may be located (press credentials or registration are rarely needed to enter a Web site's media section). To find a market research firm that's likely to have the type of data you want, search online, check the local yellow pages, or ask your local Chamber of Commerce for a referral. You might also find it helpful to speak with a market-research trade organization for advice or referrals. Two well-respected groups are the Market Research Association (Rocky Hill, CT; 860.257.4008; mra-net.org) and the Marketing Science Institute (Cambridge, MA; 617.491.2060; msi.org—registration required).

Other retailers

Before you make a final site selection, talk to at least three retailers who are familiar with the venue you're considering. Introduce yourself to store owners and managers. Ask for their opinions on a variety of issues *before* you make any final decisions. Find out what's *really* going on in the center by asking questions beyond "how are your sales these days?" Instead, ask about changes in shopper buying patterns and center management—how management helps its tenants grow, and how well management resolves conflicts. Retailers with experience selling similar merchandise lines may be able to help you estimate sales volumes (ask the leasing manager for contacts, or try a local retail association). Also ask other retailers about their rent rates, how their rents are structured (base rent, percentage rent, etc.). Ask about the center's traffic patterns: when is mall traffic lightest, and when is it heaviest? Where are the best and worst locations within the center you're considering? You may be surprised by how much information other retailers are willing to share, if you ask.

Chambers of commerce

These well-known business organizations exist not just to promote local or regional pride—they're there to help local businesses succeed. Chambers provide a great deal of information (much of it free even to non-members), business training, research, political involvement, networking opportunities, and much more. Some chambers even have staffers whose job is to help novice entrepreneurs with site selection—sometimes for free! Even if you're not a chamber member, go to as many open meetings and business-oriented events as you can ("guests" usually pay a few dollars more than members to get in). The more you're involved, the greater your access to information and to knowledgeable local business people . . . and the more you'll learn about the local market.

Economic development boards

Similar to chambers of commerce, the sole purpose of these boards (or "agencies" or "councils") is to bring in more businesses to a city and help them succeed. You may not be aware that these groups exist in your area, so ask your banker or accountant, or check the Yellow Pages. They, too, offer a wealth of information and assistance, and often hold open meetings and events that are worth attending.

Local professionals

Bankers, accountants, lawyers and other professionals are sources you can tap for advice and assistance with site selection—although in most cases, you'll have to pay for that help. Commercial realtors are also a good source of information, but they may be reluctant to help you unless you're considering a location they represent. If you're having trouble deciding between two or more locations, you may want to hire a commercial real-estate consultant. But do as much basic market research as you can in advance, or be prepared to pay the consultant for his or her research time. (Rates vary depending on locale and the nature of the research and analysis requested.)

Libraries

Business and reference librarians are professionals who are ready to help find information on your target customers, competition and industry. With their help you'll find some market data at your local branch library, but if you need specialized data or larger studies, you may have to use a big-city public library or a college or university library (even better: libraries at schools that offer business degrees). Larger libraries have a wide variety of market-data materials (some of them more user-friendly than others). But you can't take out many of these books even if you do have library privileges, so be prepared to write and photocopy. Of course, you can buy many of those books directly from the publishers, but they can cost big money (for example, Rand McNally's *Commercial Atlas & Marketing Guide* retails for almost $400). These books contain market and demographic data:

- Rand McNally Commercial Atlas and Marketing Guide (130th ed., Rand McNally & Co., Skokie, IL, 1999; randmcnally.com). Has U.S. maps plus with population and economic data for more than 128,000 metropolitan statistical areas (MSAs) with populations of 25,000 or more.

- *Lifestyle Market Analyst* (Standard Rate & Data Service, Wilmette, IL). Annual publication that outlines the demographic characteristics and lifestyle interests based on geographic region. Demographics include: age, marital status, income level, education, children at home, race, etc.). Lifestyle data include: persons in households who participate in any of 56 activities/interests (e.g., photography, gardening, specific sports, reading, stock/bond investments).

- *American Marketplace: Demographics and Spending Patterns* (5th ed., New Strategist Publications, Ithaca, NY, May 2001; newstrategist.com). Uses mostly governmental sources for raw data, but presents the information in a readable format divided into several sections: education, health, income, labor force, living arrangement, population, spending and wealth. New Strategist Publications focuses on demographic reporting, so ask the librarian what other publications are available from that company, or go to its Web site directly.

- *Editor & Publisher Market Guide* (*Editor & Publisher Magazine*, New York, NY; editorandpublisher.com). Annual publication designed for media professionals but can be very informative for retailers' site-selection questions. Analyzes more than 1,500 U.S. and Canadian daily-newspaper markets, with data focusing on: principal industries, population makeup and growth, disposable personal income, retail sales, economic climate, retail outlets, daily newspaper circulation, and market rankings and forecasts.

Your own observations

Research is important, but numbers alone can't substitute for first-hand experience and gut instinct. Walk the retail venue during different times of day and on different days of the week. Checking out the mall on a Saturday won't tell you if the center is "dead" during typical weekday afternoons.

Sit in one spot (near your potential location) for an hour or two to observe. Pay attention to how customers dress . . . even what mood they seem to be in (enthusiastic and energetic? bored? dissatisfied?) . . . what they're buying (notice the bags they're carrying). How many people seem to be just window-shopping or cruising? How many go into a store but come out empty-handed? You could talk with a few shoppers and ask why they shop there, and what kinds of merchandise they most commonly buy there. Then choose another spot and repeat the experiment. Change spots, days and times, so you get a complete snapshot.

You also can find out a lot about your competition by observing. Visit competitors to get the inside scoop. If you can swing it, talk with their customers about what they like or don't like about shopping there. Also notice any on-site advertising or marketing your competition does (newspaper ads, brochures, special events, etc.) to communicate with their customers.

Making *the* decision

As you evaluate your options, be as flexible as possible as you keep the key-site selection factors in mind. And be as dispassionate and objective as you can: don't get into a location you can't afford by believing in wishful thinking about how much business you can generate.

Armed with your market research and the input you have from various sources, you should now be ready to evaluate your potential locations and answer the final question: "Is this the right location?" The answer is in your research. If it's not, keep researching and adding to your data until it is. Or if you're up against a wall and can't see the answer clearly, consider hiring a consultant for help (check with fellow retailers or contact a retail trade association). Since you've already done so much of the work, the consultant won't have to. You'll be able to provide a good idea of what you do and don't want, and your reasons based on your research. All of this should mean a savings in time-based fees. You can find retail real estate consultants in trade directories or magazines, the Yellow Pages, or through business organizations like SCORE.

Finally, if you find the right location but can't afford it, don't give up on it yet. Try to negotiate the rent or fees with the center's management (see p. 86 for help on focusing your negotiations). And if you haven't already, you can contact a SCORE or other SBA counselor to help you locate or negotiate viable sites. (See p. 99, "Getting local assistance".)

Evaluating a Lease or License Agreement

You're about to take the next step. You've done your homework and decided that a certain location has real potential. Now it's time to get the skinny on the rent and fees you'd have to pay. At this stage, your decision about renting that space should be greatly influenced by what's in the lease or license agreement. You have to decide if its terms and conditions are favorable, and if the rent rate is reasonable (rates vary from mall to mall and region to region). But there's more to the money commitment than rent: miscellaneous fees can turn what looks like a good deal into a financial burden. You don't want any surprises, so unless you have a great deal of experience with commercial contracts, get professional advice to help you sort it out. Consult your lawyer or accountant (or even a real estate consultant, if you feel you need one) to help you understand what you're getting into, financially and otherwise.

Leases vs. "license agreements"

Leases and "license agreements" are legal contracts that spell out the rights and responsibilities of both the property owner or manager (the "landlord") and the retailer who occupies a portion of the property (the "tenant").

Leases are typically used for an occupancy ("tenancy") period of a year or more, often five or ten years. *License agreements* are usually for a period of one year or less, which is why they're sometimes referred to as temporary license agreements, or TLAs. License agreements are generally one to five pages long, whereas most leases run 20 pages or more. License agreements refer to the landlord as the *licensor* and the tenant as *licensee*. Leases refer o the landlord as the *lessor* and the tenant as the *lessee*.

Because license agreements are short-term, many specialty retailers start out with a license agreement rather than a lease. Signing a license agreement vs. a lease at start-up works in your favor on several fronts. A license agreement allows you to avoid the financial (and emotional) commitment of a multi-year lease during this delicate early phase of your new venture's life. Licenses also give you the ability to move quickly and easily if the facts (sales, customer feedback, etc.) show that sales would be stronger in another mall or another trade area. And it's not just slow sales that might make you decide to scope out and seize a better opportunity in another area. More than a few experienced specialty retailers use short-term carts or kiosks as "test vehicles" in different areas or different types of malls before they invest in one location (whether a seasonal cart or year-round in-line) with the best potential. Or let's say your sales are strong and you want to add a cart next to your first cart during a busy summer or holiday season. You can sign a short-term license agreement and know you're not locked in to a long-term commitment. And of course, short-term licenses allow you to take advantage of busy selling seasons, like Christmas.

On the down side, license agreements are not as negotiable as leases: mall managers are more willing to negotiate with retailers who sign multi-year agreements. In fact, some malls consider their license agreement to be unalterable, so that they won't have to invest time and money in an attorney's review and approval of any changes to the document for a short-term tenant. That's not to say you can't negotiate a lower rent or a more favorable rent structure (more on this later), but as for the terms and conditions, they may be set in stone. Another big downside is the license's "relocation clause" (see p. 83), which allows management to relocate you to a different space in the mall whenever they please. And the relocation would be at your expense, which could cost you thousands of dollars, especially in the case of an in-line store. Here are the decisions you want to make after you review the lease or license agreement:

- Are the lease/license terms favorable?

- Can you expand at this location if business is good and you need more selling space?

- What rules or limitations will there be on the operation?

- What services does the landlord provide in exchange
  for rent—for example, marketing programs and visual
  merchandising assistance?

- Can you afford this location?

Common lease/license terms

Accomplished specialty retailers know that there's more to a lease or license
agreement than rent numbers. As the adage goes, "What the large print
giveth, the small print taketh away." Not paying close attention to the "fine
print" can cost you. Here are the terms and conditions you're likely to see in
a specialty retail lease or license agreement:

Advertising fee Sometimes called a *marketing fee*, this is a set amount
paid to the landlord for promoting the entire retail center. Generally speaking, retail tenants have no control over how mall management spends
advertising and marketing funds, but these fees can be negotiated under
some circumstances, such as when the landlord needs to fill the space.

Application fee A few malls charge an application fee (sometimes called
a *registration fee*). This is a one-time payment ($100-$500) to cover the landlord's expenses that relate to the tenant's start-up (credit checks, account
set-up, etc.). This fee is generally not negotiable.

Base rent See *Rent*

CAM fee Tenants pay a common-area maintenance or CAM fee in addition
to rent to cover their share of center maintenance and utilities, property
taxes, security, parking lot lighting and other expenses. Many landlords
consider CAM fees non-negotiable.

Hours of Operation clause A retailer in a mall must be open during the
mall's posted hours, including extended hours during the Christmas holidays. An "early closing fee" or "late opening fee" (typically $25) is charged to
retailers who don't abide by the hours of operation set out in this clause.
Hours and fees are not negotiable.

Insurance Most specialty retail programs require tenants to have general liability insurance of at least $1 million, plus appropriate amounts of property, workers' compensation and disability insurance. Insurance requirements are not negotiable. (See "Insuring Your Business" on p. 161 for more about types of coverage.)

Late fees These are set fees the landlord charges if a tenant is late paying rent or any other fees/charges that are in the lease or license agreement. The amounts of these fees, which are usually not negotiable, vary from center to center. Generally speaking, however, they will accumulate until the outstanding payment is made. And in some cases, a payment that isn't received by a certain date can be considered a breach of contract or "default," and the tenant may be asked to leave the center.

Marketing fee See *Advertising fee*

Minimum rent See *Rent*

Penalties These are monetary penalties for violating lease/license terms range from fines and *late fees* to termination of the agreement. Often called "default provisions."

Percentage rent See *Rent*

Property Damage clause This clause makes the tenant liable for any damage to the property, within certain set limits. This is usually not negotiable.

Relocation clause The landlord can relocate the retailer's business if the landlord deems it necessary, usually without notice and at the retailer's expense. Typically, this is not negotiable for cart and kiosk tenants, but in-line tenants may be able to negotiate a longer notice period.

Rent In specialty retail, rent is often called "total rent" because in the majority of cases, rent is a combination of two factors: base rent and percentage rent. *Base rent* (sometimes called *minimum rent* or *fixed fee*) is the minimum fixed-dollar amount a landlord charges by the day, week, month or season. Percentage rent (sometimes called *overage rent*) is a percentage of the tenant's gross sales that exceed a pre-determined level, or the *breakpoint*, paid to the landlord in addition to base rent. Percentage rents vary by retail center, but for specialty retailers they generally range from 10-25 percent of gross sales above the breakpoint. Base and percentage rates are set by the landlord based on factors that include the going rates, the center's current vacancy rate, the individual retailer's profit potential, and the benefits the retailer can bring to the center, such as increased traffic, unique products or entertainment value. As a general rule, total rent for specialty retail locations selling a retail product (as opposed to a service) should equal no more than 15 to 18 percent of gross sales. Some retailers negotiate a low base rent in exchange for a higher percentage rate. Other retailers do the opposite. A few even pay high base rent in exchange for no percentage rent at all. What you decide to negotiate will depend on your financial circumstances, your long- and short-term goals, and mall management's desire to land you as a tenant.

Right of First Refusal clause This provision gives the tenant the first shot at renewing a lease or license on a space before anyone else gets a chance at it. More specifically, the tenant gets the "right to refuse" the use of current space before the landlord is permitted to offer that space to another prospective tenant. This clause is much more common in leases than in license agreements.

Reporting and Record-keeping clauses These spell out methods the center requires for your record-keeping, how frequently the tenant must report sales results to management (e.g., daily, weekly, or monthly), and how these figures are to be documented, usually with numbered sales receipts or non-resettable (i.e., includes *all* transactions made) cash-register receipts.

Santa Raises Rents!

Rent in the average mall during the Christmas crunch (November 1st to December 31st) can be three or four times the rent charged during the rest of the year. But the foot traffic during this period far exceeds the average for the rest of the year. Similar patterns apply to tourist locations: rents can double or triple during the peak season, the timing of which depends on that venue's geographic location and purpose (for example, summer in Cape Cod, winter in Palm Beach).

Security deposit The amount and other details about security deposits depend on the nature of the center. For specialty retailers in a typical mall, security is usually one month's rent, payable at the signing of the lease or license agreement. Security deposits are sometimes negotiable. If the tenant is in violation of any terms of the agreement (such as unpaid rent or vacating the premises before the termination date) at the end of the lease term, the landlord can keep the deposit. These and other specifics of the security deposit must be spelled out in the lease.

Termination clause The landlord can terminate the agreement after giving the retailer notice (typically 3 days).

Use clause This defines the "use" of the space in terms of the types of merchandise (or services) the tenant is approved to sell. This clause is intended to prevent conflicts among a center's tenants by clearly spelling out who's supposed to be selling what.

Utility Fees clause The center reserves the right to charge for the amount of electricity a tenant uses that's above a specified "normal" or "regular" level. That level should be specified in the agreement, so that you know at the start how much energy you can use without being billed for "overage." (This clause usually applies to leases rather than license agreements.)

Even though license agreements are less complicated than leases, it's still a good idea to have your attorney and accountant review any agreement you're thinking of signing, so they can point out potential pitfalls and answer your questions before you sign anything.

Pitching your concept

Some mega-malls get dozens of applications a month from specialty retail entrepreneurs, so you want to stand out when you make your pitch. The way to score points with a leasing manager is to provide as much information as you can about the strength of your concept plus your skills and experience in business—they want an entrepreneur with vision who will do what it takes to succeed. At the least, management will want you to provide:

- Your business plan

- Your visual merchandising plan (with sketches, if possible)

- Supporting information showing what makes your concept unique

- Product samples and/or quality color photos of your products

Product shots Obviously, product samples are better than product pictures because leasing managers can put their hands on the actual items. If you can't provide samples, send the highest quality photos possible. You may be able to get professional product photos from your suppliers or manufacturers at little or no cost. If not, and if you aren't experienced with taking "tabletop" product shots, hire a professional photographer who is. And be sure to label your photos appropriately (place a label on each photo identifying the date, place, what's in the picture, your store name, your name and contact information).

One other option: Digital photos sent by e-mail or on CD. If you send a photo CD, label it (store name, your name, etc.) and include a typed list of the photos and their corresponding file names. If your products are small or intricate, digital pictures may not be a good choice: The details may not come through if the leasing manager views the photos on screen, or doesn't have a good color printer handy for printing them.

Focusing your negotiations

Leasing managers want to attract and keep good specialty retailers, so don't underestimate your bargaining power. If you're not comfortable negotiating, lean on the support network you've built—your SCORE or SBA counselor, banker, attorney, real estate agent—to help you. In every negotiating situation, you have to clear these three key negotiating hurdles:

1. Learning and understanding the leasing manager's current priorities and concerns

2. Addressing them so you can emphasize the benefits you bring to the center

3. Knowing what's negotiable and what's not, so you can focus on getting the best *possible* deal. (See "Common lease/license terms" on p. 82 for more on what's usually negotiable.)

The last point may be the one that causes inexperienced entrepreneurs the most headaches. Trying to haggle over a non-negotiable item like insurance minimums not only makes you appear uninformed (which means you lose credibility and bargaining power); it also sidetracks you. If you're busy banging your head against a wall of stone-clad terms and conditions, you simply can't clear hurdles #1 and #2 and tailor your pitch accordingly.

You'll be dealing with a leasing manager whose job is to create a dynamic specialty retail program that attracts consumers to the center, keeps them shopping as long as possible, and generates the highest sales-per-square-foot possible. Managers give preference to entrepreneurs with retail experience. But new specialty retail entrepreneurs who clearly demonstrate how they can help a leasing manager achieve those goals can gain preference over other potential tenants, even experienced ones . . . and also get the best lease deals. So with preparation and perseverance, you can counter objections (such as being "unproven") and score a good lease deal.

Before you start haggling over anything, ask the leasing manager:

- What products or services does the center lack?

- Does my venture fit into/complement your current mix?

- What kinds of retail businesses or products would be on your "tenant wish list" for this center?

- What are your top three leasing goals?

- What are your top three leasing challenges?

- How does my venture address one or more of those goals or challenges?

For example, let's say you have a demonstration product, and you discover the leasing manager is trying to improve the center's reputation for offering "ho-hum" merchandise. Then stress how your product draws crowds and creates excitement. (But remember, leasing managers hear this a lot, so back it up!) Or suppose you're selling high-end products, and the leasing manager wants to capture market share from a new upscale center nearby. Then focus on your products' appeal to the target upscale consumer. Of course, if the leasing manager is struggling to fill vacancies, you're in a strong negotiating position no matter what your product. But be wary of deals that sound too good to be true. If you get the feeling the landlord's giving away the proverbial store, find out what's behind the generosity. Talk to at least three retailers in that center (and a few former retail tenants, if you can) before you sign. Ask them about sales (recent and over a time period, such as the past three years), foot traffic, tenant mix, the drawbacks/benefits of being there, and anything else they might be willing to share about that center.

Negotiating the rent Sometimes you can negotiate a low (or zero) minimum rent in exchange for a high percentage rent, or a high minimum rent in exchange for a higher breakpoint/lower percentage. You and your accountant can crunch the numbers to see which rent structure works best for you, but remember: percentage rent, which fluctuates with your sales, is harder to budget than base rent, which is fixed. If you can, negotiate a cap on your percentage rent.

You may also be able to negotiate other perks, such as a rent-free "fixturing" period—a set length of time to build out your space and get it ready for opening day; or "tenant inducements" such as free or heavily discounted materials (carpeting, shelving, partitioning, etc.).

 Start-up Tip

If you're negotiating your first lease with a national developer and you hope to expand into other properties in their portfolio, negotiate it with care and a nod to the future. How you negotiate now may set the tone for future lease negotiations with that developer for many years to come.

Negotiating do's and don'ts

Although you may use different negotiating approaches with different leasing managers, these basics of effective negotiating always apply, and always work to your advantage:

Do's

- Analyze the center's strengths and weaknesses as they pertain to your venture.

- Emphasize the benefits your presence brings to the center.

- Discuss your plans for growth.

- Talk to other retailers and center management to check your assumptions.

- Allow enough time for your attorney's review.

- Summarize your understanding of terms and conditions at the appropriate points.

- Submit your operating and visual merchandising plans before you sign the lease.

- Demonstrate excellent bookkeeping and organizational skills.

- Use clear, direct and simple language.

- Show a professional attitude at all times. And be polite.

- Display your commitment to success.

Don'ts

- Don't let management dictate all terms and conditions. (Remember, you need to negotiate what's negotiable!)

- Don't read the agreement (or any contract) in a hurry.

- Don't try to make someone look bad or prove someone wrong at the negotiating table.

- Don't judge your lease/license entirely on rent numbers. (Remember those fees!)

- Don't verbally agree to modifications in the lease without getting it in writing first.

- Don't get "stuck" on the location if the lease terms aren't favorable—look for another location.

- Don't negotiate before you're ready—get the information you need before you sit down at the negotiating table.

- Don't assume management defines terms the way you do. If you have any doubts, have definitions included in the agreement.

- Don't lose your cool if negotiations aren't going your way.

- Don't rush your decision.

- Don't sign anything before your attorney reviews it.

And finally, don't act as if the space is "yours" before you actually and legally have it. You never know: it could get scooped up by someone who's willing to pay more or commit to a longer term before your lease or license agreement is signed and finalized. In other words, don't go buying custom fixtures until your lease or license agreement is signed by both sides.

□ □ □

Creating a Solid Business Plan

B uilders have construction plans. Interior designers have décor plans. And entrepreneurs have business plans.

A business plan can be critical to the success of your business, even if you don't have to produce one to secure start-up financing from outside sources or lease space in a high-traffic mall (many of which now require business plans). But that's not all a business plan will do. It will help you:

- clarify your goals

- discover weaknesses or strengths in your business concept you may not have considered

- anticipate difficulties and identify new opportunities

- avoid being undercapitalized

- easily see if you're meeting your financial goals later on

- develop effective strategies for managing your start-up and future growth

Your plan can be an invaluable resource for years to come, especially since you'll modify it as your business expands and grows. Anytime you look for financing, lenders and investors will ask to see your business plan. It will illustrate that you've taken the time to thoroughly study your market and develop clear, realistic business goals and viable ways to reach them—and make a profit. Your business plan shows that you're in control of your venture, and that lending to your business is a wise investment. Lenders and investors see countless proposals, so while your business plan may be a labor of love and vision to you, to lenders it's just one of many. So yours has to be thorough and well written—otherwise, it won't survive a first reading.

Pre-writing

Many people find the thought of writing a business plan to be intimidating, partly because it involves a great deal of thinking things through, and then writing it so that it covers all the bases adequately and accurately. But good news: the information you need to write a great plan is at your fingertips. For example, if you aren't sure what your marketing strategy is, take another look at the notes you made for "Finding the Right Product," "Finding the Right Location" and "Marketing Your Business." The questions in those chapters are designed to help you zero in on an effective marketing strategy (among other things). If your answers have enough detail and are based on reliable information, all you really have to do is turn the thoughts and opinions in your notes into well-written sentences for your business plan.

But, before you write a word, go to the library or online for at least a few samples of business plans you can study for depth of information and writing style, tone, etc. You can easily find at least a dozen retail-oriented plans online. You should also consult your accountant and lawyer during the research and writing process. Because your business plan will include extensive financial and legal information, they'll be invaluable in helping you make sure you include everything you need, including documentation.

Be prepared to buckle down: it takes more than an afternoon to develop a solid business plan. You need to include information about your products, operations, marketing strategies, the legal aspects of your business, and financials—both business and personal—for a complete picture of your financial standing.

Outlining your business plan

If you ask 10 professionals how to write a business plan, you'll get 10 variations on the order it should be in. But the essential *content* elements will always the same. Having the right information in your plan is much more important than what page it's on (plus, you'll have a Table of Contents to help the reader find it).

Most business plans have three main sections: a description of the business, the marketing strategy, and the financials. In addition, your plan will also have a cover page, a title page, a management plan, and an executive summary. This is the order in which these components typically appear, followed by a description of each one:

- Cover page

- Title page

- Table of Contents

- Executive Summary

- Business Description

- Marketing Strategy

- Management Plan

- Financials

- Appendices

Cover page The cover page starts with the title—*Your Company Name's Business Plan*—followed by your name, your business name (again), business address, and contact information (phone, fax, e-mail, etc.) further down the page. If you have a logo and/or marketing slogans (tag lines), put them on the cover page, too.

Title page The title page repeats the information on the cover page, plus the names and contact information for all of the other owners or investors, the date the plan was completed, and the time period it covers (e.g., one-year start-up plan, five-year plan, etc.).

Table of Contents You know what this is—but here's one caution: after you print the final version, cross-check each page number listed there to make sure the pages didn't shift when you made final edits to the text.

Executive Summary The executive summary, sometimes called a "Statement of Purpose," summarizes the business plan in one page. The summary is extremely important: it's the first item lenders look for because they use it to decide if they want to keep reading. As with the rest of your plan, the summary should be clearly written and businesslike, and include brief descriptions of:

- your business concept

- the reasons you believe your venture will succeed

- the legal structure of the business

If you're seeking a loan, the summary should also include:

- the amount and purpose of your loan request

- how and when you will repay the loan

- what you're offering as collateral

- how the loan will help your business succeed

Business Description This section of your plan provides a detailed description of your products and business concept, including:

- your business goals (financial and otherwise)

- how and why you believe your business will succeed

- the skills and experience you bring to the business

- the overall strengths of your industry

- the strengths of the specific market you plan to tap

- trends that are likely to contribute to your financial success

- the marketing methods you'll use show the unique nature of your business or products give you a competitive advantage

This section also has details about your location, including:

- the reasons you chose this location

- how the space will meet your needs

- the cost to improve the space

- the location's hours of operation

- the equipment you need to purchase to create a fully functioning retail presence

- the trade area and regional market data that point to your location's potential

- neighboring competition you expect to encounter, and the methods you'll use to minimize the competition's effects

- the terms and length of your lease or license agreement

And finally, you have to state and document that you have (or will soon have):

- the necessary business licenses and permits

- the necessary insurance, including types and amounts of coverage

- a description of the legal structure of your business

Marketing Strategy This section has two parts: a marketing analysis and a competitive analysis. It's a good place to include your market/competition statistics and research (and the sources of your data).

In the *marketing analysis* part, go into detail about:

- your customers/target market

- the growth prospects for your market

- the percentage of the market you plan to capture

- the distribution and inventory-management systems you'll use, plus associated costs

- your pricing strategies

- the advertising, promotional and customer-service programs you plan to implement

If your new business is a turnkey program (see p. 28) explain the areas of support the company provides (e.g., advertising, training, etc.) and how each of them will help you capture your target market.

In the *competitive analysis* part, go into detail about your competition:

- identify direct and indirect competitors

- show how your products and/or services differ from theirs

- analyze your competitors' strengths and weaknesses

- explain how you can capture market share despite the competition, or due to the competition's weaknesses

Management Plan In this section, describe how the company will be run on a day-to-day basis, including:

- the number and type of employees (part- or full-time) you plan to hire

- the business-oriented profiles of key people (you, your partners and managers), highlighting their education, skills and experience

- the duties and responsibilities of key people and staff, including the qualifications needed for each key job and how your team meets or exceeds those qualifications

- any obvious management weaknesses, and your strategies for addressing those issues

- your hiring policies, training program, and any employee

benefits you plan to offer (now or in the future) to attract and keep experienced talent

■ details about the professionals who provide you with supporting services—your accountant, attorney, banker, SCORE counselor, etc.

If you're opening a turnkey business, fully describe the management or training support the company provides.

Financials The estimates and other financial data you prepare for this section will clearly indicate your venture's ability to succeed—or not. Now isn't the time to go it alone: enlist the help of your accountant, especially if you're not accustomed to reading (and understanding) financial statements, developing budget projections and the like. Experienced lenders and others who review your plan can tell the difference between your "guesstimates" and the realistic, concrete estimates your accountant develops. (In fact, don't be surprised if a lender turns to your financial section first.) The strength, clarity and accuracy of this section can mean the difference between a yes and no loan decision. (For more about loans, see p. 112 in Chapter 6, "Finding Start up Capital.")

The financial section of your plan has two parts: a narrative explanation of certain financial aspects of your business, and complete financial documents. In the *narrative explanation*, go into detail about:

■ the sources and amounts of start-up financing you have secured (collateral, equity capital, partners, etc.)

■ the methods of compensation for yourself, key people, and staff

■ the break-even point, and how you established it by using realistic sales projections

■ your personal financial status (loan-repayment history, current assets and liabilities, etc.)

- a lender's expected return on investment

- a confirmation of your commitment to repay all loans

- your financial contingency plan if sales are not realized as anticipated

In the *financial documents* part, you need to include three basic documents: your balance sheet, income statement, and cash flow statement.

Your *balance sheet* is a snapshot of your business's health: assets, liabilities, and net worth (assets minus liabilities) on a given day. Your *income statement* (also called a profit and loss or P&L statement, earnings report, and operating statement) details your projected revenues and expenses for a specified time period. (You'll replace those projections with actual figures after you open your doors.) Your *cash flow statement* indicates how cash flows in and out of your business: cash in from selling goods (or receiving financing), and cash out for expenses (or investments) required to operate and grow. Although these financial documents aren't particularly complicated, your accountant can be invaluable in calculating the true value of an asset or liability, or correctly classifying an expense.

Free forms online You can find many of the financial documents mentioned on the following pages online. Many Web sites offer free forms, and some offer low-cost access to thousands of legal, financial and other forms (a search for "free downloadable forms" google.com brought up more than 3,600 results). You can also go directly to office-supply sites such as officedepot.com and download or print free forms, or order forms at low cost. Also, the Web sites of many trade associations and trade publications have free forms for their members or subscribers. In addition, some of the software that's pre-installed on computers (such as the ubiquitous Microsoft Word) can generate a variety of forms, so take a look: you may already have many of the forms you need.

Appendices A business plan usually has more than one appendix. Typically there's a separate appendix for each of the following: résumés of the owners and managers, personal financial statements for all of the owners and partners, letters of reference, letters of intent from potential suppliers, copies of the lease or license agreement, proof of all permits and licenses, and any other relevant legal documents, any drawings or schematics, research sources, and the like.

Append it!

Market-research data can make a business plan more interesting and convincing—or it can be very distracting and get in the way of readability. If you want to include lengthy market analyses or complicated statistics, put them into an appendix rather than forcing them into the body of your business plan. Just remember to refer to the right appendix.

Getting local assistance

Several organizations offer information and assistance with writing a business plan. Call or visit the local branches of any of these, or visit their Web sites:

Small Business Development Centers (SBDCs) The Small Business Administration (SBA) administers these centers, which offer assistance at branch locations in every state and online. With a network of almost 1,000 sub-centers and satellite locations, SBDCs tap the talents of full- and part-time staff members, volunteers and consultants who have expertise in a variety of fields such as retail, law, banking, marketing, and even highly specialized fields such as engineering and product testing. Some SBDC staffers have years of experience with professional and trade associations. To find an SBDC in your area, call the SBA (800.8.ASK.SBA) or go online (sba.gov/hotlist/sbdc.html).

The Service Corps of Retired Executives (SCORE) This is a not-for-profit association of volunteers—retired business people who share their knowledge and experience with aspiring entrepreneurs. A resource partner with the SBA, SCORE has almost 400 chapters nationwide that offer free counseling and low-cost workshops. To find an office in your area, call SCORE (800.534.0245) or go online (score.org).

Business Information Centers (BICs) These centers work with SCORE volunteers and the SBA to provide valuable business-related resources to entrepreneurs. With locations in every state, BICs offer computer hardware and software, training videos and seminars, market-research databases, libraries of resource materials, and counseling. To learn more about BICs or to find one in your area, call the SBA or go online (sba.gov/bi/bics/bicfact-sheet.html).

Using business-plan software

If you're not comfortable with your writing skills or you just want to speed up the process, it's worth looking into business-plan software. For $50 to $150, you can buy a software package that guides you through the process of writing a business plan. Generally speaking, the more expensive the package, the more features you get. The better packages (at around $100) usually include dozens (sometimes hundreds) of sample business plans, outlines, templates (you just fill in your specific information), "wizard" functions that suggest wording to use, examples of tables plus instructions, and automatic chart and graph capabilities.

These software packages are available in most office-supply stores, computer supply stores, and online, either to order from a supplier's site or to download. Some packages are available as a free demo, either online or on a trial CD the supplier will mail you. But shop around for prices. Because of the way the software industry is structured, you often get a better price if you buy from a secondary source, either an office- or computer-supply store or an online retailer, rather than directly from the manufacturer. In any event, check out one or several of these software packages:

- Business Plan Pro 2002, or Business Plan Pro 2001, Canadian version (Palo Alto Software, Inc.; 800.229.7526; paloalto.com)

- Business Plan Toolkit 7.0 for Mac (Palo Alto Software, Inc.; 800.229.7526; paloalto.com)

- Ultimate Business Planner (Atlas Business Solutions, Inc.; 800.874.8801; abs-usa.com)

- My Business Plan Starter (MySoftware; sold through thousands of physical and online office- and computer-supply stores)

- Officeready Business Plans (Canon; sold through thousands of physical and online office- and computer-supply stores)

- PlanWrite Business Plan Writer Deluxe (Nova Development; 818.591.9600; novadevelopment.com)

Packaging your business plan

At last! You've done the research, the number-crunching, the writing—and now you have a plan! One more step, though: the packaging. Your business plan has to look professional: it has to look like it means business. So it has to be carefully formatted and flawlessly typed. It should be on premium $8^1/_2$ x 11 white or off-white paper with a smooth finish, printed on a very good printer—your own (preferably laser) or a print shop's. And finally, it should go into an attractive, quality binder with your company name on the front and spine, with labeled tab sheets inside to separate the different sections. Packaging your business plan this way adds to your credibility. And *that* helps insure your future as a specialty retailer.

□ □ □

Finding Start-Up Capital

It comes down to money. Even if you choose the hottest products, secure the highest-traffic location, make a 24/7 commitment and work countless hours, your dream will fall apart if you don't have sufficient capital to start *and sustain* your enterprise.

In this chapter are resources for debt-based financing (such as loans, credit cards) and equity-based financing (such as venture capital, partnerships). Each financing strategy has benefits and drawbacks. You need to carefully examine most if not all of them with the help of experienced financial professionals. Sources of help and information include your accountant and lawyer, government agencies, lending institutions, private organizations, and other entrepreneurs. In particular, lean on your accountant and lawyer, the people who are most familiar with your financial circumstances, your short- and long-term goals, and your tolerance for risk.

When it comes to tax laws, interest rates, credit cards, retirement and insurance laws and many other complicated factors that will influence your start-up financing options, you can count on one thing: *change*. Never assume that what was true six months ago or even six weeks ago is true now. While it's important to have trustworthy sources of information in print and online, it's equally important to go to the experts for accurate, up-to-date information *as it applies to you*. (Remember, if you don't have experts yet, *now* is the time to cultivate those relationships, not after you open.) Their advice helps ensure that your understanding and assumptions are correct *before* you take any action that will affect your business and your finances for years to come.

Start-Up Costs Worksheet

Use this sheet to estimate your start-up expenses.

Advertising/Promotion	$_____		Graphic design (logo, other graphics)	$_____
Books, trade magazine subscriptions	$_____		Dues (trade/merchant associations)	$_____
Car expenses; travel	$_____		Hiring/Training (e.g., ads, search firm, verification)	$_____
Deposits, set-up fees:				
Bank account set-up	$_____		Insurance	$_____
Credit-card merchant account set-up	$_____		Inventory	$_____
Lease deposits/ advance rents	$_____		Payroll	$_____
Utilities deposits/ phone, electric	$_____		Supplies:	
Equipment:			Bags	$_____
Cash register/POS system	$_____		Cash for cash register	$_____
Computer, file cabinet, etc	$_____		Cash for petty cash	$_____
Phones	$_____		Postage	$_____
Safe	$_____		Printing (e.g., business cards, brochures, flyers, etc.)	$_____
Signs	$_____		Other _____	$_____
Visual merchandising: Fixtures, props, fabric, etc.			Other _____	$_____
			Other _____	$_____
Installation	$_____		Other _____	$_____
VM Designer fees	$_____			
Fees:				
Accounting	$_____		**Sub-total**	$_____
Legal	$_____		Unexpected expenses: 10% of sub-total	+ $_____
Licenses, permits	$_____		**Total start-up expenses**	$_____

Being "undercapitalized"—not having enough money to open and run your business—is a sure route to a failed start-up. So even if you have enough cash to pay for your starting inventory and other major start-up expenses, the big question is: Do you have enough capital or *access* to enough capital, to sustain your business through the first year or, if you're a seasonal retailer, for the first season?

If you crunch the numbers and the answer is no, you're undercapitalized, so stop right there: you have to find an infusion of the additional cash you need (or access to it) before going any further with your start-up. In fact, even if you think you have enough, entrepreneurs often underestimate expenses and overestimate sales. When experts list the top ten reasons businesses fail, "lack of capital" routinely ranks in the top five. Fluctuations in consumer buying patterns hit under-capitalized retailers harder than those with enough money to weather shifts in the market. So it's worthwhile to have a backup plan. Well-capitalized retailers can take advantage of these shifts and emerge with even stronger businesses.

Cash crunch

According to the SBA, half of all failed small businesses owe money to creditors after the businesses closed.

Tapping personal assets

The most common way to finance your start-up is by using personal assets. And the easiest and most obvious source of cash is your personal savings.

You may have assets you can borrow against: a 401(k) or other retirement plan, life insurance, stocks and bonds or home equity. In addition, you may have personal property (such as jewelry, antiques or other valuables), stocks, bonds or real estate you can sell outright (including your house—it's been done!).

Personal property

If you're willing, you can sell some of your personal property and/or real estate to increase your pool of start-up capital. From yard sales to online auctions, you can raise funds by selling:

- art, collectibles, antiques

- jewelry, sterling flatware, other valuables

- furniture items

- "fun" car or motorcycle sitting in the garage

- the garage itself (along with your house)

- your vacation home or time-share unit

Make a list of your personal assets and note the fair market value and *collateral* value of each one to secure a loan (see p. 116). Are there assets you can live without and would be better invested in your new store? If you're having trouble putting a value on them, ask your accountant or local lender to help you analyze the numbers.

You can also consider downsizing: trading that costly, high-maintenance import car or big SUV for a more economical model; or selling your current home and buying a smaller one.

Home security It's an extreme move, but if you *are* considering selling your home to raise start-up capital, proceed carefully. The key question is how much net profit will actually land in your pocket. Your house may actually be more valuable if you hang on to it and use it as *collateral* for a long-term commercial loan. (For more about commercial loans, see p. 119.)

Paper into cash It can be worthwhile to convert investments in stocks, bonds and other securities into cash. You can do this by selling them out-right, or borrowing against them in certain circumstances. Check with your accountant to review your options.

Home equity You may be able to finance your venture through a home-equity loan (second mortgage), either as a lump sum or a line of credit. Home equity is the difference between how much your home is worth on the market (current market value) minus what you still owe on it. Most home-equity loans equal a percentage of the equity, typically 50 percent to 80 percent. Unlike commercial loans, they're are easier to get because the lenders are less concerned about the viability of your business—they have your house as security. The length (or "maturity") of these loans can be 5, 10, 15 or even 30 years. Interest rates, which fluctuate with the financial and housing markets, are usually low (2-3 percent over prime) because the loan is secured by real estate. As with your first mortgage, there are likely to be closing costs. (Find out how much in advance, and keep an eye out for hidden fees.)

The big benefit: on home-equity loans, your loan interest payments may be *tax-deductible*, just like your first mortgage. Check with your accountant first to make sure you structure the loan such that the interest is tax-deductible. The downside, of course, is that you're putting your house on the line. Again, get solid advice from your accountant first.

Shop around
Shop for the lowest possible interest rates. Hundreds of home-equity companies are online. Some, like The Lending Tree (thelendingtree.com) provide online quotes from multiple lenders.

Life insurance loan

You may be able to borrow against your life insurance if it's not a "term life" policy. (Term life insurance, which is cheaper than "ordinary life," has no value other than paying death benefits.) "Ordinary life" policies—whole life, variable life, universal life—build up cash value over time: a certain percentage of each premium payment is set aside as cash value. You can borrow against a portion your accumulated cash value (though not 100 percent of it); the percentage depends on the policy you have. However, borrowing against your life insurance could result in a premium increase. Check with your insurance agent about loan limits and payback structures before you sign the loan papers.

The downside: You may be compromising your family's financial security after you're gone. Any outstanding loan amount will be deducted from the face-value benefit that goes to your beneficiary.

401(k) loan

If you plan to start your business while you're a full-time employee and you're a member of your employer's 401(k) retirement plan, you may be able to borrow from that plan, up to 50 percent of the vested portion of your current 401(k) account balance (ask your account administrator to explain your plan's vesting rules).

The maximum 401(k) loan is $50,000 for up to five years. Since you're really borrowing from yourself, there's little paperwork but you may have to pay an application fee (usually $100 or less). You may also have to pay a small monthly or yearly maintenance fee. Interest rates are usually one or two points above the prime rate, published in *The Wall St. Journal.* That's a better deal than you might get on a conventional bank loan. Most 401(k) plans make you pay it back in monthly installments or through automatic payroll deductions.

On the downside: You're putting your retirement funds in jeopardy. And because your 401(k) plan is designed to defer federal income taxes on your contributions as long as they're in the plan, borrowing has several drawbacks:

- Investment considerations: Depending on how you invested your 401(k) money, you might be taking your money out of high-earnings investments and putting it into a low-interest loan to yourself.

- Tax consequence #1: You'll pay back the loan with *after*-tax dollars, which means the cost of the loan is even greater. If you're in the 28 percent tax bracket, for example, it will take $1.39 to pay back every $1 you borrowed from the plan. And you pay tax on that 401(k) money *again* when you withdraw it at retirement.

- Tax consequence #2: If you don't pay back a 401(k) loan plus interest within five years, the outstanding loan balance will be treated as a pay-out ("distribution"), which is taxed as income. And if you're younger than $59^{1/2}$ when that happens, you may also be hit with a 10 percent early-withdrawal penalty.

- Pay on demand: If your 401(k) is with your employer and you leave your job before you pay back the loan, the plan may require you to repay the entire outstanding loan in as little as 30 or 60 days. If you can't, the outstanding balance will be treated as a distribution and the early-withdrawal penalty may kick in. Again, check with your 401(k) plan administrator to find out about your plan's loan terms.

Some banks now offer 401(k) credit cards that allow plan members to charge as much as 40 percent of their vested account balances, up to $100,000. The interest rate equals the prime rate, and the bank gets a monthly fee of three to four percent of the outstanding loan balance (which is how the bank makes its money). To find one of these banks, search online for "401(k) credit card," or ask your accountant, local lender or your employer's 401(k) plan administrator.

IRA withdrawal If you have an Individual Retirement Account (IRA), you may be able to withdraw (not *borrow*) from your account, but only for 60 days. And the money you withdraw is tax-free and penalty-free—until day 61. Any of that money that's not back in your IRA by then is considered a distribution, which means it's subject to tax and penalties. Even though it's short term, the good news is that because it's not a loan, you don't pay interest. Contact your IRA administrator or financial advisor for an explanation of your options.

Attracting "love money"

If you're lucky, friends and family will kick in some "love money" to help you get your new business off the ground. Love money can be great. Family and friends may not charge you interest (or a very low rate). And if you have trouble with a payment or two, the people who love you are likely to be much more patient and understanding than the bank, and won't charge you a late fee like your credit cards will. And, sometimes, even a small amount of love money is all you need to get that bank loan or initial inventory shipment.

Love money can also cause problems. If you're planning on borrowing from friends and family, be sure to outline your plans in detail for them, and put all final loan arrangements in writing. Spell out the terms and anticipated return on the loan, as well as the conditions of default. Most friends and family are willing to kiss their money goodbye if your venture doesn't succeed; if that's the case, make sure you have that in writing. If the love money is a gift, make sure that's on paper, too. Putting love-money loans on paper might seem awkward and inappropriately formal when it comes to your friends and family, but in the long run you'll find doing so will make everyone feel more comfortable.

Let me count the ways

Love money can be nice, but a co-signer on a bank loan may be nicer. Before you ask a family member or friend to co-sign, though, ask your accountant to review all of your options with you.

The downsides: A loan from family or friends can put a strain on your relationships. One common effect is that even as you re-pay the loan on time, you feel a sense of indebtedness (after all, you *are* indebted) until it's paid off. Even more common (and troublesome): the people lending you money feel they now "own" a piece of your business and have the right to influence or even control your business decisions. Make sure everyone involved is clear about the conditions of the loan, legally *and* personally.

Using credit cards

You can take one of three basic routes for using your credit cards for start-up capital: charge on the credit card(s) you have; get one or more new cards with lower rates (or a low introductory rate); get a cash advance from current or new cards.

Cards you have Using a credit card you already have is your most straight-forward option. It gives you an immediate interest-free loan for up to 30 days, depending on the card—without putting up collateral, and without filling out any loan papers. Of course, on day 31 (or the first day after your card's billing/grace period—read the fine print!), you'll be charged interest ("finance charges") on any portion of the balance you haven't paid by that date.

But before you start charging start-up expenses, call the credit card company to negotiate the best possible rate, even if you plan to pay off the balance in time. That way, if you decide you can't make a full payment, you'll have a lower rate. While you're on the phone with them, negotiate a better cash-advance rate, too, so that if you do need it, you'll have the best rate lined up.

To the max
By law, the highest interest rate a credit card company can currently charge is 24.9 percent.

New cards You may also want to get a new credit card (or more than one) that offers a low "teaser" rate for an introductory period, usually six months. Some card companies offering rates as low as zero, but only for a very short time. After the introductory period, rates typically skyrocket, and can even go higher than the rates on your existing cards.

Points and perks
If you apply for a new credit card, get one that rewards you for using it. Look for a card that gives you points to redeem for free (merchandise, services, or frequent-flyer miles) or various discounts—whatever you think you'd use the most.

Banks offer a variety of *business* credit cards, many of which also have low introductory rates. These cards also offer various services, such as access to lines of credit, online account management, quarterly usage reports, and discounts on business products or services (supplies, shipping, travel, insurance, phone rates, etc.). Some business cards go even further, offering phone or e-mail access to a network of business experts who are available to answer all kinds of small-business-related questions. For example, CitiBank's CitiBusiness Card (800.750.7453; citibusiness.citibank.com) comes with access to The CitiBusiness Resource network. A lot of other cards are out there: to find out more about them, call your lender or search online.

If you do get a card with a low introductory rate, read the rules so you understand the downside of not paying off the balance within the introductory period. And make a big red notation on your calendar at least two weeks before the date the intro rate expires, so that you won't miss it.

Cost of a cash advance

If you take a cash advance, you'll pay a hefty interest rate, typically 18 percent or more. Interest starts the moment you get the cash, so even if you repay the entire amount with the first bill, you'll still pay interest based on the number of days you have the advance—that is, before your payment is posted. In addition there may be fees. For every credit-card check you write (to yourself as a cash advance or to pay someone else), you might have to pay the greater of a percentage of the amount of the check up to a maximum (like $50), or a flat $2-$5. And when you use an ATM, you may be paying ATM fees that can add up to several dollars per hit.

Getting trade credit

Trade credit is a certain period of time your suppliers give you to pay for an order. It's similar to charging your credit card, except that it's a supplier instead of a bank. Suppliers offer trade credit for 30, 60 and sometimes 90 days, depending on the size of the retailer's typical order, payment history, credit rating and the like.

Admittedly, it's likely to be difficult to get trade credit for even 30 days during start-up. But suppliers often make these decisions on a case-by-case basis, so it's worth calling to find out what their credit guidelines are, and perhaps make a case if you don't quite fit them yet. (For more about trade credit and how to get it sooner rather than later, see p. 47 in Chapter 3, "Buying from Suppliers.")

Securing commercial and government loans

Commercial and government lenders sometimes complain that first-time entrepreneurs are poorly prepared for the rigors of borrowing: that they lack a basic understanding of how the system works. It's crucial to have all your financial ducks in a row when you look for loan money from banks or the government. If you're prepared and organized, if you're armed with in-depth financial information and a well-thought-out business plan, you'll greatly improve your chances of getting financing from any source, whether it's a national bank, Uncle Sam, or even Uncle Bernie.

Professional help Not familiar with the choppy waters of commercial or government lending? Call your accountant. The fastest way to get turned down is to apply for a loan without getting advice from experienced financial professionals first. You need to involve the right people who understand your business plan and your market before you ask a lender for a dime. Search online and in business magazines for articles about borrowing. Meet with your local banker to ask preliminary questions before you ask for money. Find other entrepreneurs to see how they secured financing during their start-ups.

Or turn to Uncle Sam The SBA offers financial-advice services, plus educational programs for new business owners through a variety of organizations and funded in part by the SBA, including the Service Corps of Retired Executives (SCORE) and Small Business Development Centers (SBDCs) in every state. These organizations don't lend money directly, but they're in constant contact with lenders, and can help you find the right type of lender for your venture. To find SCORE in your area, call 800.634.0245, or go online (score.org). To find an SBDC in your area, look the blue pages of the phone book under "U.S. Government", or call the Small Business Answer Desk (800.8.ASK.SBA), or go online (sba.gov; for a list of SBDCs that have their own Web sites, go to sba.gov/hotlist/sbdc.html).

> ### On your team
> If you let a lender know that you're working closely with a team of advisers, the lender will feel more comfortable making the loan. Don't hesitate to bring one or more members of your team of advisers with you when you meet with a lender. Having your financial pro with you to explain the sometimes complicated details can help in a number of ways.

Credit report and FICO score

Before you look for a loan from banks or investors, get a copy of your credit report and your FICO score. Your FICO score is a number that lenders use to decide how credit-worthy you are. "FICO" stands for Fair, Isaac and Company, the credit-research firm that devised the credit-scoring system now used by more than 75 percent of institutional and conventional lenders to evaluate risk.

Until recently, your FICO score was a "secret." Few if any lenders revealed the number to loan applicants or explain how the score was calculated. A FICO score is a number between 300 and 850. The lower the score, the higher the credit risk, and the less likely you are to get a loan or one with the best rates. According to The Lending Universe (lendinguniverse.com), here's a general breakdown of FICO scores and corresponding credit ratings (A through D-):

- 620 or higher: A rating

- 581-619: B+ to B- rating

- 551-580: C+ to C- rating

- 550 or lower: D+ to D- rating

According to The Lending Universe, some lenders assign different letter grades or different definitions based on their own method of evaluation. In fact, TransUnion and Experian, two of the three largest credit-reporting agencies (see p. 115), currently use their own systems. In any case, while your credit report and score may vary from company to company, your score will likely suffer if any of these occurs:

- You've had payment delinquencies or collections filed
  against you. (The more recent they are, the more your
  score will drop.)

- Your balances are too high in proportion to your credit
  limits on your credit cards. (In other words, you've used
  too much of your available credit.)

- You have too many new accounts, or too many accounts
  with unpaid balances.

A credit report with FICO (or similar) score currently costs $12.95 or less, depending on your state and the credit-reporting agency. (And it's free if you're turned down for any type of loan, including credit cards.) The three main credit reporting agencies are Equifax (800.685.1111; equifax.com); Experian (888.397.3742; experian.com); and TransUnion (800.226.6214; tuc.com).

You can also order your credit report *free* from Web sites that offer them as part of a "trial demo" of their service. One of these sites is consumerinfo.com; you can find others by searching online. They hope you'll see an error or two on the report, get it corrected, and then re-order your report to make sure it's been updated. When you do, you'll either pay their credit-report fee or subscribe to a service that lets you check your credit report for a year.

"The six Cs of credit"

The best thing you can do when you want a loan is put yourself in the lender's shoes. You need to understand the loan officer's key concerns, address those concerns with confidence, and convince the lender you are committed to repayment. To help you get inside your lender's head, here are "The Six Cs of Credit" that all lenders look at when analyzing a loan application.

1. Character A subjective measurement to be sure, this is about you. Based on your credit history and other financial information, "character" is about how the lender sees your commitment to repay debts, your dedication to your retail business' success, and (here's where it really gets subjective!) your sense of moral obligation to repay the loan.

2. Capacity to pay This is based primarily on the lender's analysis of your financial statements, both personal and business. Your cash flow estimates and other financial documents in your business plan will weigh heavily in this category.

3. Capital Lenders pay close attention to your "debt-to-equity ratio" (in simplest terms, how much you owe vs. how much equity you have), to determine if your business has enough capital to pay outstanding debts. Generally speaking, lenders want debt-to-equity ratios of between 1:2

and 1:1. A lower ratio (the thinking goes) means the business may not be able to weather downturns or raise new capital for growth.

4. Collateral Assets that a borrower pledges to a lender against loan default are "loan collateral." Loans made without collateral—"unsecured loans" are rarely made to small businesses. How much collateral you need depends on the loan and the lender. In general, though, the closer the collateral amount is to the loan amount, the better. The value of your collateral to the lender isn't necessarily its appraised value or original cost—in most cases, it's quite a bit less. But if you have recent appraisals handy, it couldn't hurt to show them to your lender.

5. Conditions This means the economic conditions of the retail industry, as well as general economic data, both nationwide and regional for your area. The more data you can give the lender to show favorable conditions for your business or product, the better.

6. Confidence The level of confidence your lender has in your ability to repay the loan will depend on a number of factors. The most important is your professional demeanor. Your lender will have increasingly high levels of confidence in you if your loan application is well-prepared and organized . . . if you have a reputation for honesty and a good credit history . . . and if your cash flow estimates are reasonable and your business plan is sound (this one may be the biggest factor of all). Successful borrowers take every opportunity to instill confidence in lenders every step of the way.

> ### Be prepared
> *Whenever you ask someone for money, be prepared with all of the necessary documentation—and wear a suit.*

Rules of the loan game

Entrepreneurs who are new to the loan game often get a "no" when the answer could have been a "yes" simply because they ignored one or more of the basic rules. Here are the do's and don'ts so that you won't make the same mistakes:

The do's:

Make realistic projections. Feel free to view your new business through a rosy filter as you fall asleep at night . . . but when you're preparing a loan proposal, you have to look at your business as objectively as possible. Lenders are fluent in the language of financial statements, and they'll examine all the projections you've made very carefully. Overly optimistic estimates the lender *notices* will count against your credibility. The ones the lender *doesn't* notice can be even worse: they can come back to bite you later—for example, if you can't make loan payments because sales didn't come in as estimated.

Keep the focus on financials. Lenders will be interested in the fact that your retail concept is viable and that you plan to give shoppers a unique (or at least satisfying) experience. But the fact is, what really interests lenders are your ability to repay the loan, and the interest they make on it. So be prepared to answer a lender's bottom-line questions: Why is the loan good for your business? Why do you need this money/what are your other funding sources? How will you use the money? How will you repay the loan? When? If you stay focused on answering these questions as you prepare, you'll be able to answer them when the lender asks you, and your credibility will skyrocket.

Cross-reference your numbers. The documents you submit for a loan must be consistent. For example, if the figure for estimated sales appears in more than one financial document, the figure should be the same in each instance. At the very least, inconsistent numbers reflect poor bookkeeping skills—not a good sign to someone considering lending you money. To be sure the numbers match, cross-reference all of the documents you submit.

Leave enough time for approval. There's no sense cutting it close when it comes to your financing. After you submit the paperwork for applying for a loan (which will take more time and effort than you might think), allow 60 to 90 days for processing (SBA loans can take less time). Lenders often declare a loan application "complete," only to ask for more information later, and that can delay approval. So rather than waiting for the lender to call you, check in periodically to see if they need additional information.

The don'ts:

Don't expect to borrow 100 percent. No lender is going to give you 100 percent of the money you need to finance your venture. Generally, lenders expect you to put up 25-50 percent of your start-up funds. For collateral-based loans, each lender has its own definition of acceptable collateral. Be aware of the lender's general loan requirements *before* you turn in your loan application (just ask!).

Don't list a big salary for yourself. Lenders don't like financing what they consider to be your personal lifestyle while you're starting a business. For that reason, they look less favorably on loans that include big owner salaries. If possible, leave salaries out of your business plan and loan proposal entirely. If you can find another way to pay your living expenses while you get your new business off the ground, you'll be much more likely to get the loan.

Don't borrow more (or less) than you need. If you're thinking you need $20,000 so why not ask for $30,000 and have a $10,000 cushion, don't. Lenders aren't interested in lending you more than you *absolutely need*. The "cushion" strategy is likely to work against you because it tells the lender that you don't know how to estimate your true funding needs. Likewise, if you're thinking you need $20,000 but will borrow just $15,000 because the lender will think you're being financially responsible, don't. What the lender will think (or even know) is that you're underfunded and therefore less likely to succeed in the long run. Plus, the lender has to go through the same loan process for a $15,000 loan as for a $20,000 loan—and gets a smaller return on the smaller loan.

Don't request a loan amount based on your collateral. Don't ask for $20,000 because you have $20,000 in collateral to offer. The lender doesn't want your collateral—the lender wants to know that the loan can be repaid from the cash your business generates. The amount you request must have a direct correlation to the financial needs reflected in your business plan.

Don't assume your loan will be approved. If your chances are 50-50 (be honest!), allow yourself enough time to find another financing source if your loan request is turned down. Or apply at several banks at the same time.

Commercial loans 101

Contrary to what many entrepreneurs believe, commercial lending institutions (banks, credit unions, etc.) really do want to make loans. It's how they make their money. But many of them don't make small loans because they often cost as much to analyze and process as large loans do: thorough investigation or "due diligence" has to be done no matter what the loan amount.

Due to consolidation in the banking industry in the last decade, loan officers are under intense pressure to keep loan defaults in check. In essence, the loan officer you speak with will have to "sell" your loan to his or her higher-ups and convince them of its merits. That can happen only if you already sold the loan officer by providing as much information as possible.

Increasing your chances These are the most common reasons for loan denial from commercial lending institutions:

- The borrower has inadequate collateral.

- The business is too new and therefore too risky.

- The business owner has no previous relationship with the lender.

- The business owner isn't prepared with the proper documentation.

As a borrower, your job is to put the lender at ease in each of these four areas. If you've been in business for yourself before or you have accounts with that bank, stress those facts.

But the heart of the matter is the paperwork. You have to provide in-depth financial information (projected cash flow statements, etc.), most of which you can pull from your business plan. However, those documents don't take the place of the loan application, which you'll complete and sign for the loan to be processed. It's a good idea to get a copy of the application in advance and complete it at home (where you can take your time, and make changes if you need to) and deliver the final version when you meet with the lender.

Here's what the loan officer will want to see in writing:

General information:

- Description of the business

- Amount of the loan

- Purpose of the loan

- Sources and terms of repayment

- Available collateral

Management information:

- Owner's experience

- Key staff, including roles and experience

- Support staff (e.g., your attorney, accountant, insurance agent)

Market information:

- Products/services

- Competition ("competitive analysis")

- Suppliers: information and costs

- Potential customers: information and market analysis

Financial information:

- Balance sheets and income statements (monthly for the first year; annually for two additional years)

- Projected income statements (monthly, for at least 12 months forward)

- Projected cash flow figures (monthly, for at least 12 months forward)

- Tax returns for the past three years (business, if any, and personal)

- Personal financial statement

As mentioned, most of this will come from your business plan, which is one of the reasons you take the time to write it in the first place (see "Creating a Solid Business Plan" on p. 91). After you've reviewed the loan application and related documents with the loan officer, offer to take him or her to your potential place of business for a tour if you can. Again, the goal is to make the lender familiar with your business, and more comfortable with you as a borrower.

Finally, keep in mind that loan approval isn't the last step. You also have to close the loan– that is, meet with your loan officer to sign the loan papers (contracts) and pay any closing fees.

Before you close
Call the lender before closing day to make sure you have all the documentation they need. And of course, have your attorney and accountant review all loan documents before you sign anything.

SBA loans 101

Some first-time business owners are surprised to find out that SBA loans are made through commercial lenders. In 1999 hundreds of these lenders processed more than 40,000 SBA-guaranteed loans totaling more than $10 billion. SBA loans, especially 7(a) loans, are for people who can't secure financing on reasonable terms through normal lending channels. To get a 7(a) loan, technically you have to have been denied a commercial loan, but in reality all this means is that your lender must certify to the SBA that it could not provide funding on reasonable terms except with an SBA guaranty. However, not all lenders handle SBA Loans, and some handle only certain types.

Most commercial lenders will deny a loan based on insufficient collateral, but with an SBA loan, a government guaranty acts as collateral, allowing the commercial lender to recoup as much as 90 percent of the loan principal from the SBA if the borrower defaults. The SBA charges the lender "guaranty fees" to offset the expense of the program, and the lender in turn charges you. The amount of the fees is determined by the amount of the loan guaranty, but they typically range from 2 to 3.5 percent of the guaranty. In addition, loans are frequently subject to a 50-basis point (0.5%) annual servicing fee, which is applied to the outstanding balance of SBA's guaranteed portion of the loan.

SBA loans usually have higher interest rates than typical bank loans but are less restrictive when it comes to collateral and equity investment. SBA loans do require an owner's equity investment to be at least 25 percent. SBA loans also require a *personal guarantee to repay* from all of the owners of a business who have at least a 20 percent stake in that business. At a minimum, to qualify for an SBA loan, the your business must:

- be for-profit

- be independently owned and operated

- be engaged in, or propose to do business in, the U.S. or its possessions

- have reasonable owner equity to invest

- use alternative financial resources, including personal assets, before using SBA loan funds

Big lender
With a portfolio worth more than $45 billion, the SBA is the nation's largest single financial backer of small businesses.

SBA loan maturities (durations) vary, depending on the type of the loan, the purpose of the proceeds and the borrower's ability to repay, among other considerations. Most SBA loans are for seven years. Interest rates, either fixed or variable, are negotiated directly between the lending institution and the borrower, but the SBA has published interest maximums for many of the loans it offers. Interest rates on SBA loans are usually prime plus to two to five percentage points, depending on the loan type and amount.

According to the SBA Web site, the borrower's ability to repay the loan from cash flow is "a primary consideration in the SBA loan decision process, but good character, management capability, collateral, and owner's equity contribution are also important considerations." To contact the SBA for a loan application, literature, or answers to your questions about the SBA, call 800.ASKSBA, or go to their Web site (sba.gov).

Certified and preferred

Thousands of commercial lenders service SBA loans, but the SBA designates the most active and expert as "certified lender" or "preferred lender." This gives those lenders partial or full authority to approve loans, which means faster service from the SBA once the loan application is submitted. Certified and preferred lenders are on the SBA site (sba.gov/financing/lender.html).

SBA Loan Document Checklist These are the items you need when you apply for an SBA loan:

- loan request statement (loan amount, purpose, and description of your business)

- your résumé and those of your key managers

- statement of your investment capabilities (i.e., how much money you plan to contribute for start-up, where the money's coming from, etc.)

- current financial statement of all personal liabilities and assets

- projection of revenue statement

- documentation for an existing business (for example, articles of incorporation)

- balance sheet

- income statement for previous year(s) and current year to date

- personal financial statements of all owners/partners

- list of collateral

The lender you contact for an SBA loan will help you through the process, and will also tell you if any additional paperwork us needed.

To find a lender that handles SBA loans, call your local banker (who can tell you what financial institutions in the area do handle SBA loan if that bank doesn't), or contact the SBA.

SBA loan programs for start-ups

Some SBA loan programs are targeted to small business start-ups. Here's a brief description of the programs you should investigate:

(7)a loans The (7)a Loan Guaranty Program is one of the SBA's primary lending programs for small-business owners. The SBA considers a 7(a) loan as "small" if it's for $150,000 or less, and the will guarantee 85 percent of the principal. (The SBA guarantees 75% of these loans if they're more than $150,000.)

Maximum interest rates for fixed-rate 7(a) loans:

Up to $25,000..................less than 7 years......Prime + 4.25%
Up to $25,000.................more than 7 years ...Prime + 4.75%

$25,000-$50,000.............less than 7 years......Prime + 3.25%
$25,000-$50,000.............more than 7 years ...Prime + 3.75%

$50,000 or more.............less than 7 years......Prime + 2.25%
$50,000 or more.............more than 7 years ...Prime + 2.75%

Rates for adjustable-rate loans fluctuate as the prime rate rises or falls. For specific rates, check with your lender.

Low-doc loans The Low-Doc ("low-document") program is actually part of the 7(a) Loan Program, but it's designed for rapid turnaround with less paperwork than the typical 7(a) loan requires. The process is the same, though: You meet with a lender who will determine your need and eligibility for a Low-Doc loan. If your loan request is for less than $150,000, you then submit a simple one-page application form. If it's for more than $150,000, you submit an Income Tax Schedule C, or the front page of corporate or partnership returns, for the last three years. According to SBA literature, applications are processed "usually within two to three business days." The SBA guarantees up to 80 percent of the loan amount. Interest rates for Low-Doc loans follow the same schedule as 7(a) loans.

Express loans Similar to the Low-Doc program and also under the (7) a loan umbrella, the Express Program has an even faster turnaround—36 hours. ("Count on it!" says the SBA Web site.) Lenders can use their own loan forms to apply for an Express loan, which streamlines the process considerably. The maximum Express loan is $150,000. Lenders receive only a 50 percent SBA guaranty, but they may approve unsecured lines of credit for up to $25,000 with the SBA's approval.

Current Express loan interest rates:

More than $50,000..........less than 7 years.........Prime + 2.25%

More than $50,000 ....more than 7 years ......Prime + 2.75%

Contact your lender for rates on Express loans of under $50,000, which may carry higher rates.

Microloans These are small loans of less than $35,000 that are specifically for start-ups, newly established businesses, or small businesses. The average microloan is $10,500. The maximum loan duration is six years. They're made through non-profit "intermediaries," lenders with the authority to make these loans through the SBA. Interest rates are determined by the intermediaries and negotiated between the lender and borrower. Each intermediary sets its own lending and credit requirements, but generally require some type of collateral and a personal guarantee of repayment from the business owner.

In return for granting intermediaries the ability to make microloans, the SBA requires them to offer start-up assistance to business owners. Each intermediary is required to provide business training and technical assistance (from help with writing your business plan to advice on handling employee issues). In turn, people applying for an SBA Microloan may be required to fulfill training requirements even before the loan is considered.

Who makes these loans? In March 2000, the SBA published a report listing the top microloan lenders by state. "Micro-Business-Friendly Banks in the United States" was based on a June 1999 study of 541 such banks with "significant activity in loans of less than $100,000." Survey results were ranked according to several factors, including the total number of microloans the banks made, that number vs. other business loans, and the average microloan amount. The report lists the top two lenders in each state, and is available on the SBA's Web site. You can also order a copy by calling the SBA, or your bank may have a copy handy.

Pre-qualification programs: women, minorities and veterans These loans are specifically for business owners in these categories. In this program, you work with an SBA-designated intermediary to develop a business plan and complete a loan pre-qualification application. The intermediary submits it to the SBA, which reviews the application and, if they approve it, issues a pre-qualification letter stating the agency's intent to authorize a loan guaranty to you. The SBA usually makes a decision within three days after receiving the application. Interest rates are usually about the same as 7(a) loans.

> ### Women's Business Center Online
> *This Web site (onlinewbc.gov) details SBA loan programs and assistance for women entrepreneurs. It will soon have information on topics such as reading financial statements, borrowing and lending, banking, capital alternatives, bookkeeping, accounting, record-keeping, budgeting, and financing a growing business.*

Here's the best part: After you receive the pre-qualification letter from the SBA, you're free to shop around for the intermediary lender with the best rate. The intermediary you choose to process your pre-qualification application may charge a fee for one or more pre-qualification services, so check their fee schedule before you submit paperwork. To find intermediaries, call the SBA or go to the SBA Web site.

Bringing in an equity investor

If you can't finance your start-up with personal assets or a loan, you might consider attracting equity money by offering an "ownership position" in your company to a Small Business Investment Company (SBIC), an "angel"(an individual investor), or some other type of partner.

SBICs Licensed, regulated and partially funded by the SBA, SBICs are privately owned, for-profit organizations that make capital available to small businesses mainly through equity investments (less frequently through loans). The SBIC program currently has 315 licensees with a total combined financial investment pool of $7.7 billion, according to the SBA. Since 1958, SBICs have invested nearly $17 billion in more than 100,000 small businesses.

Some specialize in funding companies within certain industries or with certain products, but they can't own a *controlling* interest in any business they invest in. And many provide in-depth management assistance to small, unproven companies in the start-up stage. To find an SBIC in your area, call the SBA, or go it the SBA Web site (follow the SBIC investor links). The SBA has identified several SBICs that concentrate their investments in women-owned businesses:

> **Axxon Capital**
> Boston, MA
> 617.722.0980; axxoncapital.com

> **Bon Secours Community Investment Fund, LP**
> c/o Smith Whiley & Company
> Hartford, CT
> 860.548.2513

> **Capital Across America**
> Nashville, TN
> 615.254.1515; capitalacrossamerica.org

> **Women's Growth Capital Fund**
> Washington, DC 20007
> 202.342.1431; womensgrowthcapital.com

Milepost Ventures
San Francisco, CA
415.391.8950; milepostventures.com

Angels These are investment-minded individuals in your community you may know personally or professionally. Studies show that more than two million individuals in the U.S. have enough discretionary net worth to make angel investments. According to the SBA, there are more than 250,000 active angels in America, who have invested $20 billion to $50 billion in more than 30,000 small businesses. Most angels, experts say, will want between 20 and 50 percent equity in your business. Unlike venture capitalists (who usually invest at least $1 million in a venture), angels are likely to invest $10,000 to $150,000 (although some do prefer to invest $500,000 to $1 million). Like venture capitalists, angels frequently bring a great deal of business expertise and experience that can benefit you tremendously. But because angels are sophisticated business people, you need to be prepared when you pitch your business as an investment opportunity to a potential angel—just as you would with a commercial lender.

Look for angels in your backyard first; the closer the investor is to your business location or headquarters, the better. In fact, studies show that the typical angel prefers investments within a 200-mile radius of where they live.

Angel investors come in several varieties:

Entrepreneurial angels Entrepreneurs in their own right, these angels want to help other visionaries make their business dreams come true. Because of their success, entrepreneurial angels tend to take bigger risks than other angels. And they're often too busy running their own companies to take an interest in your day-to-day operations. They're more interested in providing "big picture" advice, suggesting options you may not know about, or giving guidance on overall business strategies. To find entrepreneurial angels, ask your local Chamber of Commerce if it hosts any investor groups (many have Chamber affiliations); ask other entrepreneurs in your area if they know of anyone; call attorneys and accountants in your area (they know who the investors are); or contact a Small Business Development

Center to see if they maintain an angel-investor list. Also keep an eye on the business section of your newspaper to see which new companies are getting started and who the investors are. If those people don't want to invest in your business, they may be willing to refer you to people who might. Keep networking until you find the right one.

Enthusiast angels These are usually retirees who have an interest in a certain area and want to help a business in that area grow. Think hobbies: enthusiast angels typically don't want a role in daily management—they just want to be part of a business that has a connection to a personal interest of theirs. To find enthusiast angels, research hobby and collector groups that focus on your type of business or product line. Join those groups or organizations and network. Don't hesitate to make it clear that you're looking for an investor. Ask everyone you contact to suggest possible angels. You might even be able to create your own enthusiast angel. Turning a hobbyist or collector into your own private angel may not be as difficult as you think if your need for capital is minimal.

Corporate angels These are active or retired business executives who want to lend their extensive business experience to start-ups in an active way. They may want a formal role (or job) within your business, or may want to wear many hats, helping out wherever they're needed. Retired corporate angels may take more of a management interest than active executives with less time. (Be aware, though, that corporate angels can sometimes be micro-managers: they "know" exactly how your retail business should be run.) To find corporate angels, start by researching local business organizations. Find the professional speakers are in your area, or ask local executives, lawyers, accountants and other professionals to point you in the right direction. Attend every business function you can, including Chamber of Commerce events. Keep notes and follow up on each lead until you have good prospects to contact.

Professional angels These are individuals or groups who are primarily interested in the return on their investment. Caring little about the business on a daily basis, they're in it for the money. Many of them have general business experience, but few have the time or inclination to help you run your business. They're often lawyers, accountants, doctors and other professionals busy running their own companies or practices. To root out the professional angels in your area, call the Chamber of Commerce; several venture capitalists (they're likely to know which companies or individuals invest as angels); the editor of your local business publication or local paper's business editor; your banker and your own accountant, attorney and insurance agent. You can also do an online search for companies that match entrepreneurs with professional angels, often for a fee of 5-10 percent of the investment.

Partnerships

Another way to raise start-up capital is to bring in a partner with funds and perhaps business expertise. Of course, you'd have to give up something in return: control, profit, or perhaps the freedom to make your own decisions without consulting others.

Many of the principles that apply to angels (written agreements, a clear understanding of duties and responsibilities, etc.) apply to any equity partner. Even the most informal partner (e.g., a business colleague or friend) will share in your profits and losses, so expect to report your store's financial status to your partners on a regular basis. Before you sign any agreements, make sure their investment goals are consistent with the goals of your business. Also determine exactly how involved the partner wants to be on a day-to-day basis. Be clear about your business's goals (and potential for losses). Discuss and then put in writing what would happen if the company needs more money from additional sources in the future: will additional financing be limited to debt financing vs. offering an equity interest to another party?

Also, know your partner's "exit strategy"—how he or she wants to cash in on the equity, and when (for example, by being bought out at the end of three years) and under what conditions. That, too, should be in writing.

Protect yourself

No matter how you raise start-up capital, always consult your attorney and accountant. When it comes to angels, partners and other investors, get professional advice before making final decisions about how the investment will be structured (loan, stock, etc.), and how much equity the investors receive. The wrong partner or a poorly structured deal can turn your business-building dream into a nightmare. But the right partner—SBIC, angel or friend—and the right deal can launch you beautifully.

☐☐☐

Forming Your Company

Before you form your company, you'll have to decide what to call it, which legal structure benefits you the most, and which government regulations apply to your business.

Choosing a name

There are general guidelines you can follow for naming your company. They aren't set in stone, but they reflect what works, so they're a good place to start. In general, you want to create a name that:

- Indicates the products or services you offer
- Emphasizes your key strategic advantages (price, selection, services, etc.)
- Is easy to spell, read and remember
- Evokes a positive mental image the customer can relate to
- Is sensitive to gender, race, religion, culture and language

Spend a week or so paying attention to company and business names around you. Read the phone book, too. You'll soon realize just how many companies—and their brands—don't seem to follow the guidelines. In fact, a walk through just about any mall in America will likely yield a few examples, two among many: Gap and The Limited. Neither name indicates what the store sells, elicits anything that could be considered a "positive mental image"—in fact, it's just the opposite. Both have a *negative* connotation. In the world of online retailing, Amazon.com managed to turn a seemingly nonsensical (or at least arbitrary) name into what is arguably the most widely recognized brand in the world today. But like Gap and The Limited, Amazon spent millions of dollars on marketing and advertising to "brand" itself. You may wonder whether that was a good use of marketing budget, when perhaps a less arbitrary, more descriptive name might have been less costly. So take it as a lesson: a name that works on its own won't require additional marketing money to explain it. But it also proves that the naming "rules" can be broken. So consider the guidelines as you brainstorm a name for your business, but don't let them hamper your creativity, either.

Brainstorming tips

Experts who study creativity for a living say the difference between people who are creative and people who aren't is that *creative people believe they're creative*. They don't necessarily have more creative ideas (or more *of* them) than "non-creative" people. The reality is that the people who don't think they're creative simply don't give themselves permission to brainstorm. They don't allow themselves much wild and crazy thinking, and when they do have ideas, they don't give them enough credit to put them down on paper, so most are lost forever. And without any "evidence" of their ideas, they have no record and therefore no sense of their own creativity. So if you're one of the "non-creative" people, follow these three steps and—violà!—now you're a *creative* person about to start the process of creating a great name for your company. And you will.

- **Brainstorming Step 1:** Tell yourself you're creative.

- **Brainstorming Step 2:** Keep a pad or notebook and pen handy at all times so you can capture your ideas (all gems!) on paper before they're lost.

- **Brainstorming Step 3:** Don't judge anything (yet).

The key to is to get as many ideas on paper as possible and leave the "good or bad" analysis for later. Think of as many names as you can off the top of your head (but don't share them with anyone yet). Ask friends and relatives for suggestions (just jot them down—don't comment). Notice other retailers' names, especially your competitors', and ask yourself what their names imply (low prices? huge selection?) and what images they evoke (fun? elegance?).

Need more idea-starters? Grab a dictionary, a thesaurus, magazines. Cruise them for words that pique your interest or convey a certain message, or words you just "like." Add them to your brainstorm list.

For a name with a regional flair, start by looking through a few books about the area. Jot down 30 to 50 words that keep coming up—actual place names as well as something that evokes the essence of the area. Is any part of your name on that list? If not, choose a few of those words and see how you might build your name around them.

Inventing a name Want to get really creative? Invent your own word. One new naming trend is to invent, or coin, a word that has no actual meaning. (High-tech companies lead the pack with this.) Coining a word as your business name has advantages: you'll have no trademark issues, no translation problems (maybe it's worth checking, though), and a distinct name that no one else is using. On the downside: coined names aren't usually descriptive, they may be difficult for consumers to read or pronounce, and they're much harder to introduce to the market. Research shows that most people are confused, annoyed or turned off by words that have no accepted meaning.

> **Tag it!**
> *Do you like your potential name but you feel it needs a little explanation? Consider adding a tag line that sums up your business. For example,* "Bob's Blues" *could be blueberries, all-blue products, sad poems, or who knows what. But the tag line,* "Your Music Connection," *gets the point across.*

Testing the name

Once you have a list of possible names, you're ready to try your ideas out on the people in your life who are dying to put in their two cents. Take the names you like best (but no more than six or eight) and ask friends, relatives and colleagues to tell you what image or feeling each name evokes for them. (Also ask them not to comment on whether they like it or if they think it will "work.") Keep a written record of their responses; you can even make up a simple worksheet. Then ask yourself if those are the images you're aiming for. For example, "Nina's Sweaters" will evoke different images and impressions than "Nina's Cashmere Treasures" does.

To test the *clarity* of your name ideas, ask this one question: "If you saw a new store in your area named [one of your name ideas], what would you assume they sell there?" If you're concerned about people being able to spell your business name correctly (so they can find it in the phone book), ask friends and relatives to spell the name you just told them. If only a few of them get it right, pick another name. (And if you ever plan to have a Web site, know that ease of spelling is key to finding you!) To determine how *memorable* your name is, call a few people, tell them the name and call them back in a day or two to see if they've remembered it.

Foreign words Using a foreign word or phrase can be especially problematic when it comes to consumers spelling, pronouncing and remembering your name. If you're inclined to use a non-English word (even if it's your name), be sure there's enough upside to compensate for the downside. Then (assuming it isn't your own name, of course), make sure you spell and accent it correctly. If you're not fluent in that language, ask someone who is to check it for you. (Countless retailers, salons and restaurants make that mistake in an effort to seem elegant or continental.) Many people know a mistake in Italian, French, Spanish and so on when they see or hear one, and will remember you for the wrong reasons.

Culture clash

No matter whether you sell here or abroad, differences in culture and language come into play, and it's easy to get tripped up. Even big companies fall into the trap. A classic example: marketing for the Chevrolet Nova failed in Mexico. Why? "No va" in Spanish means "It doesn't go." Not good for a car company. So for someone selling aromatherapy products in an area where a significant number of customers speak German, it's helpful to know in advance that "mist" in German translates to "manure"— which means a name like "Mandy's Mists" might not evoke the image Mandy was aiming for. The lesson: do a little homework first.

Online help   The Namestormers (namestormers.com) sells consulting services and sophisticated naming software ($200-$500). If your budget doesn't allow for that, the company also has an online-only naming service NameWave. For $15 per "naming session," they will generate up to 40 company names based on one or two general ideas you want to get across. For example, "Easy, Simple, Handy" and "Fun, Wild, Crazy, Exciting' are two "categories" you can choose from. If you don't see any names you like on the list it generates, you can run another request for up to 40 more name ideas. You can repeat the process up to five times for that same $15, thereby giving you as many as 200 possible names. The site also provides a free *Naming Guide* for entrepreneurs.

How it looks   One more little thing to consider: how does the name translate typographically? In other words, will it work as a logo? How will it look on a sign? On a tag or a bag? In an ad? For starters, you can play with the name by doodling with colored markers or on your computer. (One-color lettering is cheapest to produce, by the way.) You can then take your doodles or just your ideas to a graphic designer for some preliminary renderings. If the name looks good, go to the next step with it. If not, reconsider either the name or the design.

Is it available?   Once you settle on a name, you need to check its availability to be sure you don't infringe on someone else's established rights to the name. This means doing a trademark search. The best way: hire a trademark attorney or trademark search company to do it for you. It's money well spent. (You could do the search yourself, but that's not advisable.) If it turns out the name isn't available, search your next favorite name. (Or you could try to see if the taken name is for sale first.) For more on trademarks, see "Copyrights, Trademarks and Patents" on p. 146.

Choosing a legal structure

To inc. or not to inc.? The legal structure you choose for your business will affect how and when you pay taxes, what types of taxes you pay, what liabilities you have and a host of other financial factors. It might not be the most *exciting* decision you make during start-up, but it will be one of the most *important* ones.

Where to get advice There's really only one good way to determine what the best legal structure is for your business: Ask your attorney and your accountant. For advice that takes your specific needs and financial situation into account, there's no substitute for your lawyer and your tax preparer. Again, it's money well spent. Then for *general* information and advice, you can consult a SCORE or SBA counselor, community resources (local government, local colleges, chamber of commerce, business bureau), your bank, other retailers, and even Aunt Minnie if she knows a thing or two.

Common legal structures

The four most common legal structures are: sole proprietorship, partnership (general or limited), corporation ("C" corporation and "S" corporation), and limited liability company (LLC). Each structure has its own advantages and drawbacks.

Sole proprietorship This is an appealing option because it offers you total control of your business. Start-up is simpler and taxes are filed as part of your personal income tax return. You will have to make quarterly estimated tax payments, however, and you'll have to pay self-employment tax. Sole proprietors also put their personal assets at a risk because they are responsible for any business debts. Furthermore, it can be difficult to raise capital for sole proprietorships.

General partnership, limited partnership Either of these may be a better option if more than one person will own and run the business. General partnerships are simpler to form, and are similar to sole proprietorships in that the partners have full control of the company's management. A limited partnership has both general and limited partners, with the limited partners playing an inactive role, serving only as investors. One advantage of partner-ships is that, while they must report income, the partnership itself pays no income tax. The taxes are paid by each partner on his or her individual tax return. However, as is the case with sole proprietorships, the general partners are liable for any debts incurred, and the start-up costs of a partnership are higher.

Corporation Incorporating provides business owners with liability pro-tection because the company is a stand-alone legal entity: in other words, the company is separate from the business owners themselves. Liability protection is one of the chief advantages of incorporating. Corporations are owned by investors who "buy" shares (stock), each share being worth x dol-lars. This is another advantage: corporations can raise money through the sale of stock. Shareholders elect a board of directors to run the company, and on other major issues that come up. One drawback (although often more an irritation) is that corporations must keep written records (minutes) of regular board meetings, and must file annual reports. Corporations are governed by both federal and state laws. Because state laws can vary, some people choose to register their corporation in a state other than their own, which is perfectly legal. (Delaware, for example, is known for its advanta-geous corporation laws.)

There are two types of for-profit corporations: "C" corporations and "S" cor-porations (the names come from the subsection of the tax code that defines them.) "C" corporations usually aren't recommended for start-up businesses, largely because of taxes. Not only does the corporation pay federal income tax, but shareholders are taxed individually on their earnings from the cor-poration. In effect, it's a case of double taxation. "S" corporations are usually a better structure for a small businesses because it avoids double taxation: taxes are paid not by the corporation but by the individual shareholders.

On the downside, business owners have less control of their business under corporate structure, and the cost of incorporating can be high. Because of the complexity of incorporation, ongoing accounting costs can be high, as well.

Incorporating through an attorney Until recently, you needed to hire an attorney to set up your corporation, and many people still prefer doing it that way. An attorney will draw up your articles of incorporation, provide the paperwork, file the necessary papers with the appropriate agencies, and hand you a package that includes copies of everything, shares of your corporation's stock, your corporation's seal, and often templates for filing meeting minutes. It costs you not just the filing fees, and but also your attorney's fees, and it's costlier than using a kit, but the extra expense may buy you the peace of mind of knowing that every *t* is properly crossed.

Incorporation kits Or you can do it yourself with an incorporation kit. Dozens if not hundreds of companies now offer inexpensive kits for do-it-yourselfers, which are accepted as valid by most if not all state governments. To find these companies, do an online search or check with a retail trade association, Chamber of Commerce, or a retail trade directory or publication. Some of these companies, like The Company Corporation (800.818.0204; thecompanycorporation.com), also have an "incorporate online" option on their Web sites. A word of caution: Once you settle on one of these services and fill out the papers, have your attorney and accountant review everything before you sign on the dotted line. It's worth it to pay them to spend an hour to two to review the paperwork and the incorporation process the kit is offering, and to offer advice and/or give you a thumbs up or down and an explanation.

Limited liability company (LLC) This option offers some of the advantages of both corporations and partnerships: LLCs are separate entities like corporations, thereby providing liability protection. Taxes are paid by the individual members. And LLCs can raise funds more easily than a partnership can. Unlike limited partnerships, any member in an LLC can participate in business operations, and there's no limit on the number of shareholders, as there is with an "S" corporation. Unfortunately, because LLCs are state-chartered organizations, the start-up costs are high compared to partnerships or sole proprietorships.

Government regulations

New entrepreneurs are often surprised to learn how many laws and regulations apply to cart, kiosk and in-line retailers. Some people are so overwhelmed by the process that they cut corners—which invariably leads to problems down the line. The SBA cautions you to "avoid the temptation to ignore regulatory details . . . Being out of compliance could leave you unprotected legally, lead to expensive penalties, and jeopardize your business." The last thing you need at this crucial time is to have your attention diverted by regulatory issues—so follow the rules. You'll need to:

- Obtain the required business licenses and permits from your city, county and/or state government.

- Contact the relevant government agencies to get your business ID or tax ID numbers. You'll need this to collect and pay sales tax as well as federal, state and local taxes; hire employees; get business insurance. An ID number is sometimes required to open a business checking account, too.

If you want to avoid the time and effort of obtaining the forms or if you're in doubt about which regulations apply to your business, ask your attorney and accountant. They can give you specific advice targeted to your venture, and get the government forms you'll need—all in one place. Again, you're likely to find it's worth the cost of a few hours of their time to help you navigate the regulatory maze. But if you do want to do it yourself, here are some of the resources to go to:

Federal The IRS's annual *Small Business Resource Guide* has everything you need to know about federal taxes, including instructions and forms. Order a copy in print or on CD (a single copy is free). The full text is also on the IRS Web site. The CD version (which is in a number of formats that will work on just about any computer) also has valuable business information from various government agencies. To order the *guide* or any federal tax forms, call the IRS at 800.TAX.FORM and ask for Publication #3207, or go to the Web site (irs.gov/plain/bus_info/sm_bus/smbus-cd.html).

State For information on state laws and regulations, go to the state's Web site. Every state has one, and the address is usually *state* plus the two-letter state abbreviation plus ".us" (Florida's site, for example, is state.fl.us). Or just key the state's name and "government" into a search engine.

Local   Your area's Chamber of Commerce, SBDC or SCORE chapter can point you to the right person in the right agency for whatever local licenses, permits and tax forms you need. To find local offices of federal, state and local agencies, check the phone book's blue pages (if your local book doesn't have them, look under "Government" in the yellow pages). Or go online to find their Web sites—many city and county government Web sites are information-packed, if a little slow.

How long will it take to get the permits and licenses? Some general guidelines are on the following pages. But to play it safe, try to allow time for glitches along the way—lost paperwork, overburdened staffers, and who knows what. Knowing when to apply for a license or permit can be tricky sometimes. For example, your obligation to pay taxes starts as soon as you receive your federal tax ID number from the IRS—so you don't want to apply for that number too early. Again, your accountant and attorney can help you determine not just what you need, but when. That said, here's the rundown.

Licenses, permits and ID numbers

Here are details on the most common licenses and permits specialty retailers have to have before opening day. Application fees vary, depending on the type of business, location, number of employees, projected income (in some cases) and the type of license or permit you require.

Business license   You need a business license to operate legally almost everywhere. If your business is within city limits, you have to get a license from the city. If you're outside the city limits, then you need a license from the county if your county requires it (some don't). Most cities and counties charge a minimal fee for a business license ($10 to $50). Contact the tax and license division in your city or county.

Certificate of occupancy   A certificate of occupancy (or CO) is what you get when the local zoning or building-code enforcement agency inspects your space and approves it. If you're in a location that requires a CO, you can't open for business until you have one. Good news: if you're in a mall, chances are you don't need a CO. As a cart or kiosk-based retailer you don't need one. Nor will you need one even if you're in an in-line store unless you make major changes to the space (structural, electrical, etc.). If you plan to operate in a location that requires you to have a CO, contact your local zoning department, or the retail district management. Fees and processing times vary, depending on your geographic area, the nature of the construction you need before you occupy the space and open for business, and the types of inspections required.

Employer identification number A federal employer ID number (EIN), sometimes called a tax ID number (TIN), is a nine-digit number you have to use when reporting, depositing and paying business-related taxes. In the majority of cases, you need a federal tax number even if you don't have employees, so you can collect and pay state taxes. If you're in a tax-free state, consult your attorney and accountant for guidance. The IRS suggests getting your federal tax number before you open so that you'll have it when you make your first tax payment. (However, if you don't have it by then, you can send in the tax payment and write "EIN applied for on [date]" on the tax return.)

You can apply for an EIN by mail, fax or online (instructions are on the form). Allow four to six weeks to get your number by mail, two weeks by fax, and less than a day by phone. Contact the IRS online or call 800.TAX.FORMS and ask for Form SS-4, "Application for Employer Identification Number." Some states also require you to have a state or local ID number. To find out if yours is one that does, call your state's department of revenue.

Sales tax number States that collect sales tax require every retail business operating in that state to have a sales tax number, sometimes called a "seller's permit," "certificate of authority," "certificate of resale" or "merchant certificate." (At present, Alaska, Delaware, Montana, New Hampshire and Oregon don't have sales tax.) You can get a sales tax number plus instructions for sales tax collection, monthly reporting and payment, from your state's department of revenue. Some states issue sales tax numbers for free, while others charge a fee (usually around $20). Allow two to four weeks to receive your number.

Fictitious business name This is the business name you file with the appropriate government agency in your area. Every state has its own definition of a fictitious name, also known as a DBA ("doing business as," often written as "dba" or "d/b/a"). Some states define it as a name that doesn't include the owner's surname, but some states don't make that distinction: you have to file a fictitious name even if the name isn't fictitious. So if you set up your business under your real name, you'd have to file as "Mary Doe dba Mary Doe" in one of those states. As always, check on the law in your area. In any event, you must file a form called something like "Petition of Fictitious Business Name" with the county and pay a fee (usually $10 to $50). However, each county has its own definition and rules, some stricter than others, so check with your county government. Contact the County Clerk for an application, rules and guidelines, or ask your attorney. After you file your fictitious name, most states require you to publish it once a week for four consecutive weeks in a general-circulation newspaper in the county where the business is located. (Again, different locales may have different rules.) Publication costs vary, so if your county has more than one newspaper, shop around for the best rates, but be sure that newspaper is state-approved for fictitious-name publication. Then within 30 days after your published notice first appears (in most cases), you'll file an "Affidavit of Publication" with the County Clerk.

Health permit If you sell pre-packaged food items, you won't need a health permit. But if you plan to sell "open" (that is not pre-packaged) food or beverages to the public, you need a health permit from the county. You may also be subject to additional state and/or federal rules and regulations. Permit fees vary, but every county requires food retailers to have access to a commissary (water, sink, drain), and abide by all food-sales regulations (such as wearing latex gloves). Contact your state's health department for the rules, and instructions on how to apply. At some point after receiving your application, the county will send an inspector to your premises before issuing the permit.

Samples and permits
If you plan to "prepare" that food item—anything from cooking it, adding water to it or even just unwrapping it—and then hand out samples, you have to have a health permit first.

Sign permit Whether you'll need a city or county sign permit depends on your location. If you're in a mall, you won't (although mall management has rules for signs). If you're in a strip center or a storefront on a street, you may need a sign permit. Most cities and counties have restrictions on the size, location and sometimes the materials and even the look of signs you can use outside your business. The permit ensures that your signs conform to local codes. Contact the city or county clerk for an application and regulations (and get your landlord's written permission) before you have signs made and installed.

Other regulations

Minimum wage Almost all businesses are subject to federal and some-times state laws governing minimum wage, overtime and child labor. You can get information on these and related laws from your accountant, or go online to the Department of Labor Wage and Hour Division site for federal laws (dol.gov) and state laws (dol.gov/dol/esa/public/minwage/america).

> ### Online help for employers
> FirstGov (employers.gov) is a site that was created by various government agencies to provide employers with resources and cross-agency information.

Employment eligibility and immigration Under federal law, you must verify the identity and employment eligibility of anyone you hire for employment in the U.S. This includes citizens and non-citizens. You need to complete the Immigration and Naturalization Service (INS) Form I-9 for every employee you hire. Complete the form (instructions and mail-to address are on the form), sign and send it, and keep a copy in your files. You can get the forms from your attorney or accountant, or by calling the Forms Hotline (800.870.3676) or Employer Hotline (800.357.2099), or go to their Online Forms Index (ins.gov/graphics/formsfee/forms/index).

Workers' compensation Every state requires that employers carry workers' compensation insurance to provide protection for those injured while on the job. For more about workers' comp, see "Insuring Your Business" on p. 161.

Unemployment insurance tax Every state also requires businesses to pay unemployment insurance tax if the business has at least one employee for 20 weeks in a calendar year, or paid gross wages of $1,500 or more in a calendar year. Go to your state's Web site to check the amounts for your state, or check with your accountant. (For more about unemployment insurance, see Chapter 8, "Accounting and Taxes.")

Employment discrimination The U.S. Equal Employment Opportunity Commission (EEOC), as well as state and local civil rights enforcement agencies that work with the Commission, prohibits companies with 15 or more employees from discrimination in all employee-related practices, including recruitment, pay, hiring, firing, promotion/job assignment, training, leave, layoffs and benefits. In addition, the Americans with Disabilities Act of 1990 (ADA) makes it unlawful for employers to discriminate against any qualified individual with a disability. The ADA is also enforced by the EEOC (for more about anti-discrimination laws, go to dol.gov).

In-home offices In recent years some taxpayers have taken the IRS to court over the definition of "home office" (and many have lost!). The IRS considers a home office deductions legal only if your home office is your "primary place of business." In other words, if you're in your retail store all day and do your paperwork at home during your spare time, the IRS may balk when it comes to your home-office deductions. When in doubt, check with your attorney and accountant before taking these deductions.

Copyrights, patents and trademarks

Copyrights, patents and trademarks are designed to protect the hard work of their creators. As a new business owner, you not only want to protect your work—you'll also want to make sure you're not infringing on anyone else's rights. And you want to do so well before you open. MarksOnline (marksonline.com) and NameBase (namebase.com) are two online companies that conduct trademark searches and registration services.

Domain names

You can check to see if a domain name (Web address) is available by checking with an online registration service (such as register.com, domainit.com, or networksolutions.com).

Copyrights Copyrights protect the thoughts and ideas of authors, composers and artists. A copyright prevents illegal copying of written matter (such as a brochure or catalog), works of art or computer programs. Contrary to popular belief, the U.S. Copyright Office (part of the U.S. Library of Congress) requires no registration of the copyright; it is automatically secured when the work is created in a fixed "tangible form of expression" (published or unpublished). Nevertheless, in many instances there are advantages to registering your copyrights, which you should explore with your attorney, or contact the U.S. Copyright Office (202.707.3000 or loc.gov/copyright). Fees vary, depending on the nature of the material, but in most cases it costs about $30 to register a copyright.

Patents New and useful inventions can be protected by a U.S. patent—either a utility patent on how something works, or a *design* patent on how something looks. Because patent-application procedures are detailed, technical and often costly, in part because they involve a patent search, consult an experienced patent attorney before you apply. Only attorneys and agents registered with the U.S. Patent and Trademark Office (USPTO) may perform patent searches in the patent office. (Be particularly cautious of companies offering to handle your invention, including patent application and search, for you.) A patent search is done to see if one already exists on "the same or nearly the same device," according to the USPTO. If it doesn't, you're free to proceed. For more on applying for a patent and related costs, contact the USPTO (800.786.9199; uspto.gov).

Trademarks and service marks These "marks" are actually words, phrases, symbols or designs that identify the source (e.g., owner or manufacturer) of the product or service, and distinguish that source from others. Marks include your company name, logo and any slogans or tag lines that accompany your logo or your ads. You can register trademarks and service marks with the state for a term of 10 years. But you have to conduct a trademark search first, to be sure yours is available. You can hire an attorney or a trademark search firm to search your mark; or you can do a search yourself, either online (http://tess.uspto.gov) or by going to the Trademark Public Search Library (2900 Crystal Dr., 2nd Floor, Arlington, Virginia; 800.786.9199; uspto.gov). The cost to register a name with the USPTO is $325, and you can apply online. For more about applications for registering trade or service marks in your state, contact your state government or the USPTO.

□□□

Accounting and Taxes

Y ou don't need degrees in accounting and tax law to run a successful specialty retail operation, but you do need these two things: a working knowledge of basic accounting principles, and a good accountant. Find an experienced certified account you trust, and who understands your business. Then learn the basics of Accounting 101. Even if your accountant keeps your books and track your finances on a regular basis, you still need a solid familiarity with accounting so you'll know what you're looking at on a P&L statement or balance sheet, and the questions to ask. Your accountant is likely to be more knowledgeable about the latest tax laws than a general-practice attorney may be. In short, it's crucial to find an accountant who has your best interests at heart as well as solid experience with small retail businesses.

Finding the right accountant

Finding and hiring an accountant is not unlike buying a computer: the first question you have to answer is, "What do you want to do with it?" Knowing what you want an accountant for—that is, the types of services you need an accountant to perform—is your first step in finding the right accountant for your business. Do you need help with start-up costs? Start-up financing? Keeping monthly accounts? Calculating taxes? Once you've identified your needs, you can look for the right accountant by asking around. For example, if you need help primarily with taxes, ask three or four retailers for the accountant who prepares their taxes, and if they're satisfied with the services they received. If your primary need is generating documents to secure start-up financing, you might ask several bank managers for their recommendations, or for any names they frequently see in new business proposals. You can also ask your attorney, SBA advisor or SCORE counselor and, of course, family, friends and business associates, especially if you're looking for general accounting expertise. In any case, try to build a list of at least six possibles.

Once you have your list of names, call two or three to schedule a meeting. Nearly all accountants are willing to meet briefly with a potential client for the first time free of charge. (If you find someone who won't, you've just gotten a glimpse of that accountant's billing strategy—move on to another name.) In that initial meeting, ask about the accountant's experience with retail as well as general business tax issues, start-up financing, and any other concerns you have. Ask if the accountant works with a number of retailers in the area, and whether those retailers are similar in size to your business. An accountant who does work for large corporations, for example, will have a different approach from one who serves small-business owners. Ask if the accountant will work on your account personally, or if the work will be passed down to his or her staff (other accountants, bookkeepers, etc.). If staff work is acceptable to you, then ask if you'll be paying a lower fee. In any case, get a good explanation of the fee structure, preferably on paper so you can review it later and compare the rate to others you'll gather.

Also make sure that accountant can communicate complex financial issues so that you understand them. Not fully understanding your financial status or where your money's going can be disastrous, so you can't afford an accountant who can't explain complex issues clearly. To test that ability, ask a few questions, perhaps definitions of financial terms or something in the course of writing your business plan.

Finally, ask for references. And call them. Ask how long have they've used the accountant, the services performed, whether the client was pleased with the work, and if there were areas they were disappointed with. And if there were problems, did the accountant address them quickly and efficiently? Ask about billing issues, too: have the bills been what they expected? If the invoices were higher than expected, what was the reason given for the discrepancy, and was the reason satisfactory?

If in the end you're not comfortable with any of the accountants on your list, start a new search for the right accountant—someone who can ultimately save you time, aggravation and, yes, money. It also helps if you find an accountant who is familiar with retail business or advises other retail entrepreneurs.

Recording business transactions

Nobody likes paperwork, of course. But it's less painful and time-consuming if you get organized early. So before opening day, create a record-keeping system you can use throughout the year. Having easy access to complete records will make life easier by allowing you to do all of these necessary tasks:

- Track the progress of your business from day to day, month to month, and year to year.

- Prepare clear, complete financial statements so you can analyze your growth, secure financing, etc.

- Know the amount and sources of your income.

- Track your expenses.

- Prepare complete, accurate tax returns you can support with backup documentation.

Creating financial documents

A good record-keeping system allows you to account for all of your income and expenses. It also allows you to generate the following financial documents for yourself and, in some cases, for your accountant:

Balance sheet A snapshot of the financial health of your business in terms of *assets* (everything the company owns), *liabilities* (everything the company owes), and *net worth* (assets minus liabilities) on the day the report is generated. How often to generate: As often as you think is necessary, or whenever your accountant asks for one.

Cash receipts A summary of cash receipts, which is usually calculated by the cash register/POS system. If there's no register, the sales slips are totaled. How often to generate: Daily, weekly, monthly and annually.

Cash flow summary A statement that indicates how cash flows in and out of the business: cash comes in from sales of goods (and/or financing received), and goes out to pay operating expenses, debts, and/or investments to finance growth. How often to generate: Monthly.

Income statement, profit-and-loss (P&L) statement A statement that details revenues and expenses for a specific period, indicating how cash is flowing in and out of the business. Also called "earnings reports" and "operating statements." How often to generate: Monthly and annually.

Disbursements statement A record of all disbursements (payments) made on a daily basis, usually taken from individual entries in the business checking account, and from the cash register/POS system for payments made from the till—the cash in the register. (Note: It's a good idea to avoid paying with cash, because cash doesn't leave a record of the disbursement, except for funds taken from petty cash, of course.) Also record bank-account fees you may not have written a check for. (Most banks deduct fees from the account balance every month, so check your account statement for the amount.) How often to generate: Monthly, to check against your checking account register; annually for your accountant.

Employee compensation record A summary of the number of hours employees worked during a specific period, the total pay for the period, and the amounts of deductions and withholding. How often to generate: Monthly and annually.

Setting up a checking account

Before you open for business, open a business checking account. Order checkbooks that give you enough room to write in the sources of deposits (such as income and loan funds) and types of expenses (such as phone, rent, wages, credit-card fees), so you can identify the income and outgo months later. (Avoid writing checks payable to "Cash" because that gives you no record of the expense.) And balance your checkbook every month.

Using accounting software

Are you flinching at the thought of producing financial documents on your own? Good news: you can use one or several of the dozens of software packages for keeping records and generating reports. Most of these packages are great for people with little or no bookkeeping or accounting experience, and some of these programs even help users decide how to categorize receipts or expenses. All of the software provides fully automated report-generation functions that summarize a variety of transactions by category. Many programs are available as a free demo as a download or on a trial CD that's mailed to you. Expect to spend $100 to $300 (the more features, the higher the price).

Free demos!
AccountingShop.com offers free demos of the top 20 accounting packages.

Currently, the two most popular and best-known programs are QuickBooks (Intuit, 800.782.9430; quickbooks.com) and Peachtree's Complete Accounting (Peachtree, 800.247.3224; peachtree.com), which you can find online or through computer- or office-supply stores. These two programs, as well as many others on the market today, allow you to manage accounts receivable (money you expect to receive) and accounts payable (money you expect to pay), write and print checks, locate customer information, create invoices and purchase orders, and print financial statements.

Shopping for software
Buying direct from manufacturers can cost more, not less. Their prices are usually much higher than those you'll find at computer- or office-supply stores. The biggest bargains are usually online, but buy from a reputable supplier.

Paying taxes

Paying taxes: the "patriotic duty" everyone loves to hate. And now that you're starting a business, you have to do even more of it. Your accountant will be a tremendous help to you in this regard, and—believe it or not—so will the IRS.

Establishing your tax year

One of the first things you need to do is establish your *tax year* (also known as "accounting year"). It's the 12-month accounting period on which you'll calculate your taxable income and file a business income tax return. There are two types of tax year: *calendar* year, and *fiscal* year as defined by the IRS. A calendar year is January 1st through December 31st. A fiscal year is 12 consecutive months ending on the last day of any month except December (that would be a calendar year).

Ask your accountant which option is best for you, or if there are tax-year regulations that apply to your business. For example, if you operate as a sole proprietor, the business tax year must be the same as your individual (personal) tax year. Special rules apply to partnerships and "S" corporations. In any case, you must establish your tax year within the time limit (not including extensions) for filing your first return, as set by law. Plan carefully, because once you establish your tax year, you may have to get IRS approval, plus pay a fee, to change it. (For more information, request IRS Publication 538, "Accounting Periods and Methods.")

Paying federal taxes

When it comes to paying your federal taxes, much depends on the legal structure you choose when you form your company (e.g., sole proprietorship, partnership or corporation—see p. 138 for more). Here's the information you'll need to understand each type of tax as it pertains to your business structure, along with a tax table that explains which forms you'll need from the IRS. As always, when in doubt, ask your accountant!

Hello, IRS?

To request forms, publications or other information, contact the IRS at 800.829.1040, or irs.gov.

Income tax

The IRS requires all businesses, except partnerships, to file an annual income tax return. Sole proprietorships and corporations are required to file tax returns, plus they have to make quarterly estimated tax payments if they expect to owe more than a certain amount of taxes when they file. For sole proprietorships and "S" corporations, that amount is $1,000 or more. For all other corporations, it's $500 or more. (For more information, request IRS Publication 505, "Tax Withholding and Estimated Tax.")

Partnerships have to file a Partnerships Return of Income (Form 1065), an informational return that's used to report the profit or loss of the partnership. No payments are sent in with the form: if any tax payments are due, they're reported on and sent in with each partner's individual income-tax return.

Driving down the tax bill

If you use your car or truck for business, you can deduct all or part of your costs to run and maintain it—either your actual expenses or the IRS standard mileage rate. Ask your accountant to explain the pros and cons, and which method will give you the bigger deduction. (Or request IRS Publication 463, "Travel, Entertainment, Gift and Car Expenses.")

Self-employment tax

For individuals who work for themselves (including sole proprietors), self-employment tax is the Social Security and Medicare tax. Currently, the total self-employment tax rate is 15.3 percent: 12.4 percent for Social Security plus 2.9 percent for Medicare. (For more information, request IRS Publication 533, "Self-Employment Tax.")

Half off

You can deduct 50 percent of your self-employment tax as an adjustment to income on Form 1040.

Employment taxes

If you have employees, you'll have to pay certain taxes, including federal income tax withholding, FICA (Federal Insurance Contributions Act) and FUTA (Federal Unemployment Tax Act) taxes. Here's more about each of these.

Federal income tax Generally, you must withhold federal income tax from your employees' wages. To figure how much federal income tax to withhold from each wage payment, you'll use the employee's Form W–4 (instructions are on the form).

FICA Social Security and Medicare taxes pay for benefits that workers and their families receive under the Federal Insurance Contributions Act (FICA), so they're commonly known as "FICA taxes." Employers withhold part of these taxes from the employees' wages, and also pay a matching amount. FICA tax rates vary, depending on the amount paid and several other factors. To determine how much FICA tax to withhold, ask your accountant or request IRS Publication 15. These taxes are reported on Form 941, "Employer's Quarterly Federal Tax Return."

Unemployment (FUTA) The Federal Unemployment Tax Act (FUTA) established the federal unemployment tax that pays unemployment compensation to employees who lose their jobs through no fault of their own (for example, through corporate downsizing). You pay FUTA tax separately, and from your own funds: employees don't pay this tax or have it withheld from their pay. You'll report FUTA taxes on Form 940, "Employer's Annual Federal Unemployment (FUTA) Tax Return." Or if you qualify to do so, use the much simpler Form 940-EZ (ask your accountant, or request IRS Publication 15). Depending on where you operate, you may also be required to pay state unemployment tax. Check with your accountant.

For more about how federal employee taxes work, request Publication 15, Circular E, "Employer's Tax Guide," which explains your tax responsibilities as an employer. If you're not sure if the people working for you are classifiable as "employees," request Publication 15–A, "Employer's Supplemental

Tax Guide," which can help you determine if they are "employees" or "independent contractors" according to IRS definitions.

Employee forms You and/or your employees have to complete several IRS forms, which you'll keep in your files. Each employee must fill out an I-9 (proof of eligibility to work in the U.S.) and a W-4 (the employee's filing status, deductions, etc.). By the end of each January, you must send every employee a completed W–2, "Wage and Tax Statement" for the previous calendar year if they worked for you during any part of that year. You must also send copies of those W-2s to the Social Security Administration. For more information, request Publication "20xx Instruction for Forms W-2 and W-3" for that prior calendar year (e.g., "2002 Instructions for . . .").

Depositing taxes

Chances are, you'll have to deposit certain taxes—employment taxes, corporate income taxes, estimated taxes, etc.—before you file your annual tax return. If so, you'll complete IRS Form 8109 ("Federal Tax Deposit Coupon") to indicate the deposit amount, the type of tax being paid, the period for which you're making a deposit. You'll include the form with your deposit, which you'll mail or deliver to an authorized financial institution ("depository"). Mailed deposits must arrive at the depository by the due date. (The IRS can charge you a penalty for late deposits.)

The IRS will send you a coupon book five or six weeks after you receive your employer ID number (EIN). If a deposit is due and you have your EIN but not your coupon book, you can get a blank coupon (Form 8109-B) by calling the IRS (800.829.1040). If you haven't been issued an EIN yet, don't use Form 8109: instead, mail your payment with an explanation to the same IRS Service Center you send your annual tax returns to (take a look at last year's return if you aren't sure).

In either case, make your check or money order payable to the United States Treasury. The IRS suggests that you also write the following on it: your name (exactly as it appears on your Social Security card) and address, your EIN (or the date you applied for it), the kind of tax being paid, and the period the tax payment covers. Doing this helps ensure that they accurately credit your tax payment to your account.

This IRS table shows the tax forms that each "type of business" must file:

Type of Business	Tax Liabilities	IRS Form
Sole Proprietor	Income tax	1040 + Schedule C or C-EZ
	Self-employment tax	1040 + Schedule SE
	Estimated tax	1040-ES

	Employment taxes:
	   Social Sec., Medicare and
	   income withholding
		941

	FUTA	940 or 940-EZ
	Depositing employmt. taxes	8109 (except electronic deposits)

Type of Business	Tax Liabilities	IRS Form
Partnership*	Annual return of income	1065

	Employment taxes:
	   Social Sec., Medicare and
	   income withholding
		941

	FUTA	940 or 940-EZ
	Depositing employmt. taxes	8109 (except electronic deposits)

*Separate additional filings are required by each partner.

Type of Business	Tax Liabilities	IRS Form
Corporation	Income tax	1120 or 1120-A
"S" corporation	Income tax	1120S
All corporations	Estimated tax	1020-W + 8109

	Employment taxes:
	   Social Sec., Medicare and
	   income withholding
		941

	FUTA	940 or 940-EZ
	Depositing employmt. taxes	8109 (except electronic deposits)

Tax-preparation software

Tax-preparation software packages won't make paying taxes fun, but they can make the process easier and quicker. Most of these programs rely on the "interview" method: they ask the user a series of questions, make calculations based on the user's answers, and plug in the data on IRS-approved forms. Some packages, including Intuit's Quicken Turbo Tax, can import data such as wage payments from a user's other software (e.g., money-management or spreadsheet programs), further streamlining the tax-prep process.

Some programs even provide access to experts. H&R Block's TaxCut gives users access by phone or e-mail to one of their tax preparers who can answer any question at $20 per "solution." You can also pay H&R Block to review your completed return electronically ($30 per submission) before you file. And when you file, many programs give you the option of paying the IRS electronically by credit card.

Prices for this kind of tax-prep software range from $50 to $100. You can find these packages in computer- and office-supply stores, or online. The three most widely used programs are:

- **TurboTax Business** (Intuit/Quicken; 800.782.9430; quicken.com). Specifically for "C" corporations, "S" corporations, LLCs and partnerships. Guides users through business tax returns step by step, includes "Business Deduction Finder," "Depreciation Expert" and "Audit Flags" features, and generates IRS-approved forms.

- **TurboTax Home and Business** (Intuit/Quicken; 800.782.9430; quicken.com). For sole proprietorships and individuals. Guides users through returns, provides expert tax advice especially for small businesses and includes "Tax Savvy for Your Small Business," "Business Deduction Finder," "Business Tax Planner" and "Home Office Expert." Generates IRS-approved forms for contractors and employees.

- **TaxCut Platinum Home & Business Edition** (H&R Block; 818.779.7223; taxcut.com). Has complete instructions and forms for filing home and business taxes, including Form 1040 for sole proprietorships, Form 1120 for corporations, Form 1120S for "S" corporations, Form 1065 for partnerships, and payroll return Forms 940 and 941. Lets users plan ahead and maximize deductions with the built-in "Tax Planner."

Paying state sales tax

The only states with no state sales tax are Alaska, Delaware, Montana, New Hampshire and Oregon (although some, like Alaska, may have local sales taxes). Retailers in every other state must collect, report and remit sales taxes to their state's department of revenue, monthly or quarterly. Every state issues sales tax numbers to retailers in order to collect sales taxes (and track delinquents)—which is why you'll use that number every time you report and send in the sales tax you collected. Each state has its own instructions for collecting, reporting and remitting sales tax. To request a copy of these instructions, call your state department of revenue; the number will be in the blue pages of your phone book. (For more on how to apply for a sales tax number, also see "Forming Your Company" on p. 133.)

> ### By any other name
> *A sales tax number is sometimes referred to as a "seller's permit," "certificate of authority," "certificate of resale" or "merchant certificate."*

□ □ □

Insuring Your Business

Before you open for business, you have to have the right insurance. And your coverage levels have to be adequate, at least. Failing to protect yourself from risk exposes you to unexpected costs that could be enormous: in fact, they could shut you down.

That's one side of the issue. The other side is making informed decisions about buying insurance. The last thing you want is to pour large sums of money into coverage you don't need. So before you buy anything, you need to gather as much information as possible, including rate quotes, so you can choose the types and amounts of coverage that are right for your business.

How much? How much insurance should you buy? The short answer: as much as you need (and can afford), and no more. As a general rule, you want to be insured against major risks. But being "over-insured"—having too much coverage or trying to cover every little thing—isn't cost-effective. That's why it pays to do some insurance homework first.

Mall requirements Insurance is so important to financial survival that malls and other retail venues include non-negotiable insurance require-ments in their leases and license agreements. The requirements for types of insurance and minimum levels of coverage vary from mall to mall, but count on management to require you to have liability (at least $1 million in coverage), and Worker's Compensation if it's required by state law. Mall management may also have additional requirements—for example, that the property owner and the management company are listed as "insureds." Contact the leasing manager for a full explanation of the center's insurance requirements. And check to see that they're spelled out in your lease or license agreement before you sign. (For more on leases and license agreements, see p. 80.)

That said, there are some types of insurance you'll need no matter what. This section covers insurance "must-haves," plus additional types of coverage you might want, and how to find an insurance company that's right for you.

Insurance "must-haves"

No question about it: These are the types of business insurance you must have: property, liability, and auto. If you have employees, you must also have Workers' Compensation.

Liability

This coverage protects you from the financial consequences of being sued for injuries that happen to others as a result of your business. There are three main types of liability coverage: general liability, product liability, and "umbrella" coverage. Here's a look at each one:

General liability insurance General liability coverage protects you from the cost of lawsuits resulting from accidents or injuries that occur on your premises. If an accident happens at or because of your cart, kiosk, store or other retail space, you could be sued and held liable, depending on the circumstances. And defending yourself in a suit, whether you're found liable and have to pay a judgment, could prove extremely costly. That's where your general liability insurance comes in. It provides you with legal representation and, if you lose the lawsuit or settle out of court, the policy will cover the amount of the judgment award or settlement up to your coverage limit. However, liability policies typically list many exclusions, so review yours with your insurance rep so you know precisely what it covers and what it doesn't.

Product liability insurance Product liability coverage isn't just for manufacturers—retailers may need it, too. Product liability protects you if an item you sell is faulty and causes an injury, and someone files a product-liability lawsuit against you. For example, your supplier ships you a product that needs to be assembled at your store or altered in some way before it's sold. According to law, that may mean that you as the retailer "participated in the product's manufacture." As a result, if a consumer is injured by that product, you may be held liable. Talk to your insurance rep about product liability for your business, so that you can be adequately covered if you need it.

"Umbrella" coverage An umbrella policy basically picks up where your general-liability or auto-liability policies coverage leaves off. For example, if the amount of a judgment against you exceeds your liability coverage, your umbrella policy will kick in to make up the difference, up to your maximum umbrella-coverage amount. Many umbrella policies have minimum requirements for the "underlying" liability policies (general and auto, for example), so you want to be sure your underlying policies dovetail with your umbrella policy. Ask your insurance agent to make sure all of that is taken care of before you buy, so you have no gaps in your coverage.

In most policies, everything is written in legal language with technical jargon, which means most people find them practically incomprehensible. Some insurance companies have tried to put policy language into plain English, but even that isn't always "plain." So before you sign, ask your insurance agent to explain every paragraph and every clause so you understand their meaning. If you don't quite get it, keep asking until you do.

The insurance "policy"

An insurance policy is the contract that spells everything out. Every policy has three main sections:

- inclusions: losses the policy covers

- exclusions: losses the policy doesn't cover; and the circumstances under which the policy won't pay for losses it would normally cover (for example, the familiar "acts of God" exclusion)

- general terms and conditions: what's required for the policy, or the particular provisions of the policy, to stay in effect

Property

Property insurance covers damage and loss to the permanent structures and the contents of your business due to certain causes under certain circumstances. Read the inclusions and exclusions carefully, since they will spell out exactly what type of losses are covered and which are not (policies vary widely). Property insurance usually covers damage and loss by fire. If yours doesn't, buy a separate policy to cover it. Property insurance policies usually don't cover damage from events such as hurricanes, floods and earthquakes. (Your state may have laws requiring coverage for these. More about this type of coverage starts on p. 169.) Many policies also exclude "acts of God," and as a result of September 11th, many now also exclude "acts of terrorism." If you want coverage for those kinds of events (if it's even available), you have to buy separate coverage.

> ### Replacement value
> Consider buying coverage based on "replacement value" and not "current cash value" or "depreciated value." Replacement value means the insurance company pays for covered losses based on the cost of replacing them at the time of the claim. Rates may be slightly higher, but it will make a great difference to your wallet if you ever need to make a claim.

Home office If you have an office in your home, you'll also need insurance to cover that space and the equipment in it. Even if you already have a current homeowner's or renter's policy, you'll have to buy a separate policy to cover your home office, or at least your business equipment. Check with your agent.

Auto

If you have a car, you already have car insurance; but if you plan to use your personal car or truck for *business* purposes, you'll need to modify your existing personal car insurance policy because, it doesn't cover business-related driving like deliveries, pickups and trips to the bank. And it doesn't matter who's doing the driving (you, the car's owner, or your employees). A personal vehicle that's used for company business is referred to as a "non-owned auto," which means "not owned by the company." Ask your car insurance agent about a non-owned-auto policy, and explain how you plan to use it for business purposes: how many additional miles, how often, and who may be driving. On the other hand, if you plan to use a *company-owned* car or truck for business and your employees may drive it, make sure your policy covers that.

Workers' Compensation

Workers' Compensation insurance covers lost wages and medical bills if an employee is hurt on the job or has a work-related illness, and death benefits if an employee dies of a job-related cause. Workers' Comp also provides a business with legal representation if an employee files a work-related injury lawsuit. This coverage is required by every state in the U.S., although each state has its own rules and requirements for rates and benefits. In most cases you'll purchase Workers' Comp through an insurance company rather than a state's insurance fund. Ask your business-insurance agent for the latest requirements, and whether you purchase your coverage through an insurance company or the state fund. Or you can contact your state's Department of Insurance or Insurance Commissioner (listed in the phone book's blue pages and on your state's Web site) to request this information.

If your business is a corporation Some states consider the owners of corporations to be *employees* of that corporation, which means you'll be required to carry Workers' Comp even if you don't have other employees. (Sole proprietors and owners of partnerships are not considered employees.)

Other business insurance

Other types of insurance are widely available, and while they may not be "must-haves" for everyone in business, some of them may be worthwhile protection for yourself and your assets.

Business interruption Property insurance will cover goods damaged in a disaster, but if you have to close the business to make repairs or replace merchandise, property insurance won't cover your continuing business expenses such as salaries, taxes, lost earnings and certain other expenses.

That's what business interruption (BI) insurance is for. It's designed to cover ongoing costs like those, as outlined and defined in the policy (as always, review it carefully!). If BI insurance doesn't seem like a necessity, you should know that many small businesses never reopen after disasters because they don't have the money to survive the downtime. Many coverage options are available, and policies can be easily customized to meet your needs; ask your insurance agent. In some cases, you can buy BI coverage as part of a larger insurance package like a "business owner's policy."

Business owner's Small-business owners often choose a business owner's policy (BOP) because it bundles property insurance, liability insurance and, in most cases, business-interruption insurance (but not Workers' Comp: you have to buy that separately). BOPs usually have these two advantages going for them: they offer substantial savings on coverage costs; and they can be tailored to a business owner's specific situation. As you compare BOPs, take into consideration the same issues that govern your purchase of liability and property insurance: coverage amounts, what's covered, what's excluded, and the like.

Disability

Although Workers' Compensation covers lost pay due to work-related injury or illness, it doesn't cover lost pay during a disability that's *not* work-related. That's where short- and long-term disability insurance comes in.

Short-term disability (STD) This insurance covers short absences—a specified number of consecutive days or weeks—due to illness or injury. Most business owners feel they can weather a short-term loss of income and find this coverage isn't cost-effective, especially at start-up.

Long-term disability (LTD) This insurance, on the other hand, could be a financial life-saver if you have an illness or injury that keeps you out of work—and out of income. It's designed to replace a portion of your actual or "assumed" future income (usually 45-60 percent).

Insurance companies define both "long-term" and "disability" very narrowly (read the fine print!). If your disability meets all of the policy's conditions, these plans are usually set up to start paying you periodic benefits at the end of an "elimination period." That's typically defined as the length of time (anywhere from 30 days to several years) after the start of the disability. While you're disabled, LTD coverage usually pays a percentage of your annual income as monthly benefits for a certain time (or sometimes up to a certain age). Read these policies closely for definitions, benefit calculations, and the terms and conditions of policy renewals.

It's a *very* good idea to buy LTD insurance for yourself. Even though your health insurance pays your covered medical expenses, the loss of income due to a prolonged illness or injury can financially devastate you. Check with your insurance agent for the ins and outs of LTD coverage, and how you might reduce the cost of coverage by means of a longer elimination period and/or a lower benefit percentage. (Just be prepared to cover the gap and/or supplement a lower benefit percentage.) And although it's not likely that you would make LTD insurance available to hourly or commissioned employees, it might be wise to provide or offer it to key members of your operation. Your agent can tell you more about your options and costs.

Business overhead expense (BOE) Another type of insurance that can come to your aid if you become disabled is business overhead expense coverage. It can cover 100 percent of your ongoing business expenses such as employee pay while you're disabled. Ask your insurance agent for details.

Employee dishonesty

Let's face it: some employees aren't honest. Employee dishonesty insurance can protect you from losses due to their sticky fingers. This coverage is designed to pay benefits only if you file a police report and the employee is charged and convicted of stealing from you. Most small-business people don't think about this coverage at start-up, but it might be worth it, depending on the value of your merchandise, how many employees you have and how well you know them. Ask your insurance agent about the cost of this coverage: it may be less than you think.

Theft

Retailers experience many types theft, the most common being robbery, burglary, shoplifting, and employee dishonesty (covered above). If you're concerned about theft, ask your insurance agent to explain coverage that's available through a general or special policy. Whether you need this type of coverage depends on several factors, such as your product (i.e., how easy it is to steal and how valuable it is), and how much financial loss you could suffer. Your agent can help you determine if this coverage is worth it for you.

Health

Sure it's expensive, but considering that one accident, major illness or surgery can run up tens of thousands of dollars or more in medical bills (a single x-ray can cost hundreds!), health insurance is worth it. If you don't already have health insurance get coverage at least for yourself. Some insurance companies also offer "small employer group" coverage, usually for a minimum of two or five people. This may require jumping through hoops when you apply, but if you qualify, it could mean lower rates or better coverage. And "employer-sponsored" insurance may also give you some legal advantages as the insured (for example, some states don't allow employer-sponsored health plans to exclude "pre-existing conditions"). As your business grows, you may find it worthwhile to offer group health insurance for your employees, which can help attract and keep good people. (However, if you have more than 20 employees, additional laws and regulations govern your health plan. At that point, you should check with your attorney for advice.)

Whether individual or group coverage, a good health insurance plan is expensive, so shop around for the best rate. And to help keep rates down, consider high deductibles and/or eliminating certain coverage you know you won't need. Again, your insurance agent can help, or you can start by going direct: all of the big companies have Web sites with basic consumer information.

Business-association group health

Many small-business associations offer their members group health insurance. Here are three you can look into:

- *U.S. Federation of Small Businesses (800.637.3331; usfsb.com)*
- *Northeast Business Trust (800.464.0039; nbtgroup.com)*
- *Small Business Service Bureau (800.222.3434; sbsb.com)*

Key person, partners, buy-sell

Key person insurance What happens if a key staff member becomes disabled or dies? Your business can suffer; operations could even come to a standstill. But if you have key person insurance, it will pay all or part of that employee's salary if he or she becomes disabled, and death benefits if that person dies. This coverage can be important for a small business, where the loss of a key employee can limit or stop operations. And if you have a business loan, your lender may require you to carry key person insurance and/or partner insurance so that the loan will be repaid in case of disability or death.

Life

Life insurance will protect your estate and family from your creditors in the event of your death and provide for them in the future (if you purchase enough coverage, that is). If you borrow money from a lending institution, you will likely be required to purchase life insurance (for yourself and other partners/co-owners) that will pay back the loan in the event of your death. The two most common types of life insurance policies are term life and whole life. As the name implies, term life insurance covers you for a specified period of time, which may be more appropriate if you want coverage until you have paid off a loan. Whole life insurance is more expensive, but it accumulates a cash value over time as premiums are paid.

Earthquake, flood, hurricane: "peculiar risks"

Every retailer is at risk for losses due to all kinds of unforeseen events, some retailers face "peculiar risks" such as earthquakes, floods and hurricanes because their locations are in areas that are prone to them. If you plan to locate in a high-risk area, ask your insurance agent to review your options and calculate the cost of a policy that protects your assets against those events. In many cases, earthquake, flood and hurricane insurance are separate policies that are purchased through specialist insurance companies. For any of the peculiar-risk policies below, your own insurance agent can analyze your risks and explain your options.

Earthquake insurance People often shrug off the possibility of an earthquake happening—even in areas where quakes occur, most notably parts of California. But here's a sobering fact: in January 1994, a 6.8 earthquake hit southern California and caused more than $10 billion in damage—including extensive damage to the North Ridge Fashion Center. Windows were shattered throughout, Bullocks department store collapsed, and many other retailers suffered heavy losses. So if you locate in an area that's earthquake-prone, consider adding earthquake insurance.

Flood insurance Even if you aren't in a flood-prone area, heavy rains can cause widespread flooding almost anywhere. According to estimates, more than one-third of flood-loss claims are for property that's located *outside* flood-prone areas. The main source of flood insurance for small businesses is the National Flood Insurance Program, which issues policies directly or through one of many insurers that are licensed to sell this coverage. In some high-risk areas, you may be required to have flood coverage; but even if it's not required and you locate a flood-prone area, consider adding flood insurance.

Hurricane insurance As with earthquake insurance, hurricane insurance can be crucial if you live in a hurricane-prone part of the country. Case in point: in September 1999, Hurricane Floyd hit North Carolina, not just the coast but inland, as well. Damages were estimated at $3 billion to $6 billion; but government reports showed *insured* losses at only $1.3 billion. Many businesses, including retailers, lost everything. Owners with hurricane insurance were the ones who had the best a chance at recovering.

Your insurance agent

Company rep or independent agent? Company reps (sometimes called "direct writers") are *agents who usually represent and sell for one insurance company such as Nationwide or Allstate (among many others). Independent agents usually sell for several (sometimes many) insurance companies.*

Finding the right agent or company

Chances are you already have insurance of some kind, so the best way to start is to contact that insurance agent. Set up a meeting to discuss the types of insurance he or she offers, and how you can get the best rates (e.g., by choosing higher deductibles). Once you know which policies you need, you can shop around for the best coverage and rates available.

If you need help finding an insurance company that offers the types of insurance you need, you could ask other retailers for their agents' names and/or insurance companies. Also ask about the retailers' experiences with that agent and insurer. You can also ask your leasing manager for leads and background. Other sources include industry associations, chambers of commerce, and local business groups. Many trade associations offer various insurance plans for their members, and the association's group buying power may also mean lower premiums.

"Cart and kiosk" insurance

Insurance for carts and kiosks may be hard to find, but these two companies offer short-term liability policies—even as short as one month— in all 50 states:

- *Arizona Central Insurance, Tucson, AZ (800.678.0062; azcentralins.com)*

- *Shahinian Insurance Services, Inc., Tustin, CA (800.457.2231; shahinianinsurance.com)*

The quality of service an insurance agent gives you is as important as good coverage and competitive rates. You need someone in your corner who can answer your questions and look out for your business's welfare—someone who is familiar with your business. An agent who will be active in resolving any problems, especially in the claims process, and not leave you to fend for yourself with the claims adjuster—the person who scrutinizes and then approves or denies claims.

Your agent should also try to have your premiums reduced by suggesting changes you could make in your business that reduce certain risks, such as installing a security system to reduce the risk of burglary. Your agent should also be on top of changes in the insurance industry, especially as they affect you, and periodically review and re-evaluate your insurance needs with you. And finally, you want someone you like and trust—not just because your money's involved, but also because you may have to spend a fair amount of time with that person during stressful moments if ever you need to make a claim.

But you don't want "duplication of coverage," which can happen without knowing about it, but which you're paying for. Chances are, there's less likelihood of duplicate coverage if you use the same insurance agent for all of your policies. Ask your agent to review your policies for coverage duplications. If you have any questions about what's covered and what's not, ask your rep for a full and complete explanation *before* you sign anything.

Buying tips

Before you buy any insurance, use these tips to get the best insurance products at the best rates:

- Ask about the insurer's and the agent's track records for paying claims and then do your own research by contacting a rating agency, which you can find online or in the phone book. Online, ratings are available at a lot of sites, including A.M. Best (ambest.com/ratings/info.asp) and Insure.com (insure.com), one of the many Web sites where you can also buy coverage.

- Confirm that your insurance company and your agent are licensed in your state to sell the type of insurance you're buying. For example, your agent may be licensed to sell car insurance in your state but not general liability or life. To confirm any agent's or insurance company's license status, contact your state's Department of Insurance or Insurance Commissioner (check your local phone book's blue pages or your state's Web site).

- See if you can get a better deal by staying with one insurance company or agent for all of your insurance, or splitting your policies among only a few companies.

- Consider increasing your deductibles or lowering your coverage limits, to lower your premiums. Only you can determine how much risk you're willing to take.

- Ask what types of package policies are available (e.g. Business Owner Policies) that may reduce your insurance expenses.

- Review all of your policies, being careful to read what's covered and what's not, and keep an eye out for any duplications of coverage.

As the old song says, you gotta shop around, especially for insurance. It takes an informed comparison shopper to find the best insurance products ith the best coverage for your business, and at the best rates.

□ □ □

Taking Credit Cards, Debit Cards & Checks

T hirty-plus years ago, when the credit card industry was in its infancy, most consumers paid for everything with cash, or by personal check if they had a relationship with the retailer. Today, the landscape is very different, cash may be an endangered species, and retailers who don't accept the entire array of payment options—credit cards, debit cards, personal checks and travelers checks—are at a distinct disadvantage. Here's what you need to accept money from your customers, no matter what form it takes.

Credit cards

Today's currency is plastic, and Visa, MasterCard, American Express and Discover are the big four. These are the cards you need to accept. Americans charged an all-time high of more than $1.5 trillion to their credit cards in 2000. Clearly, you want a share of that bounty.

For many new retail entrepreneurs, the "merchant" side of credit cards is a mystery. So here's a primer: Cards like Visa and MasterCard are sometimes called "bank cards" because they're issued by banks (and other financial institutions). The banks set up and maintain the merchant accounts for these cards. American Express and Discover, on the other hand, are issued not by banks but by the card companies themselves, who set up and maintain the merchant accounts. The banks and card companies make money by charging interest/finance charges on cardholders' unpaid balances (as everyone knows only too well) . . . and by charging merchants various fees for accepting the card as payment.

Is it worth it to you as a merchant to accept credit cards? You don't have to believe the credit-card companies' studies showing that after retailers start accepting credit cards, sales increase from 30 percent to 200 percent. You don't have to believe it, but it certainly drives home the point about how valuable credit-card sales are to a retail business, and how important they are to customers. If you want to do a quick, unscientific "study" of your own, spend an hour near the cash register of any store in any mall, and you'll see that customers *expect* to be able to pay with plastic. And in retail, as you know, customer expectations are everything. Retailers who don't meet, let alone exceed, customers' expectations lose sales in the short run, and have a much harder time building a repeat-customer base in the long run. And because the cost of acquiring new customers is much greater than the cost of keeping current customers, the profit potential suffers. So the short answer is yes, it's worth it.

AmEx on top

American Express says that, on average, their cardholders spend more than four times per American Express card than bank card holders spend per bank card.

Credit stats

Here are some remarkable facts about credit cards in 2000, from the U.S. Federal Reserve's Division of Consumer Affairs:

- Card issuers sent out 3.5 billion direct-mail solicitations, and got a response rate of 0.6%. (Not bad: 1%-2% is generally considered a good response to direct mail.) That's a lot of potential new credit card accounts.

- Consumers used 1.4 billion credit cards—an average of roughly nine cards per cardholder—to buy nearly $1.5 trillion in goods and services.

- Consumers made more than 20 billion individual credit-card transactions . . . and owed nearly $675 billion on their credit cards by the end of the year.

The benefits

The repeat-customer issue aside, here are the benefits of accepting at least the four major cards:

Credibility By not taking plastic, a retail business gives customers bad vibes: it signals a "here-today-gone-tomorrow" feel, a "bush league" aura, and customers simply don't like or trust it. If you don't accept any credit cards, customers will wonder why, even if they don't ask. They may wonder how stable your business is, or how committed you are to it.

Multi-channel sales You can't take orders by phone, through the mail or online if you don't take plastic (at least not without the hassle of invoicing, or using a payment service for online sales). It's even difficult to make sales at retail events like craft shows or street festivals if you only take cash and checks. Think of the sales you could be making if you were set up for credit cards . . . and the sales you can't if you aren't.

> ### Visa dollars?
> Visa says its cards are accepted at more than 16 million locations in 300 countries and territories, "making Visa the closest thing there is to a universal currency."

Better customer service One aspect of good customer service is making the buying process as convenient as possible. If you don't accept credit cards, you'll inconvenience some of your customers who can't or don't want to pay by cash or check. Because the vast majority of credit cards have reward ("affinity") programs that give users airline miles, points, restaurant and travel discounts and other perks, some consumers use their credit cards just for the "freebies" value. You don't want to stand between your customers and their free airline tickets!

Quick payment Credit cards allow retailers to receive payment fairly quickly (within 48 hours in many cases) without having to wait for customer checks to clear.

Competitive (dis)advantage A decade ago, small retailers could still gain a competitive edge by accepting credit cards. But since plastic is now ubiquitous, you're at a disadvantage if you *don't* take credit cards.

The drawbacks

Set-up hassles If you want to explore all of your options—computer-based cash-register processing, swipe terminal lease vs. purchase, full-scale point-of-sale systems with integrated credit-card processing software—you'll have to make more than one phone call (limited information is available online). At American Express, for example, you might end up speaking with three different divisions: the software division, to find out about computer-based processing options; the equipment division, to discuss the cost of lease vs. purchase; and the rates/account set-up division, to find out what it will cost to accept the Amex card and what you have to do to get a merchant account.

Regulation C A federal consumer-protection law, Regulation C protects all deposits and payments made with credit cards, giving consumers the right to a refund if the merchandise doesn't measure up (for example, if it's defective, or if what's delivered isn't the exact merchandise the customer ordered) and the merchant refuses to give the customer a refund or credit. Under these circumstances and if the cardholder made a written complaint to the credit card company, the company will remove the charge from the cardholder's account, mark the funds as being "in dispute," and contact the merchant to resolve the issue. If the merchant can't successfully argue his or her side of the issue, or if the transaction was processed in a way that violated any of the terms of the merchant-account agreement, the merchant has to repay the amount of the sale to the credit card company, plus a "chargeback" fee.

> ### Avoiding chargebacks
> The best way to avoid chargebacks is to make sure your customers are fully aware of your return policy when they make their purchases. Your return policy should be posted at the point of sale—in the same place as your check-acceptance policy—and printed on your receipts below the signature line.

Fraud Chances are, someone will slip you a stolen credit card at one time or another. But if you use the best equipment that includes automatic authorization (or always call for authorization if you process cards manually—

see p. 182) and you follow the card issuer's suggestions to avoid fraud, your risk of getting burned will be greatly reduced.

Costs Credit-card companies charge retailers a percentage of each sale charged. Known as the "discount rate" (explained below), this is usually between 1.5 percent and 4 percent of the sale. In addition, miscellaneous fees push the actual cost of accepting plastic higher.

Discount rate

"Discount rate" may sound appealing, but when it comes to credit cards, it's not. The discount rate is what the retailer is charged for processing a credit-card purchase. The rate is a percentage of the total amount of the purchase, tax included, which the merchant pays to the bank or credit card company. The rates vary from about 1.5 percent to 4 percent, and are based primarily on these four factors:

- the total amount of credit-card sales per year (current or estimated)

- the amount of the average credit-card sale (current or estimated)

- the retail channel (retail location, direct mail, online)

- the method of processing (electronic "swipe," manual key in, etc.)

The higher the yearly sales volume and average sale, the lower the discount rate. For example, a retailer whose sales volume is greater than $50,000 and whose average sale is $50 might get a discount rate in the range of 2-3 percent. A retailer who makes the majority of sales from a Web site—even if they also sell through a store—will pay a higher discount rate. Why? Because when you sell on the Web, you can't see the cardholder or the card at the time of purchase, so you and the card company have less protection. As for the method of processing, retailers who use electronic card-swipe terminals sometimes (depending on the card) pay a lower rate than those who don't and have to key in numbers manually on a keypad (PC-based or otherwise).

Other fees

That's just the discount rate. Fees and miscellaneous charges can add up. Here are the most common fees you're likely to encounter as you shop for the best deal:

- Application and/or set-up fee: an up-front, flat fee of $50 to $500 charged to review your merchant-account application, run a credit check, process the application, and/or open your account.

- Transaction fee: a flat fee of 5¢ to 15¢ per transaction.

- Chargeback fee: a flat fee of $10 to $25 for each disputed transaction.

- Membership fee: a one-time or annual flat fee of less than $100.

- Monthly processing fee: a flat fee of up to $40 charged monthly to process your credit-card transactions. This is *in addition* to per-transaction charges.

- Minimum monthly processing fee: a flat fee of $10 to $30 charged if the total discount-rate fees collected for one month don't meet a pre-set minimum.

- Service fee: can be anything (read the fine print!), but may be tied to whether you leased or purchased the authorization equipment.

- Equipment fee: a monthly fee of $25 to $50 to lease the equipment you need for processing transactions. This doesn't apply if you buy the equipment outright.

- Statement fee: a flat fee of $5 to $10 charged for each monthly statement.

Sometimes these fees are negotiable, so shop around to get the best total deal, not just the lowest discount rate. And, you can ask for a lower discount rate and other fees once you've been operating for a while. And definitely ask once your sales increase to certain levels. In fact, it's a good idea to ask for a "rate review" every six months, or so.

Watch what you say

Credit-card companies have rules about what a retailer can say to a customer regarding a credit-card purchase. For example, you can't tell a customer you prefer cash to credit cards that cost you a percentage of the sale. If it's discovered that you did, the company can terminate your merchant account.

Applying for a merchant account

Assuming you want to accept the four major cards (Visa, MasterCard, American Express and Discover), here's how to go about getting your merchant accounts:

Visa, MasterCard You can apply for these merchant accounts either through a bank or independent merchant-account provider. You might get the best rate from the bank that handles your business accounts, so start there. If they don't handle merchant accounts, they can point you in the right direction. You can find an independent account provider online (search for "accept credit cards" and you'll find hundreds of providers), or through the SBA, SCORE or a retail trade association. Or you can ask retailers or leasing managers for the names of the account providers they use.

American Express, Discover You can apply for these merchant accounts either directly from American Express and Discover or through an independent merchant-account provider. To go direct, contact American Express Merchant Services (800.528.5200; americanexpress.com) and Discover Card Merchant Accounts (800.347.7996; discovercard.com).

Trade association discounts

If you're a member of a retail trade association or a chamber of commerce (or you're thinking of joining one), ask if they offer members a merchant-account discount. In fact, some chambers and trade associations offer so many member-discount opportunities (insurance,

travel, supplies, services, even restaurants)
that the membership fee may be well worth it.

Equipment

In addition to merchant accounts, you'll need an authorization terminal to process your customer's credit card purchases via phone lines. The terminal lets merchants capture the buyer's credit-card information (either by manual key-in or "swiping" the card) and dial into the credit-card processor's database to verify that the card isn't counterfeit and hasn't been reported lost or stolen, and that the cardholder hasn't reached or exceeded the pre-set credit limit. If the processing company approves the transaction, it gives the merchant an authorization code, and the purchase can be completed. (Each credit-card company has guidelines on how to proceed if authorization is denied.)

Dozens of terminal models are on the market, many of which have built-in printers (if you don't get one of those models, you'll need a separate printer). For $500 to $700, you can buy a terminal that will process and authorize the four major cards. Or you can lease one from the bank or processing company for around $25 to $50 a month. If you plan to sell in venues like festivals and craft shows, where your access to phone lines may be limited (or non-existent), consider buying or leasing a wireless terminal.

Processing software If you plan to use a PC as your cash register, you can buy credit-card authorization software to process transactions instead of using an authorization terminal. These packages, which cost $300-$600, process all the major credit and debit cards. American Express has its own "Purchase Express" software for $450 plus $95 a year for tech support (required).

Manual processing You can avoid the expense of buying or leasing a credit-card authorization terminal by using a manual imprinter and calling in each purchase instead. The downsides: Manual processing at your end is labor-intensive (read "costly") for the credit-card companies, so they'll charge you higher transaction fees and discount rates; and it can take longer for the money to be credited to you.

✔ Start-up Tip

No matter which method you use to process credit card sales, practice ringing up a few before opening day. Doing that will prevent making your customers wait as you try to figure out what key to hit next.

Setting up merchant accounts

You can set up your merchant accounts over the phone, although many processing companies may also want to visit your place of business to make sure you're an established retailer. To set up your merchant accounts, you'll need to provide information that includes:

- your name and Social Security number

- the name of your bank

- the account number the funds should be deposited into

- the bank routing code for that bank account

- basic sales information: estimated annual charge volume, and average transaction amount

Debit cards

With debit cards gaining in popularity, you may want to accept them, too. Debit cards, draw directly from the cardholder's checking or savings account. If you want to accept them, you need one more piece of equipment: a PIN pad. It's what customers use to key in their personal identification number to authorize the debit transaction. You can buy a PIN pad for around $200, or you can lease one for around $6-$10 a month. You may be in luck, though: since some credit-card authorization terminals already have a PIN pad built in, you might be able to avoid that extra expense if you buy or lease the right terminal. Ask your merchant-account provider to review your options and, as always, shop around and crunch the numbers.

Checks

"Will you take a check?" How many times have you asked a merchant that question, or overheard someone else ask? Customers will ask you, too. Will you or won't you? There are pros and cons either way. Obviously, you could get stuck with a bad check, but if you don't take checks, you could lose sales from customers who don't have (or don't want to use) credit cards or cash.

If you want to accept checks, ask your bank about the steps you can take to reduce the chance of getting a fraudulent or other bad check. For example, some standard ways to protect yourself are to insist on:

- checks that have the customer's name and address imprinted on them (no counter checks), plus get home and work phone numbers

- the check number above 400 (or whatever number you choose)

- a government-issued photo ID (e.g., driver's license)

- a check written for the amount of purchase only

- no third-party checks

- no pre-signed checks—the check must be signed in front of you (and signor must be the name printed on the check)

- return policy: only after 10 business days for items paid by check, so the check has time to clear first

You must post these check-acceptance policy "rules" at your point of sale so that customers can read them easily (and so that there's no dispute either at your location or if you ever need to take legal action). And if you charge a fee (usually $20) for "returned" checks as most retailers do, post that rule, too. Just make sure the fee you charge is within the limit set by state law (ask your bank or accountant).

Also ask your bank how long it takes for checks to clear. In-state checks usually clear in three to five business days; out-of-state checks usually clear in five to seven business days, sometimes more. Also ask the bank how to collect on checks that bounce due to non-sufficient funds, or "NSF." You can try to deposit the check again.

Check verification   If you expect a large number of customers to pay by check, you can protect yourself against bad checks by using one of two methods. One is to invest in a point-of-sale (POS) system (see p. 210) that includes check-verification features. Similar to credit-card authorization, the system dials into a national database of checking-account holders to verify that the check is good, and that the account has sufficient funds to cover it. The other method is to contract with a check-verification service, which does the same thing. But if you go it alone and you do get a bad check, hundreds of companies specialize in helping you collect. To find check-verification or check-recovery companies (some firms do both), check with your bank, your accountant or merchants association for recommendations, or search online.

Travelers checks

Travelers checks are basically the same as cash. You'll see checks issued by companies like American Express and other major credit cards, banks, and travel companies like AAA and Thomas Cook. And they're easy to accept. Customers present a pre-signed check and then sign it again in front of you. (You can ask for a phone number, and depending on the company's rules, you may also be permitted to ask for photo ID.) When change is due (and there often is: the common denominations are $20 and $50), you give it to the customer in cash.

These checks are easy for you to process. With American Express, for example, you don't have to sign a contract, set up a merchant account, or pay a discount rate. You'll deposit the checks into your bank account just as you would personal checks. (Some banks have a handling charge; ask them for details.) As long as you follow the issuing company's guidelines for accepting travelers checks (such as American Express's "Watch and Compare"program), you're guaranteed full payment. For more about accepting travelers checks and what to do if signatures don't match, go to the companies' Web sites, or search online for "travelers checks" (or "cheques").

Gift checks

Some companies that issue travelers checks also issue gift checks, like American Express Gift Cheques. They're like travelers checks someone bought for someone else, and work the same way.

□ □ □

Hiring and Managing Employees

For a new business owner, hiring employees may be one of the most daunting tasks. Consider what it takes to hire someone: the time and expense to find and train that someone; the tax and accounting issues to pay even one employee; and the legal do's and don'ts you have to navigate. No wonder new business owners are intimidated by it all. And once the new employee is on board, there are management issues: even the best employee might challenge your management skills from time to time, and a bad one can not only make life difficult but can seriously hurt your business.

But good employees are among your best assets. They can make your business succeed in ways you could never achieve on your own. They can bring skills to your business that you don't have. If they have good sales skills, they can significantly increase your profitability. And best of all, they can make work more fun, exciting and rewarding for you.

First, you have to decide whether you even need employees in the beginning (most people do) and if so, how many. Considering your hours of operation, most malls are open at least 65 hours a week (from 10:00 a.m. to 9:00 or 10:00 p.m. Mon.-Sat., and 11:00 a.m.-6:00 p.m., Sun.) and the size of your business, do you need part-time to help year-round, or just for the holidays? Do you need a full-time employee who can take on managerial duties? Or do you need several part-timers to give you greater "coverage" and scheduling flexibility? To decide what you need, define the job you need an employee (or more than one) to fill and the tasks you need them to do.

Holiday help Specialty retailers put in especially long hours during the holiday season, especially in malls. Malls usually have extended hours, sometimes staying open past midnight during November and December, when shoppers come out in droves. The holiday season can account for a big chunk of a year-round retailer's sales (and, obviously, 100 percent of a Christmas-season retailer's sales). And because the Christmas crunch can be a make-or-break proposition, most owners are on-site from opening to well after closing. But you can't do it all, all day and all night. Even if you already have employees by the time the holiday buying season rolls around, you must continue to gauge your staffing needs throughout the holiday season.

Writing a job description

It may seem tedious or simplistic to write a job description for a salesperson—doesn't everyone know what a salesperson's job entails? In the long run, though, the energy you invest in analyzing and outlining a job's requirements will be more than worth the effort. A clear understanding of that job will enable you to simplify the interview process, clarify applicants' expectations and hire the right person. It will also make training that employee easier, and reduce the potential for turnover. And here's another plus: if you ever have problems with an employee, a specific job description will make it much easier to iron out conflicts—or defend your position if you have to.

For each job you want to fill, list the job's major and minor responsibilities (see the checklist on p. 189 for ideas). Start with the obvious ("selling merchandise"), then move on to the nitty-gritty details (like "restocking, organizing, dusting, tidying"). Describe the physical tasks (e.g., lifting heavy boxes, making deliveries), any specific knowledge or skills the employee must learn on the job (e.g., operating the cash register or computer system); work days (which days of the week? days or nights? weekends? flexible/rotating shifts?); total work hours per week; and rules for breaks (e.g., one 20-minute break per 4.5 hours worked; 30-minute meal break for full-time employee;) or time off (vacation/sick time policies, whether paid or not). If there are any potential job-related hazards (e.g., using machinery to customize products), include them, too. Next, create a job title and state who the employee will report to (that's probably you, at least at first). You also have to decide what the job will pay—that is, what your business will pay an employee in that job, and if it will be hourly or salaried, and with or without commission. Finding out what you should pay to be fair and competitive may take a little market research on your part. (You can get help with both the job description and the going rate for various jobs from other retailers, your SCORE or SBA counselor, or a retail trade association. Or do an online search.)

Finally, list the skills and qualities you want in an employee. Include education (high school grad? some college? college grad?), types and length of experience, any computer skills, etc. Also list certain personal skills that are needed for performing the job well (e.g., outgoing, well-groomed, well-spoken, punctual). Make a distinction between the abilities an applicant *must* have and those you prefer but don't require (e.g., "bilingual a plus"). This list is primarily for you to use to evaluate the applicants you interview.

Sample job duties

When creating job descriptions, you may want to include some or all of the following job duties:

- Arrange products, fixtures and displays.
- Assemble, maintain, and dismantle displays.
- Maintain inventory control systems.
- Report status/progress to management at specified times.
- Participate in employee meetings.
- Make suggestions to management.
- Arrange special-event displays.
- Comparison-shop nearby competitors.
- Operate register/point-of-sale terminal/calculator.

- Receive and check incoming stock.

- Process returns to vendors.

- Price and mark stock.

- Make and record price changes.

- Handle reserve and back stock.

- Transfer stock to selling floor.

- Process returned and damaged products.

- Wrap and package merchandise.

- Process special orders.

- Answer the phone.

- Process mail.

- Demonstrate products.

- Handle customer objections and complaints.

- Operate store equipment.

- Process phone orders.

- Make change (with and without POS change indicator).

- Complete credit-card transactions.

- Open and close out register/POS terminal.

- Complete a deposit slip, and deposit funds.

Types of employees

You now have a clearly defined job description and a list of some personal traits that fill the bill. But what's the best *type* of employee for the job slot and for your business? Full-time or part-time? Year-round or seasonal? Independent contractor or temp? Here's some information on the advantages of each type.

Full-time   Generally speaking, full-time employees are more willing to accept broader responsibilities. They're also often more reliable because their job is their sole (or at least primary) source of income, and they depend on it. And full-time employees are often more dedicated when they're included in a company's future plans to expand, making their position more a career than just a job. So if you want someone to assume managerial duties and a committed outlook, a full-time employee may be the best choice. Keep in mind, however, that if you only have one full-time employee and that person gets sick, you may have to put in many extra hours to cover for them.

Part-time   Part-time employees sometimes mean a great deal of flexibility for retailers. In shopping malls, with their long hours and fluctuating traffic levels, flexibility can be particularly advantageous. Using part-time help also gives you a large pool of "non-traditional" employees to draw from—retirees, mothers of school-age kids, and students. Retirees often have considerable experience and a good work ethic; so do mothers, who are often motivated to do something useful and interesting but not kid-oriented; and students sometimes have great success selling to younger consumers. To create a "patchwork" schedule or just cover some holes in the business day or week, part-timers can be the answer. You may also find some employees will eventually want managerial duties—if so, these are the ones you'll eventually promote to roles like "assistant manager," and the first ones you'll make full-time if you and the employee want to go that way.

Seasonal   Seasonal retailers face the daunting task of finding capable, dependable employees to work for just 8 to 12 weeks straight. But it's by no means impossible. Where do you find them? Special-interest groups (hobby clubs, collectors' associations, etc.) can be a good resource; so can church groups. Students are a good bet, so get the word out through students and teachers you know, or through campus channels. Also ask family, friends and neighbors to scout for you. And don't forget to ask your best customers—they might love to have some part-time work, especially if they like your products (and you!), and you give them an employee discount while they're employed.

Temps Hiring through a temporary-employment agency is a good way to fill employment gaps (some retailers even use part-time temps year-round). Temp agencies take some of the burden off the employer by testing skills and checking references before they send someone to an interview. Using a temp agency is also a good way to try out a prospective employee: If you're happy with the temp working for you, you can hire that person full-time. Expect to pay the agency's hiring fee, but it's worth it in the long run, which is why so may employers do it this way. Temp agencies are listed in the Yellow Pages.

Independent contractors Some retailers prefer hiring independent contractors. A large part of the appeal is that the employer doesn't have to withhold or pay payroll taxes. Generally speaking, independent contractors run their own businesses (usually sole proprietorships), have multiple clients, set their own hours, are hired on a per-job basis, and provide their own tools and equipment. In short, they're their own bosses, hired by you to do a certain job. The key word in this scenario is *independent*. The IRS has strict guidelines on the differences between employees and independent contractors—which means if you so much as set the work hours for the independent contractor working for you, you may be putting that person's independent-contractor status in jeopardy. According to the IRS, requiring work to be performed at set hours "indicates control by the service recipient [you] over the worker, and is indicative of an employer-employee relationship." If the IRS reclassifies your independent contractor as an employee, you could end up owing a chunk of back taxes and penalties. For more on these IRS guidelines, contact the IRS (800.TAX.FORM; irs.gov) for Publication 15-A, *Employer's Supplemental Tax Guide*. You can also order a copy of the parent publication, Pub. 15, Circular E, *Employer's Tax Guide*, which explains your tax responsibilities as an employer. You need a copy of Acrobat Reader to read these publications online, (you can download it free from adobe.com).

Finding good candidates

Advertising in newspapers is perhaps the most common way to attract employees, but many other effective means can be less expensive. Your first and best resource may actually be yourself. Spread the word! Tell friends, business contacts and former co-workers that you're looking for employees. Perhaps they have teenagers or retired parents who need work. Perhaps you belong to social clubs or civic organizations where you could post job fliers or run ads in their newsletters (often at affordable rates). Ask permission to post notices on boards at churches, senior centers, community centers and libraries. Trade and vocational schools, colleges, universities and some high schools have job placement programs—contact their job-placement counselors to get listed as an employer. They also have bulletin boards: ask to post job fliers in campus student centers, classroom buildings, and dorms.

Keep an eye out for upcoming job fairs, and get in on the action. Or focus your search by targeting specific groups or organizations that relate to your product line. For example, if you sell collectibles, running an ad in collectors' newsletters may attract enthusiastic applicants with a wealth of knowledge about your products. Or you could go through a well-respected employment agency. Again, you'll pay a fee, but you get the benefit of having applicants pre-screened, and there's usually a "refund" policy or "guarantee" (i.e., if the employee doesn't work out—or walks—within a certain period, you don't pay the agency).

Finally, don't forget the Net. Numerous Web sites have national and local job listings, and many trade and professional organizations have job banks. The Internet also lets you search outside your immediate job market so you can find potential employees who want to move to your area.

Writing an effective ad

A well-written ad can make a huge difference. A good ad attracts the right people for the job and deters (mostly) everyone else. A good ad is *informative*. It has the right stuff, the basic who-what-where details. Use the list you made earlier so that your ad includes:

- a concise, informative job description

- education and experience requirements/preferences

- a request for a résumé, and how to send it
  (mail? fax? e-mail?)

- instructions (apply in person, call for an appointment, etc.)

- contact information: your company, name, address, phone,
  fax, e-mail, Web site (as applicable)

Sell the job, the company and what you have to offer. Think about the people you're trying to reach and what they would find appealing. Flexible or evening hours? Advancement? A chance to learn new skills? A fun work environment? Opportunities to be creative and share ideas? You're competing with other employers to get the best people, so you need to communicate what makes your business different. That way, you attract employees who want more from a job than just a paycheck.

Two dont's

1. Don't waste expensive space spelling out the kind of person you want (e.g., "go-getter, upbeat"). You'll know if they have the personality traits you're looking for when you interview them.

2. Don't run a "blind" ad, one with no company name or info other than a PO box, fax number or e-mail address. People don't trust them, and you'll get fewer responses and fewer good applicants.

Reviewing the résumés

Résumés, like applicants, come in all shapes and sizes. Some people provide chronological job histories; others organize according to skills and tasks. Regardless of the structure, you want to see the same types of information on every one: name and contact information, education, employment history, and skills. (If a résumé is incomplete, don't bother with it.)

Job applications

You also want job-seekers to fill out an application—the same form for everyone. (You can get a pack of basic "apps" at office suppliers.) Some people, especially teens, may not have a résumé. But more important, a résumé can hide things like unexplained gaps in employment. Having the two documents lets you compare.

When you evaluate résumés, read beyond the facts to see what you can about the applicant's attitude and character. Neatness and correct spelling are obviously good signs. A résumé that's tailored to your job ad shows initiative (and good sales skills!). Good writing shows good communication skills. By the way, if you think someone else may have written the résumé for the applicant, that's not all bad: the applicant was smart enough to get help.

Also notice if applicants merely *list* their previous job duties, or if they *explain* what they learned, how they met challenges, and what they achieved. Granted, they don't have room for too many details, but good candidates find a way to make their enthusiasm, creativity and growth potential come through.

Selecting applicants to interview

Once you have the applications and résumés in front of you, go over your job description and list of desired skills and qualities. Use those criteria to decide who might fit best. The key is to be consistent: use the same job-related standards for everyone. It's not only the fair thing; it's also the legal thing. If someone were to question your hiring practices, you can demonstrate that you used the same *objective* standards to assess all of the candidates. For similar reasons, keep that job description and skills list in your files, along with applications and résumés for at least a year.

Any notes you make during interviews should be job-related only, and made on a separate sheet of paper, not on the application or résumé. Some employers also use a standardized checklist that they create from the job description and list of skills to help guide the interview process.

Interviewing the applicants

Once you start interviewing, keep your job description and skills list handy so you can stay focused on *your needs*. A lot of people talk a good game during an interview, but that doesn't mean they can do the job. Hiring someone just because you like them won't work out if they can't perform, so always keep the job requirements in mind.

Set a specific time for the interview to test punctuality. When applicants arrive, take a moment to notice if they're neatly and appropriately dressed. As you talk and listen, note whether the applicant has good communication skills. (Easy to understand? Good information? Quick-thinking?) What do you sense from his or her body language? friendliness? nervousness? confidence? evasiveness? sense of humor? Again, read between the lines to see what the applicant *isn't* telling you. Numerous books are out there written by job-placement and human-resources pros to guide you on the kinds of questions to ask—and the meanings behind the answers you get.

Interviewing can be tricky. You want applicants to volunteer information they might rather keep hidden. You're trying to read between the lines. But again, as a general rule, keep interviews relaxed and friendly, ask questions that get applicants to reveal their true selves, and pay as much attention to what they're *not* saying.

Keep in mind that just because you'll be doing a little detective work doesn't mean interviews are adversarial situations. Quite the opposite. Your best interviews will be those where interviewees feel relaxed and comfortable enough to open up and be themselves.

If your business is already up and running by the time you do interviews, take the candidate to a more relaxed atmosphere, like a nearby café, rather than your place of business. (And don't forget to bring your list of interview questions). Standing near your cart or behind a counter does nothing to put the candidate at ease. You want an environment that's relatively quiet, comfortable, relaxed, and free of interruptions (don't even *think* of turning on your cell phone). After all, interviewees are trying to sell their talents to you, just as you're selling your business to them. You want to signal that you appreciate their time and interest, and that you don't want to be distracted so that you can actively listen to what they have to tell you—both now, and in the future if they work for you.

Applicants are likely to be nervous, especially students, so start with small talk. Then ease into your questions. Jotting just a few notes during the interview can be helpful later, but extreme note-taking makes candidates self-conscious. (Plus, are you really listening, or just taking dictation? One cancels out the other.) Simply telling the interviewee before hand that you'll be taking a few notes will help to make him or her more comfortable.

Make sure you have a prepared a list of questions before the interview starts. You don't have to stick to the list, but having it will help you keep the interview structured and prevent you from accidentally skipping any important topics.

Asking questions

What should you ask applicants? The goal is to get them talking, so don't ask closed-ended "yes-no" questions. But you don't gain much by asking hypothetical "What would you do if" questions. They'll just tell you what they think you want to hear. Instead, ask what the candidate did in past jobs (or even at school). As they answer, encourage them to move from general to specific information. How did they handle certain challenges and situations, like an angry customer or not having what someone wanted at that moment. Why did they do it that way? What was the result? Would they do it that way again, and why or why not? You'll learn a lot about attitude, skills and smarts by how they answer specific questions like these.

Another good technique is to ask them what their references will say when (not *if*) you call them. If applicants have something to hide, most of them tend to think it's better for you to hear it from them first. For example, "My old boss will tell you I was a great employee. And I was very good with people. I think his only complaint was that I was late sometimes." That applicant may turn out to be a great employee—but you'll know up front that you'll have to work with that employee on being punctual.

Sell yourself

Also, take time to tell the applicant about your business. Explain what you expect from an employee. Get them to ask you questions, which often reveal as much about them as their answers to your pre-set questions. Notice what kinds of questions the candidate asks. Are they basic, or do they show a level of understanding about retail work or your product line? Do they show quick thinking? Do they show that the candidate did the homework, and is genuinely curious about (or at least interested in) your business?

Again, don't forget to sell the job. Share some of your goals. Explain what you expect of employees: that you want to work with people who are coopera- tive, enthusiastic and supportive of each other. Tell them about learning and growth opportunities. Tell them you value employee input; you encourage and reward creativity and initiative; and you always maintain good, open communication with your employees. (And you have to mean it! Otherwise you'll have a case of the proverbial revolving door.)

When the interview is finished, make sure the candidate leaves on a positive note. Ask if they have any last questions; thank them for coming; and tell them when they can expect to hear from you. Remember, even if you don't ever plan to hire them, you want them to leave with good feelings about the interview, you, and your company.

Checking references

After the interviews are over, choose the best candidates and check their references. Former employers are more reliable than personal references, but you many have a hard time getting some of them to talk, for legal reasons. If this happens, try to get them to empathize with your situation—convey the feeling that, as employers, you're on the same team. Former employers will be more likely to answer job-related questions that don't require them to share personal opinions. If all else fails, you can always go back to the appli- cant and ask that they grease the wheels, or give you new references.

Collecting institutional information can also be a bit of a hassle. High school and college admission departments are likely to refuse to release information, and many high schools don't have comprehensive computerized records. (You can ask the applicant to give or show you a photocopy of a diploma, completion certificate or grade slip, though.) If you need to do a criminal background check, you'll work through county courthouses (which can be time-consuming) or with a background-check company (find them online, or contact a retail trade association for names of companies). It's also a good idea to run a credit check on applicants, but if your decision not to hire is partially based on a bad credit rating, you have to inform the applicant. And if an employee will do any driving for your business, you should check their driving record through your state's motor vehicles department.

Informed consent

You have to tell every applicant you interview that you'll be checking references. If you plan to run a credit or criminal background check, tell the applicant and get his or her written approval in advance.

Making a decision

Think you've picked a winner? Be warned: many first-time employers make the mistake of relying too heavily on their instincts. Sure, they're a valuable tool, just like applications, résumés and interviews. But if your instincts make you disregard your pre-set job needs, you may regret it.

Keep your eyes open for employees with some skills and qualities that you don't possess. You already have one of you; don't hire a clone. For example, an employee who turns out to be an artist might have great ideas about visual merchandising; a computer enthusiast may provide you with in-house tech support. Most employees love to demonstrate their expertise, and they'll be thrilled to have lent their know-how to help you get something done or solved, especially if you compensate them for those skills.

By the way, right after you've made your decision (and the applicant has accepted the job), call all of the interviewees to thank them for their interest. It's not only courteous; if your new hire doesn't work out, you may be offering a job to one of the other applicants.

Hiring by the rules

A number of federal and state laws govern hiring practices, and many are enforced by the U.S. Equal Employment Opportunity Commission (EEOC). Private employers (vs. public ones, such as government agencies) who have 15 or more employees are bound by EEOC guidelines. But that doesn't mean you can ignore them just because you have fewer than 15. Keeping within EEOC guidelines is strongly recommended, no matter how many employees you have.

Do you have to memorize pages and pages of law and regs? No. In a nutshell, here's the golden rule of hiring: *All of your decision-making criteria must be job-related.* So if you ask questions that don't pertain specifically to job *performance*, you could find yourself in trouble. Why? Because anything that's outside of doing the job as you've already described it in writing is legally "none of your business." (Here's an example of a classic no-no: "Are you planning to start a family?") You might be surprised at how easy it is to make innocent but potentially costly mistakes, especially during the interview process.

Why? Because asking makes you look behind the employment curve at best, and sets you up for a possible lawsuit at worst: an applicant may decide he or she didn't get the job because you based your hiring decision on the answers to those questions. Here's a conversational example. You're making small talk and the interviewee mentions going to a church function last night. Your natural reaction might be to say, "Oh, what church do you go to?" which is fine at a party. But as an employer, you can't ask that question: it has nothing to do with job performance. Ditto about asking how many kids. Or the year they graduated from college. Additional off-limits topics: age, date of birth, sex, race/color, ethnic/national, religion, type of military discharge, sexual orientation, marital status, family ("maiden") name, general health, alcohol/drug-addiction/mental-health treatment history, and Worker's Comp claims or job-related injuries.

If you're not sure if a question is job-related, play it safe and don't ask. Some applicants may also resist giving you their Social Security numbers at this stage. (Many experts and even the government are widely advising people to guard it closely now.)

Questions, questions

To avoid getting in trouble by asking any illegal questions, go online or contact the EEOC directly for their anti-discrimination guidelines (800.669.3362; eeoc.gov). Another good source is FirstGov (employers.gov). Or check with your attorney.

Paying employees

Nobody looks forward to managing payroll. In addition to cutting employee checks, employers have to withhold income taxes, FICA (Social Security and Medicare), and unemployment (FUTA). The goal is to set up efficient payroll systems that become routine; stay organized; and make sure you don't fall behind in your payments.

You'll need to work closely with your accountant during the organization period, and he or she should be able to answer your questions. The following is a brief description that should help demystify the payroll-management process.

- **Employer identification numbers** (EINs) Start by obtaining one from the IRS and one from your state department of revenue. You'll use them to identify your tax accounts.

- **Form I-9** Then have each employee fill out this form, which is proof of eligibility to work in the U.S.

- **Form W-4** Also have each employee fill out this form to indicate their tax filing status, number of deductions and the like. You'll use the information from the W-4 to withhold the appropriate amounts for federal income and FICA taxes from each paycheck, plus state income tax where applicable. Employers are responsible for matching FICA withholding amounts, and making payments to a qualified financial institution or Federal Reserve Bank. You'll file employee tax returns quarterly. Unemployment taxes (FUTA) are paid separately, also on a quarterly basis. Your accountant can walk you through all of this.

- **Form W-2** At the end of the year, you have to generate W-2 forms to provide the IRS, Social Security and your employees with a summary of individual earnings and withholdings for the year.

The tax calculations and paperwork may give you a headache at first, but once you and your accountant establish a system, the process should become routine. Many business owners streamline it by using payroll-management software to generate paychecks, reports and tax forms. Ask your accountant to recommend a program that's also compatible with the one he or she uses so information can be easily exchanged.

Also ask your accountant to go over record-keeping requirements. Generally speaking, you have to keep records of employment, wages, payments, and related forms and documentation for a minimum of four years. Some states have even longer requirements, so make sure you know and follow them.

Using a payroll service

If managing your payroll sounds like a great deal of trouble, you have several outsourcing options. Your accountant may handle payroll processing; or you can use a company that specializes in payroll processing. These companies can generate employee checks, provide quarterly and annual documentation, file tax forms and make your tax payments. You can provide them with earnings information by phone, fax or online (some of these companies have their own software that you have to use for online account management).

These companies offer a variety of options and levels of control, which makes them popular among small-business owners. They can save a lot of time and headaches, especially if you have many employees. The cost varies, depending on the number of employees, how often you pay those employees, and the scope of services you require (mailing checks, etc.). Some companies provide cost quotes online with just a few clicks, but all of them provide quick quotes by phone. The two largest companies are ADP (800.225.5237; adp.com) and Paychex (800.322.7292; paychex.com). Both of these are nationwide, so they'll refer you to the representative for your area. And both companies' Web sites have online quote features.

New employees: setting the tone

You set the tone for your working relations right from an employee's first day on the job. If you're not prepared on that employee's first day, you'll send the message that being unprepared is acceptable. By contrast, if you're organized, prepared and enthusiastic, you'll let the employee know that you're excited to have them join your team, and that you expect top performance on the job.

Do some advance work before a new employee arrives: Have all the paperwork in order (tax forms, nondisclosure agreements, etc.), all ready to be filled out. Gather the training materials (manuals, videos, worksheets) you intend to use and, if necessary, make copies for the new employee. Make a list of everything you think your employee needs to know: product information, sales techniques, company policies, how to use equipment, safety procedures, and more. Then use this list to create a general outline of your training process. Specific training varies radically from business to business, so it's almost impossible to tell you what your outline should include. But here are some guidelines for getting your relationship with new employees off to a great start.

First, get the initial paperwork out of the way. Once that's done, take them on a tour of your business. (Provide a notepad and pen so they can make notes and jot questions.) Showing them where they can find equipment and supplies has a "grounding" effect that helps them relax a bit and feel they belong.

Give the new employee the training materials you prepared. New employees have to absorb a lot of information on their first day; if they have the right materials to refer to, that day can be a little less overwhelming. And take the time during (or at the start of) the training process to talk about your business: your goals, business philosophy, and expectations for employees. Explain how you want your customers to be treated, and how you handle difficult situations or emergencies. This is also an opportunity to reinforce good communications. Let them know you want their input. If they have problems, concerns or ideas, encourage them to share those with you constructively, and let them know you'll do the same. And of course, encourage questions throughout the whole training process.

It's also a good idea to take some time just to kick back a little and get to know each other. You'll be throwing a lot of information at new employees, so consider taking a break after a few hours, or taking them to lunch. But don't talk shop here—talk life! Ask benign questions about their interests, or favorites (movies, music, sports, etc.), or school (if it's a student or recent graduate), or hometown if they recently relocated—anything that shows your interest without being overly nosy (or illegal). And share a little of the same about yourself. Demonstrating that you care about your employees as people can work wonders for their loyalty and enthusiasm.

Retaining good employees

Like every other employer—especially retailers—you may be worried about keeping good employees, especially part-timers, who are much more likely to come and go than full-time employees are. And like many other retailers, you'll probably pay hourly wages without benefits, which does little to encourage stability.

But studies show that employees, even those in non-career jobs, routinely say there are many aspects of the work environment that are as important as pay—and sometimes even more important. For example, employees want their opinions heard and valued. They want to feel they make a difference, that they're an important part of the operation and success of the business, and make real contributions to it. They want to be treated with respect and courtesy. And they want to enjoy their jobs and the people they work with.

Reward good behavior You'll find countless opportunities to reward good behavior once you start looking for them, even if that just means giving a compliment. For example, if an employee handles a difficult situation well, or you notice that they're on a first-name basis with repeat customers, let them know how much you appreciate it, and why. It's also a great idea to thank your employees at the end of the holiday rush. Any time you see an employee showing initiative, whether they straighten up the cleaning supplies or read up on the latest sales techniques, rewarding them will do wonders to reinforce their behavior.

Create a good environment As a small-business owner, you may have a great advantage over larger companies in creating the kind of "team-building" environment that keeps good employees. Even though you don't offer the employee benefits and perks of a Fortune 500 company, it can be much easier for you to give your employees personal attention and use their ideas when appropriate. It's also easier for you to be flexible, which may be worth much more to good workers than just wages.

Create opportunity In a large company, employees tend to become increasingly specialized: their jobs are often quite narrow. But small-business owners can provide their employees with the chance to learn all the facets of running a business. After all, as a small business owner, you do just about everything to some degree. That means you can give employees an invaluable learning and growth opportunity, extending if not their job duties, at least their knowledge and experience. Again, if they feel they're a more integral part of your company, they're much more likely to stay.

Make it fun Perhaps the most important thing you can do to have a positive relationship with your employees, is to have fun. How many times have you seen a cart or kiosk or store where the employees seem like automatons or "shop-sitters," there just to do the job, go home at the end of the shift, and get paid. Why? Because "it's just a job" and they're bored and unmotivated. But if you turn that scenario around, if you create an environment that allows for fun and that your employees enjoy, and if you can come across as fun in your own way, employees will feel free to be themselves, and see that you *value* them that way. (That cheerful sense of freedom, by the way, is something your customers will also pick up on and respond to.)

Likewise, there's no substitute for showing interest in your employees and getting to know them. One great way is to give modest or even fun little gifts for personal milestones—birthdays, job anniversaries, graduations—and even holidays. Good employees won't be in a hurry to leave a "fun job" and a "great boss."

Show respect Treat employees with courtesy and respect, just as you want them to treat you. Be honest with them. For example, if you say you're going to do something, do it, and quickly. If you can't do something they ask or suggest, give a reason. Being the boss doesn't mean being a parent or a martinet. The "do as I say, not as I do" approach doesn't work. Giving orders creates nothing but resentment and unhappiness (and ironically, the result is often that *less* work gets done). Make yourself a visible, working member of the team, not a pit boss on a pedestal.

Encourage input and initiative When you acknowledge employees for their contributions, and when you put their ideas into action, you let them know that they're making a difference. One way to make employees feel they're an important part of the business is to solicit their views and suggestions. You get the same results when you give them the authority to make decisions. And if you happen to have an unhappy customer, let them handle it instead of calling you in every time. By empowering employees to deal with situations that call for strategy and judgment, you show you trust them with your business, and you build their confidence. (And if you can't trust an employee's judgment, it's time for more training—or a replacement.)

Remember, you set an example every time you come to work. Your good behavior can't guarantee good employee performance, but rest assured, if you set a bad example, you can't expect better from the people who work for you. If you have fun, they'll feel free to have fun, too. If you're respectful and courteous, creative and fun, hard-working and committed, they'll follow your lead. And that's exactly the kind of employee you want.

□ □ □

Managing Your Inventory

S imply put, managing your inventory means knowing what you have on hand, how much you have, which products are selling, and which ones are collecting dust. Retailers who don't have a good handle on their inventory flow have a much harder time building a thriving business than retailers who do.

Setting up a retail business without an inventory-management system is like setting up an accounting business without a calculator: you can still get the work done and get paid for it, but it's a whole lot slower and you can't sell as much. So as the old song says, "You gotta have a system."

Inventory management systems: The benefits

Whether computer-based or just a notebook and a pencil, a good inventory-management system makes it easy to retrieve the information you need when you need it. Every retailer should have a good system—and not just to prevent and/or uncover theft, as some retailers think. The best overall reason for putting in and using a system is money: you make more, keep more, and lose less money when you have an inventory management system in place. Here's what a good system can do for you at the very least:

Reduce out-of-stock/lost sales incidents The more you know about your inventory flow, the less often you have to tell customers, "I'm sorry, we're out of that right now." Every lost sale is a direct hit to your bottom line. And if you have to restock quickly to keep pace with demand, you might end up with a lower profit margin because of less than optimum wholesale costs and/or rush-delivery shipping charges.

Spot slow sellers Slow sellers cost you two ways. First, they aren't turning into money if they aren't being bought. And second, the money that's tied up in those slow sellers can't be put to use in some other way, such as paying for more product or marketing or even props. Think of your inventory as cash sitting on a shelf waiting to turn into profit. The longer that inventory sits, the less work it can do. A good inventory management system lets you spot slow sellers quickly and easily, so you can reduce their prices, get them out the door, and put better-selling merchandise on the shelf. By the same token, a good system will also let you spot *fast* sellers, so you can re-order quickly to meet increasing demand.

Schedule your staff A good inventory-management system tells you what products have been sold and *when* they were sold. This information helps you identify the peak buying periods, which lets you adjust employee schedules and even hire extra staffers when you need them most.

Reduce theft A strong system helps you spot employee and customer theft—which protects your bottom line. If you let employees know you're tracking orders, sales and returns, you'll reduce missing inventory ("shrinkage").

Analyzing your options

Specialty retailers have three basic options for creating or buying an inventory-management system: a basic cash register backed by manual inventory tracking; a combination cash register/point-of-sale (POS) system; or a fully integrated POS system. Here's what you need to know about these three options to determine which is right for your new business:

Manual inventory management

How it works: A basic cash register is used to ring up sales and calculate taxes, but inventory reductions and additions are accounted for manually by using an inventory-control form to note additions/subtractions to stock on a daily basis.

INVENTORY CONTROL FORM

Store Name: _____ **Location:** _____

Date	Product SKU/code	Opening Inventory	Inventory Received	Inventory Sold	Closing Inventory	Over/Short
12-1-02	Item #222	4	6	3	7	0

Equipment: A cash register, a pencil and an inventory-control form (like the sample above).

Cost: $150-$300 for the cash register; less than a buck for a pencil.

Main benefits: Low cost, easy to set up, easy to learn to use, minimum staff training necessary.

Main drawbacks: Keeping track of inventory reductions and additions manually can take a good deal of time, which you could be spending on increasing sales and growing your business.

Best bet for: Retailers with one or two product lines and who have mostly cash sales and don't need to track sales by color, size or other factors

Where to buy: At most office supply stores, or online.

 Start-up Tip

If you plan to manage your inventory manually, you need to track all inventory additions and reductions on a daily basis so you know what's selling and what's not. Train your employees so that they understand your inventory system and know how to track sales, returns, etc. on the form.

Combination cash register/POS systems

How it works: Some higher priced cash registers blur the line between cash register and POS system, thanks to integrated (if somewhat limited) software that can track sales and inventory automatically. When the purchase is rung up, each item purchased is automatically deducted from inventory. Also, products can be coded according to department/category (data fields can include color, size, etc.), and the system can generate multiple management reports such as: sales by day, hour or salesperson; current inventory; cash in drawer; sales by vendor, etc. Although these systems are less flexible (and less modifiable) than fully integrated POS systems (below), they can be a great buy for start-up retailers who want a good middle-of-the-road solution.

Equipment needed: Most cash register/POS systems are self-contained units that include cash register, cash drawer, receipt printer, barcode scanner, and a computer port that allows a PC or Mac to be connected to your register/POS system for additional software integration. This enables you to use the data in reports like spreadsheets or graphs. Barcode printers, which let you print merchandise tags with barcodes that the register/POS system can read, are usually sold separately.

Cost: $600-$1,500

Main benefits: Automated inventory management gives you the benefit of knowing what you have on hand without the cost of a full-scale integrated POS system. These "smart cash registers" are fairly easy to set up and learn, and often have fewer technical glitches than full-scale POS systems do. Basic inventory and financial reports give a clear picture of "where you stand" on any day.

Main drawbacks: These systems are more expensive and harder to learn than a basic cash register, and aren't as flexible or customizable as a fully integrated POS system.

Best bet for: Retailers with multiple product lines who need automated inventory management without the expense and training a full-scale integrated POS system requires.

Where to buy: Local office supply stores may carry them; online (numerous options).

✔ *Start-up Tip*

Even if the system you buy is easy to learn, take the time to give your employees in-depth training and then test their knowledge. Do they know how to process a return or how to handle a store credit? Ask your system supplier to go over the most common technical glitches with you, and then teach your staff what to do when those glitches happen.

Tracking commissions

If you plan to hire employees who are paid on commission, seriously consider getting a system that tracks sales by salesperson ID number or shift. You'll save time and paperwork over the course of the year.

Fully integrated POS systems

How it works: An integrated point-of-sale system is a combination computer/cash register that uses sophisticated retail software to track sales, inventory and purchasing. A good POS system can "suggest" re-ordering times and quantities, and even re-order automatically; flag slow sellers; and track layaways and special orders. You can generate sales and inventory reports as often as needed. Incoming wholesale orders are entered into the system as additional inventory when the goods arrive, and the system's "pricing intelligence" can track retail prices vs. cost of goods, and calculate profit margins. Using barcode software, POS systems let you price products easily and efficiently, and you can raise or lower prices with a few keyboard commands (but you'll still have to update the shelf prices!).

Equipment needed: An integrated POS system is a mix of software (usually a Windows-based package) and the following hardware: a monitor/screen;

CPU (central processing unit, the "brain" of the computer) with internal modem and an option for backups (Zip drive or CD burner); a keyboard and mouse; cash drawer; customer-purchase display screen (so buyers can see the price of the item being rung up and the total); receipt printer, and report printer; credit card reader/magnetic swipe slot; barcode scanner (scans the product at the point of sale); and barcode label printer (to price products for sale).

Cost: $1,500-$4,000+

Main benefits: Inventory additions/reductions are accounted for automatically, and reports can be generated with a few mouse clicks. POS systems also track retail prices, cost of goods, profits realized at the time of sale, and a wealth of other data, all of which can be imported into other software programs for generating spreadsheets, accounting reports, forms and/or word-processing documents. POS systems also integrate credit-card processing, and can generate reports detailing sales paid by credit card vs. cash, check or invoice.

Main drawbacks: The cost is the main drawback here, but many specialty retailers say that the time they save and the quality of information they get from a POS system makes the investment well worth it. Another drawback may be the training required to use the system efficiently. Most POS sellers provide training of some kind (on-site, at the seller's headquarters, online, or on CD). That said, though, the vast majority of POS systems can be operated even if you have little or no computer experience.

Best bet for: Retailers with multiple products lines who need fully automatic inventory control and integration with other software in order to generate accounting spreadsheets, etc. Also for: Retailers who plan to open more than one location and need networking capabilities.

Where to buy: Usually not in office-supply stores. The best place to start is online. Most POS sellers have online or downloadable demo versions that illustrate the system's features, provide sample screen shots and sample reports. Then follow up with a company representative who can answer your questions.

POS lingo A POS (point-of-sale) system that reads barcodes can read a manufacturer's UPC (universal price code) and match the UPC to the product's PLU (price lookup) code—the code that identifies the retail price the retailer assigned when the merchandise was put into the system. A POS system can also identify a product by its SKU number ("skew": stock-keeping unit), usually assigned to a product that doesn't come with a UPC code (although today 80 percent of merchandise has UPC codes). SKU numbers can also be assigned to help retailers identify products by category (e.g., size, color and style). By the way, don't confuse POS with POP (point-of-purchase), which usually refers to displays that are designed to increase impulse sales. POP displays are usually set-up near the cash register—the point of purchase.

Customer Tracking, Repeat Sales

A good POS system allows you to manage a database of customers, track their purchases, and create direct mail (postal or e-mail) that announces new products or special events, which will bring customers back and generate repeat sales.

 ### Start-up Tip

Test and re-test your integrated POS equipment before opening day. You don't want buyers lined up, and have no way to complete those sales. If your POS system supplier suggests training for you or your employees, do it! You can't be "too busy" to learn how to use this valuable tool to the max. A poorly trained cashier— whether that's you or an employee—who can't process a sale quickly and correctly will generate customer complaints instead of purchases, and lose sales instead of making them.

Easier year-end inventory

For tax purposes, retailers are required to do a physical inventory count once a year at the end of the calendar or fiscal year. Anyone who has ever done it knows it can be tedious and difficult. Good news, though: there are ways to make it easier. Here are some tips for smoother year-end counts:

- Pre-count your *backstock*—the inventory in storage—the week before. This will save time on inventory day. However, be careful not to mingle that backstock with product that's for sale before inventory day, or you'll end up counting merchandise twice—once in the back room and again out front!

- If you use a POS system that scans barcodes, ask your system supplier how to speed up the inventory count. For example, your supplier may suggest that you could speed things up by using a portable, hand-held barcode scanner, which lets you walk around zapping items rather than counting products and then keying in the information.

- If you use a manual system for year-end counts, make sure everyone involved in the count has a calculator, the kind of pen or pencil you want used (if you want every sheet to look the same), and the blank inventory-control forms (or sheets of paper) so they can write the product description, retail price, and number of units counted.

- Make sure everyone knows the rules: *Every item must be counted.* Boxes containing product have to be opened so that their contents can be verified, and cases of product have to be counted per *unit*, not per case.

- No "guesstimating" allowed. "About two dozen" isn't acceptable, and "24" has to mean that 24 items were actually, physically counted.

- Divide your cart, kiosk or store into sections or departments, and assign an employee (or the friend or family member you roped in for the day) to count that specific area.

One final survival tip: As the troops are busy counting (even if it's only one other person), you want to stay on top of the situation in order to avoid any confusion, missed counts, double-counts and so on. If you own a big store and have several people counting inventory, for example, you may want to assume the role of a caring commander-in-chief, staying close by to answer questions and give advice and direction. If you keep in mind that a miscounted annual inventory could ultimately cost you money, you'll be more inclined to do it right—methodically, carefully, and accurately. Because when you do it right, you only have to do it once . . . until the same time next year.

□ □ □

Creating Your Retail Look

E very retail business has an identity. But there's much more to it than a store's catchy name. A store's *retail identity* is the combination of elements—name, products, displays, signs, and much more—that sets the tone and creates a *positive and persuasive image* that customers respond to.

A positive, effective retail identity that's working well will serve as a founda tion of your business for years to come. So even if your displays, signs, products, layout and color schemes change, and even if they change frequently, your image—your retail identity—will remain the same.

Establishing your retail identity

To develop a retail identity for your cart, kiosk or store, you need to ask yourself a few questions about your target customers and their expectations. As you read the questions below that relate to the unique aspects of your business, grab a notebook and brainstorm for a while (for brainstorming tips, see p. 134). Jot down all of the images and ideas, adjectives and nouns, stray thoughts and fragments that come to mind. The notes you make now will help you pinpoint the retail image you want to project on opening day.

- Who are my target customers and what are their expectations for my product? (If you haven't answered this question already, see "Identifying your target customers" on p. 64.) Young mothers looking for bargains on baby clothes? Teens looking for the latest, greatest gizmo they just have to have? Collectors in search of that one-of-a-kind item or latest edition?

- What kind of shopping environment do my target customers want? (Some examples: subdued, sophisticated . . . high energy . . . high fashion . . . high-tech . . . interactive . . . urban . . . suburban . . . family-friendly)

- What thoughts and feelings are associated with this kind of environment? (Some examples: relaxation . . . romance . . . excitement . . . friendship . . . fun . . . patriotism . . . playfulness . . . youthfulness)

- What thoughts and feelings are associated with my product?

- What colors are associated with those feelings? (Some examples: silver and chrome for high-tech . . . pastels for infants . . . bright colors for fun, excitement . . . green for health, gardening)

- What mental images, words or symbols are associated with my products? With my target customer's expectations? With the feelings I want to evoke?

The last question—images associated with the feelings you want to invoke—is the hardest to answer, because it can include anything. In fact, the best thing is to list anything and everything that comes to mind—an exercise in free association can actually be fun. For example, a retailer of remote-control toy cars might have these (among others) on the list: *speed, cars, kids, dads, laughter, street, spinning tires, steering wheel, seat belt, danger, joy stick, Daytona 500, bleachers/fans, track, risk, driving gloves, helmet, wheel covers, blurred racing photos, mirrors, skid marks, racing stripes, sunglasses, Paul Newman, Velcro suit, red-yellow-green, pit crew, checkered flag.*

What identities or themes would this list suggest? Obviously something to do with race cars: perhaps a race track, or the "pit." Let's say this retailer wants to create an identity based on the thrill of speed. To carry out the theme, racing stripes in red, yellow and green can go along the store's walls or inside the cart or kiosk. The color scheme can extend throughout the store or RMU by means of fixtures, fabrics, a host of low-cost props (see p. 226 for a list of the most commonly used props), and even bags and gift wrap in those colors, with or without the stripes, for the final touch.

The answers in your own notes and the items on your list will point you toward several distinct retail identities you can create for your cart, kiosk or store. The possibilities are endless but there's just one goal, and it's always the same: to tap into and meet your customers' expectations, wants and needs so that you can get their attention.

Incorporate the images that are important to your customers throughout your venture in any way you can, from your visual merchandising (or VM) plan to you customer receipts. Before you make your final merchandising plans, check your notes to make sure you're staying focused on one unified theme you can convey.

VM Lingo

Here are a few of the visual merchandising terms you'll be likely to hear as you focus on creating your retail identity:

- **CAD, CAM (computer-aided design, computer-aided manufacturing):** Software that visual-display designers (as well as architects, engineers and others) use to design a space or a display.

- **Lifestyle presentation:** A display showing products as used in real life.

- **Merchandise capacity:** The maximum number of products that can be displayed in a certain area or space, or on a particular fixture.

- **Positioning:** Creating and reinforcing a product or brand's pre-determined image through advertising, marketing, visual merchandising, etc.

- **Sight line:** The line of vision from any given spot; used to determine where and how to display products for maximum visibility within a store and at a distance.

- **Signage:** Graphically coordinated collection or system of signs (graphics and/or text) that identify a business (or other entity), promote its products or services, and reinforce a pre-determined retail image.

Visual merchandising techniques

Effective visual merchandising involves more than neatly arranging products for sale. It requires an understanding of how the customer shops, what the customer perceives and feels, and how to display merchandise in a way that invites customers in. But first, of course, visual merchandisers have to grab the shopper's attention, and use several proven techniques to do that. Here are some of them:

Motion No doubt about it: motion attracts. Animated characters, blinking lasers, spinning fans and turning turntables—anything that moves will attract attention. Inexpensive rotating displays that hang from the ceiling or a cart's roof grid get noticed. "Spin displays" and "motion displays," self-contained fixtures that rotate products, are available from at least a dozen fixture manufacturers in the U.S. alone (for more about fixtures, see "Tools of the VM Trade" on page 224). A videotaped product demonstration makes shoppers stop and watch. Live, on-site product demonstration is low-cost, high-impact motion. The more dynamic the demonstration, the larger the crowds. And free samples, tastings, contests and the like also to draw shoppers. So if you can find a way to create movement in your store, do it!

Color The right dash of color can do wonders for your retail image and your product displays. Generate excitement and accentuate products to get that "pop!" you've been looking for with paint, paper and fabric. Strong colors get attention. Strong contrasts between background and product punch up the product's visibility. Certain colors may influence a shopper's mood. According to research, these are some common effects and associations different colors have:

- Red: exciting, dynamic, aggressive; stimulates appetite, activity, impulse; a favorite of achievers

- Orange: vibrant, warm, extroverted; a teen favorite

- Yellow: warm, sunny, cheerful; little kids' favorite (but least favorite among adults)

- Blue: calm, cool; cleansing, purity, peace; Americans' favorite color

- Purple: mysterious, regal, rich; spirituality, creativity; a favorite of artists, older teens

- Green: fresh, clean, healthful; nature, ecology; America's second favorite

- Black: sophisticated, mysterious, powerful; elegance, mourning; magic; a favorite among *fashionistas*, urbanites, intellectuals

Sometimes a lack of bright, obvious color works best for a retail display. You can use any or several of the neutrals—beige, cream, tan, gray, white—as background colors that won't compete with your merchandise.

Add shine and sparkle to any surface with high-gloss, metallic, pearlized or other special-effect paints. Some papers and fabrics contain metallic fibers or have metallic or iridescent finishes. With light fixtures set at the correct angles, shiny surfaces catch and reflect the light in ways that change as the customer moves, thereby creating a sense of motion, highlighting the product, and generating more interest for the shopper.

Texture Incorporate texture with the help of wallpapers, fabrics, colored foam-core, trims, paints, and numerous other materials that are available today. The options are as endless as your imagination. For example, add depth and perspective by painting layers of color or faux finishes on walls or display cases. Create highlight boxes around certain shelves or on the wall behind individual products for a special "Check *this* out!" presentation.

(A great deal of how-to information on eye-catching paint effects is available online, in print, and in free brochures from paint stores and home-improvement centers.)

Lighting Lighting is a vastly under utilized visual element. Simply stated, you do want to put your merchandise in "the best possible light." But there's more to it than a few bright bulbs: you can also use lighting for specific results. The right light source can guide the customers' attention, illuminate the intricacies of the merchandise—the details customers might otherwise not notice—and highlight its quality. Good lighting that's well-positioned can make a dull store window an eye-catching "event" that draws traffic. In short, good lighting can help you sell.

Recent advances in lighting have created a number of interesting and highly effective options. Fiber-optic and backlit signs, for example, add great visual appeal. New low-voltage, high-intensity halogen fixtures can highlight merchandise in a variety of ways without spiking the electric bill. Several RMU manufacturers have recently introduced compact spotlights, floods and track lights that help make single or grouped products shine. Some retailers use sequenced lighting, which creates the illusion of motion that gives customers a reason to stop and watch. And some retailers have successfully experimented with colored lights that cast just the right glow on merchandise.

Oversizing Something that's much, much larger than expected always gets noticed. Depending on the item and the context it's in, the oversized item might evoke fear (Godzilla!) or delight or wonder or surprise—*but it won't go unnoticed.* Oversized props, graphics and fixtures not only get attention, but draw attention from a distance. Shoppers who can spot your very large sign or exaggerated prop from the other side of the common area 50 or 100 feet away become consciously aware of you . . . get the message you're sending ("This is a great store! Come see!") . . . *stay* aware of you for as long as it takes to walk to your location . . . and experience the positive reaction (delight, wonder, etc.) you intended once they get there. As with all VM elements, the best oversized props or graphics reinforce your retail identity. The power of exaggerated size, along with color, texture, lighting and movement, brings customers and generates sales you may not have had without that great big prop.

Humor Putting some fun in your visual displays is a great attention-getter. Anything that makes people smile will draw them to you and create some buzz about your business. Be aware, though, that it can be a little tricky because humor, like beauty, is in the eye of the beholder. It takes a light touch, a good sense of humor (nothing offensive), a little wit or whimsy or even a dash of absurdity to make it fun.

The possibilities are endless, but sometimes the best gags use a visual "hook" that relates to your merchandise and your retail identity in some way. A few examples: an apparel retailer's mannequins cut in half and "emerging" from a wall, floor or ceiling (absurdity and implied movement in one shot!); a sunglasses retailer's oversized cutouts of cows and bulls wearing fashionable shades; a pet-adoption center's window outfitted as a cat's "furnished apartment" with many cute visual and verbal puns; the employees of a children's photographer in bright, silly costumes and hats. If you do more than one display at a time, tie them together with one oversized graphic.

Merchandising mistakes to avoid

When you create something out of the ordinary, you get shoppers' attention. And, of course, you want *good* attention. So here are a few visual merchandising mistakes to avoid:

- **Overcrowding** Crowded or cluttered displays with too much product or displays too closely packed together invite confusion and frustration, not interest.

- **Overpowering** The purpose of visual merchandising is to highlight products, not overpower them. The display isn't the "star"—the product is. Displays that compete with and overpower the merchandise will work against you. Make sure your products are the focal point, not your displays.

- **Static displays** Change your displays often, so customers always see something new and different at your cart, kiosk or store. Displays that are the same all year round say "There's nothing new here!" to passers by.

- **Hand-lettering** Unless hand-lettered signs and handwritten price tags tie into your visual merchandising theme, don't do it. In most cases, they project an unprofessional image.

- **Poor lighting** If your customers can't *see* your products, they won't *buy* them. Sometimes spending $150 on upgrading your lighting can mean the difference between browsers and buyers.

Display ideas

Need ideas? In addition to looking through retail trade magazines, head to your local newsstand or library for various consumer magazines. Fashion, lifestyle, decorating and even travel magazines are excellent sources of display ideas, even though the focus isn't on retail per se.

Tools of the VM trade

How do visual merchandising professionals create arresting, award-winning designs? They use a wide range of display props, fixtures and accents strategically placed to create excitement and interest. Certain fixtures such as shelves and grid systems (see below) are used as a foundation; props and accessories are added to build the display and complete the look. Fixtures you can use as a foundation for your displays include:

slatwall, grid and pegboard systems ∎ nesting crates, tables

shelving ∎ showcases (freestanding or tabletop)

garment racks, hat racks ∎ tubing ∎ specialty racks

wire displays, racks (book racks, earring racks, etc.)

hangers, hooks ∎ bookshelves ∎ cubes, pedestals, risers, platforms

chairs and tables ∎ islands, end caps, gondolas

dressers, armoires, other furniture ∎ mannequins, busts, other forms

Fixture lingo

VM fixtures and accessories come in a variety of shapes and sizes. The terms you're most likely to encounter include:

- **Cable ties** Similar to some trash-bag ties, used to tie items together quickly.

- **Cash wrap** A fixture with compartments for organizing items such as sales forms, bags and other packaging supplies, and the cash register.

- **End cap** A fixture that's placed at the end of a display aisle; freestanding or attached.

- **Foamcore** Inexpensive lightweight sheets with foam in the middle and a paper coating on both sides; can be cut to size and shape, and painted; also called "foam board."

- **Gondola** A fixture that allows customers to approach merchandise from all sides.

- **Grid rack, grid wall** A panel that's a network of horizontal and vertical rods, either freestanding (grid rack) or attached to a wall (grid wall), used to display merchandise or support hooks, shelving, etc.

- **Island** A freestanding fixture, usually a table-like unit, which allows customers to approach merchandise from more than one side.

- **Nesting crates, tables** Crates or tables that come in multiple sizes, designed to fit inside or on top of one another.

- **Pedestal** A fixture that stands alone and serves as a base on which merchandise is displayed; come in various heights, sizes, materials, etc.

- **Pegboard** A board with evenly spaced holes to support shelving, hangers, hooks, etc.

- **POP (point of purchase) display** A movable display near the cash wrap; typically features impulse products or merchandise on sale.

- **Riser** A fixture with various levels used to display products at various heights.

- **Showcase** A freestanding floor, countertop or tabletop display case with glass or clear plastic front or top, often fitted with lights, lock; usually for fragile items (e.g., figurines) or small items (e.g., jewelry).

- **Slatwall** (Slotwall) A board (usually wall-mounted) with evenly spaced slats (or slots) that support shelving, hangers, hooks, bins, etc., horizontally or vertically.

- **Tubing** Usually metal or plastic (PVC is popular), used alone or in multiples to display merchandise or support hangers, hooks, etc.

Certain props and fixtures can enhance your cart, kiosk or store by repeating a design element or adding a contrasting or complementary element. These include:

photos, posters ▪ pots, planters, vases ▪ statues, sculptures
antiques, art, frames ▪ plants, flowers (live or silk) ▪ shells
miniature faux fish, birds, animals ▪ mirrors ▪ columns ▪ cardboard, poster board
fabric, felt, burlap ▪ foam ▪ pallets ▪ easels ▪ baskets ▪ ribbons, trim, tassels
banners ▪ rope; cork ▪ lattice ▪ sand, stones, gravel

As you can see, high-impact displays can be very low-cost. Many of these props and accessories are extremely reasonable, and sometimes some of them are free (sand, shells, etc.). Keep your eyes open for these and other possibilities.

✔ *Start-up Tip*

The hardware and plumbing sections of home-improvement centers offer a wealth of low-cost items you can use in displays. Walk the aisles and think about how you might use items you see, such as chains, metal washers, oversized nuts and bolts—even mailboxes.

Adding the seasonal touch Try some of these props when the time comes:

- **Spring** Butterflies, birds, hammocks, flowers (tulips, daffodils), fruit (whatever fruit says "spring" in your locale), sunshine, grass, lawn sprinklers, picnics, T-shirts and shorts, fishing, baseball, budding trees, baby wildlife, seeds/gardening/bird feeders, bunnies, Easter baskets/eggs, jellybeans. Spring colors: light-bright greens, yellows, pink, lavender.

- **Summer** Bright flowers, beach, sand, seashells, beach umbrellas/chairs/towels, sunglasses, flip-flops/sandals, sun hats, parasols, sunshine, palm trees, tropics, sailing, fruit (peaches, strawberries, watermelon), ice cream, backyard barbecue, gardening, picnics. Summer colors: pastels, tropical/brights, white eyelet; gingham

- **Fall** Vines, swags, grapes, apples, harvest, cornucopias, baskets, turkey, (mini) pumpkins, gourds, autumn leaves, rake, hot cider, cinnamon, scarecrow, hay bales, Halloween. Autumn colors: yellow, gold, red, brown, bronze, rust, olive green; black-and-orange

- **Winter/Christmas** Snow, pine, pine cones, fireplace, wreaths, garland, (mini) wrapped gift boxes, ribbons/bows, holly, berries and nuts, mistletoe, Christmas tree, Santa/elves, ornaments, tinsel, stars, sleigh/sled, bells, candy canes, snowmen, hot cocoa, cinnamon/spice, potpourri, candles, string lights (white or multi), model trains, mittens/caps/scarves, skis, ice skates. Winter colors: deep green, burgundy, purple; winter white, metallic gold/silver; red-and-green; blue-and-silver; velvet, plaid wool

Getting professional help?

If you need help creating your retail identity and visual merchandising plan, consider hiring an experienced VM professional who can help you form a strategy. The right visual merchandiser can take your notes and turn them into a complete, high-impact presentation. Some visual merchandisers specialize in creating custom fixtures—that can be expensive, but they serve the exact purpose for which they were intended: to showcase and sell your products. Other visual merchandisers tend to use off-the-shelf materials for maximum effect. Before you hire a VM professional, review his or her portfolio and overall philosophy of design and presentation. As always, check references. If you need help finding visual merchandisers, check the ads in retail trade magazines, contact a retail trade association, ask your leasing manager or ask retailers whose displays and image you like.

Evaluating your image and presentation

After you've determined your retail identity and you've picked out the right fixtures and props to reinforce it and create excitement for your future customers, ask yourself these key questions well before opening day. Your answers will determine if your visual merchandising plan is on track, or if you need to do more tweaking before you open:

- What does my store say to shoppers at a glance? What image does it project? Ask friends or other retailers for their opinions and impressions. If what they tell you isn't in line with your retail identity and doesn't reflect the image you want, now's the time to make changes.

- How does my signage (the whole system, from entrance sign to price tags) reinforce the image I want to project? What about my store name, tagline and logo: do they reflect my retail identity and evoke the feelings I want them to? If they don't, make changes to these elements so that they will.

    ### Signs that work
    To attract attention, signs have to be visible and legible from a distance. Keep the message simple—just a few words will do it. For easy reading, keep the lettering simple: don't use all capital letters, and use a standard typestyle (not

script or other decorative styles). Remember, even an entrance sign with fancy lettering or graphics still has to be readable.

- Are there elements in my visual merchandising plan that detract from the image I'm going for? Are there any that might confuse shoppers? Sometimes more is less. If you have conflicting elements—too many colors, or too many props, *edit* (as designers say). Take a few out, and you'll see an improvement. Is my lighting adequate? Lights that are either too bright or too dim invite customers to leave.

- Is my cart, kiosk or store attractive and inviting?

If you can't answer with a big "Yes!" it's time to go over your notes again to come up with a new retail identity . . . or hire a VM professional to help you.

If you can't answer with a big "Yes!" it's time to go over your notes again to come up with a new retail identity . . . or hire a VM professional to help you.

Your VM toolbox

Not unlike carpenters or mechanics, visual merchandisers have toolboxes that hold the items they use the most. You can create a VM toolbox, too. That way, you'll have everything you need at your fingertips for creating and fine-tuning your visual merchandising strategy. Your toolbox should include:

tape measure ■ pencil ■ fishing wire ■ all-purpose wire

(heavier than fishing wire) ■ hooks (assorted sizes, shapes)

thumbtacks ■ Velcro ■ super glue ■ box cutter ■ scissors

all-purpose adhesive (such as Liquid Nails) ■ foamcore (several sheets)

tape (transparent, packing, double-sided, masking, duct) ■ cable ties

screwdrivers (straight and Phillips), screws ■ power drill, bits, nuts/bolts

hammer, nails ■ needle-nose pliers; standard wrenches

stapler, staple gun, staples ■ glue gun, glue sticks ■ touch-up paint

□ □ □

Advertising Your New Business

14

You've chosen a great product, found the right location and created a pricing strategy to attract customers. Now it's time to tell the world! Well, not yet: you need to be more focused than that. You need to tell your target customers the benefits they get from shopping at your cart, kiosk or store. Here's how to create an effective advertising strategy, execute it, and track the results, starting with the biggest element—money.

Setting your ad budget

"How much money should I spend?" It's one of the first questions new business owners ask about advertising. The method most specialty retailers use to answer that is a percentage of gross sales, usually between two and three percent. (The 2001 average for the entire retail industry nationwide was 2.3 percent.) Using this formula, a business that anticipates gross sales of $150,000 per year (or season) will allocate $3,000-$4,500 for advertising for that period. But it's your first season or year, which means your goals are different from those of an established retailer. You want to get noticed, draw as much traffic to you as possible, and establish a presence in the marketplace. To accomplish that, you might think about spending a little more, another percentage point or two.

Sure, you can think of 10 good ways to spend a few thousand on something other than advertising. But think of advertising as an investment: in short-term visibility and, even more important, in long-term growth.

The question isn't whether to spend the money on advertising or something else: the question is what's the best type of advertising for your business—how can you get the biggest bang for your advertising buck? The answer depends on several factors.

Focusing your efforts

Some retailers wonder where marketing ends and advertising begins. *Marketing* refers to how you want your company to be perceived in the market in terms of your products, your location and your pricing strategy. *Advertising* refers to the methods you use to convey your marketing message to your audience. The most common methods are print ads (in newspapers, magazines, newsletters) and direct mail (postcards, fliers, brochures and anything else that's mailed directly to the consumer). The best method or combination of methods for your business will depend on several factors, including:

- **Your products.** Does the nature of the product suggest a certain method of advertising? For example, if you sell impulse products from a mall cart or kiosk, you may get a boost from on-site advertising that generates sales from existing foot traffic. And you'll probably get much better response from something like fliers near the cash register advertising an upcoming sale than you would from newspaper ads. But if you're selling computer accessories, you might be better off advertising in the local newspaper's tech or business section.

- **Your target customers.** Where will your target customers look for information about your kind of products? The customer you're trying to reach will greatly influence your decision as to which media you use. For example, if you sell music CDs to teens, running radio ads on the right stations may be a good bet. But if you're selling baby clothes and accessories consider advertising in the local paper's "Living" or "Families" section.

- **Your message.** Does your marketing strategy suggest using a certain type of advertising? The ad message you need to convey is based on the marketing strategy you developed for your business plan. If that strategy keys on maintaining lower prices than your competitors, for example, you may want to run a few newspaper ads touting your low prices.

- **Your competitors.** Are your competitor's successfully reaching customers with methods that you could or should use? You don't have to mimic their advertising efforts. But because their customers will soon be your customers, you should be aware of which methods your competitors use to reach them. If most of your competitors are running full-page newspaper ads, you have to seriously consider news-paper ads. Why? Because that's where your customers are most likely looking for information about what you sell. If your competitors are there and you're not, you're invisible. And you've missed a big opportunity to lure away some business. Look at it this way: if your competition is spending big bucks to advertise in ways that work, they've already taken the financial lumps of advertising trial-and-error, and you don't have to. You can just follow their lead to where the consumers are.

- **Your budget.** What's the cost of reaching the audience you're targeting? Generally, the more expensive the adver-tising method, the more exposure you gain to a larger audience. But just because an audience is big in terms of numbers doesn't mean that audience is composed of your *target* customers. And that's the audience you really want to reach. For example, say you're selling fishing equipment and most of your customers are men between 25 and 45. You could easily spend $5,000 creating and running a full-page ad in a mid-sized daily paper, and reach more than 100,000 readers at once. Or you could spend $200 on a full-page ad in a local newsletter that reaches 1,000 fishing enthusiasts—far fewer readers but more target customers. You may get better results with the newsletter because you'll have reached the right audience.

To decide which methods to use, gather all the information you can about the advertising options in your area, and calculate the costs associated with each option (including any production costs to create the ad itself). Make your final decisions based on the overall value of each option as it relates to your marketing strategy.

Analyzing your options

You can't expect customers to know about you unless you tell them where you are and why they should buy from you, as strongly and as frequently as possible. The more you advertise, the more likely people will know about and remember your cart, kiosk or store. And the more they remember you, the more likely they are to buy from you.

No matter which media you choose for your ads, advertise as often as you can within your budget. Then track the results of your ads to refine them, and refocus your efforts on the media and methods that are getting you the best results. The following tells you more about your advertising options, from newspapers to Yellow Pages to e-mail, plus a few low-cost techniques that might be ideal for your new business.

Newspaper ads

According to the Newspaper Association of America, 55 percent of American adults read a daily paper, and 65 percent read a Sunday paper. So if you want to reach to a large, diverse audience, your local newspaper might be your best bet. Newspaper ads can be expensive: a small black-and-white ad running just one day in a major paper can cost hundreds of dollars. But if you're looking to reach a large, diverse audience, your local paper might be the best bet. Even if you want it to reach a targeted audience, the newspaper might still be a good bet if it has a section your target customers read—entertainment, sports, food, tech, local business, fashion, parenting, and more. Most papers also have special inserts that run only at certain times of the year (holidays, summer, etc.). They may be good options for your ads, too.

Calculating your costs: Factor in the paper's ad rates *plus* production costs to budget the true cost of an ad. New retailers often focus on rates but forget to factor in the cost to produce an ad. Some publications will design the ad at no additional cost. Chances are, you'll pay a modest fee if they do the design and layout. You'll pay more for an outside graphic designer or ad agency.

To get information about ad rates, circulation, reader demographics, the paper's regular sections, special inserts and more, call to ask for a media kit. (Some of the larger papers also have media-kit information online.) If you plan to advertise more than just sporadically, ask about "contract rates" if they're not already in the kit. These rates reflect frequency discounts for advertisers who sign contracts for a minimum number of ads during a specific period (e.g., 12 times in 3 months). The more frequent the commitment, the better the discount—sometimes less than half off the newspaper's regular rates.

If you want ad rates and other basic information for several different papers but don't want to make multiple calls for media kits, go to your library's reference section for a national media directory. *Gale's Directory of Publications and Broadcast Media, Bacon's*, and *Standard Rates & Data Service (SRDS)* are multiple directories that cover each medium separately: newspapers, magazines, radio, TV and the Internet. You can buy them (or access some of them online), but the prices are steep, from $200 to $700 for a *single* directory.

Radio ads

Typically sold as 30- or 60-second "spots," radio ads can be a great way to reach a target market without spending thousands of dollars. Depending on your market, you may be able to run several ads on the radio for the same or similar cost as a single newspaper ad. Plus, many radio stations reach a specific or narrowly targeted audience, which lets you zero in cost-effectively. In addition to selling straight commercial airtime, some stations accept advertising on a per-inquiry basis, where the advertiser pays the station based on the number of consumer inquiries the ad generates. To find out the advertising opportunities in your radio market, call your local stations for media kits, which have all the information you need about the station's format, programming, geographic reach, listener demographics and more.

Calculating your costs: You can write your own copy (if you know how—there's an art to creating effective radio copy), hire an ad agency (costs vary), or ask the radio station if they write copy (some even do it for next to nothing). You'll also have to pay an hourly rate for voice-over talent—the person who reads your ad. Unless you have experience and a very good voice, don't think about doing it yourself. Hire the best talent you can afford. The radio station or the sound studio that produces your spot can help you find good voice talent, and you can listen to different voices on tape before you choose. You also have to pay for studio time for recording and editing, again at hourly rates. And if you use any music or sound effects, you pay according to your selections (fees vary widely). The radio station or sound studio can tell you more.

If you need rates and other basic information for several different stations but don't want to make multiple calls for media kits, your local library should have at least one broadcast directory available for your review, or you can search online.

Television ads

At $1,000 to $5,000 or more for video production plus the cost of airtime, advertising on television is probably beyond your start-up budget's reach. Still, if you feel TV ads are a good idea for your business, look into cable: local stations, locally produced shows, or local affiliates of national channels. You may find attractive deals on rates and on low-cost production assistance. One advantage of cable is that local viewers of certain channels are targeted—for example, people with high interest in fishing, golf, cooking or travel. To find out more about advertising on cable, including rates, viewer demographics (to see if their target audience is your target market) and production assistance and costs, call the station for a media kit. Or check one of the broadcast media directories such as *Gale's, Bacon's* or *SRDS* in your library's reference section.

Newsletter ads

Newsletters produced by local organizations usually run ads from local businesses; so do those of some churches, collector's groups, hobby enthusiasts, and suburban communities. These can be good opportunities for you, often at modest costs. Before you place an ad, though, find out as much as you can about their mailing list—not so much the "how many" but the "who." Are they people who are likely to respond to your ad and spend money with you? Many of these groups won't be able to give you demographic data on their readers, but they can usually tell you something about their interests and possibly more. Also ask about the response previous advertisers received, if that information's available.

Calculating your costs: If you advertise in a newsletter, costs will depend on the nature of the newsletter (primarily the circulation level), how often it's published (monthly? quarterly?), and the size of your ad. Don't hesitate to ask about contract rates to reduce your costs.

Your own newsletter

Publishing a newsletter is a great way to advertise your business, keep in touch with (and in front of) your customers, and let them know what's happening at your store. You can use your newsletter to advertise upcoming sales or special events, give customers discount coupons toward a future purchase (thereby generating more foot traffic), or provide product information, and anything else you think fits in, to make the newsletter valuable to customers.

If you want to start a newsletter, first make sure you have the time to do the work it takes to make it an *ongoing* success—just one or two issues won't do. Better never to send the first one if you can't keep it going for the long term.

Start by determining your goals: Do you want to educate your customer about your products? Let your customers know about special store events? Next, create a graphic template—a design and layout you can use issue after issue. (Word-processing software like *WordPerfect, Word* and *Publisher* have several newsletter templates built in.) Using a template means not having to worry about the larger design choices after your first issue, and accustoms your readers to your newsletter's "look," so they're likely to recognize it and read it when it arrives. Take time to flesh out a few content categories or special sections you want in every issue, such as a "New Products" or "Great Deals" section, and decide who will be writing every issue. You must also decide on production matters like paper size and weight; whether to use pre-printed newsletter paper (available at office-supply chain stores and online—see p. 242) vs. your own design; and which color(s) you want to use (generally speaking, the more colors, the more expensive to print). Who will print it: you? a print shop? a chain photocopy store? Finally, how will you handle addresses (self-mailer, envelopes) and postage (bulk rate, first class)?

To make your newsletter as effective as possible:

- Don't exaggerate the merits of your products and/or your business. Newsletters that come across as ad hype instead of solid information get tossed unread.

- Keep the style informal and friendly, a "me to you" approach, as the greeting-card companies call it.

- Be sure your store name, location, phone number, e-mail address and Web site (if you have one) are prominent on every page.

- Keep it to four pages. Anything longer and you're asking readers to commit to a reading "task."

- Always include a coupon or promote a special. That way, your customers will always open and look through each issue.

If you're not a writer or a graphic designer/typesetter, hire someone. Ask around: mall management, other retailers, local business organizations might have names of local marketing/public relations agencies or free-lancers with newsletter experience.

Calculating your costs: If you produce your own newsletter, calculate the costs of production, writing, graphic design and printing, as well as mailing. To save money on your printing costs, consider using pre-printed newsletter papers, which are now offered by a variety of companies (see "Direct Mail" on p. 241).

Yellow Pages ads

When you set up your business phone number, the information you provide the phone company will be used for your free basic listing (i.e., company name, address, phone number with no boldface or color) in both the White Pages and Yellow Pages for your area's phone book. You won't get to proof-read a basic listing, so double-check that they have correct spellings of your business name and address before you finish ordering your phone line.

If you want something more than the basic listing, from a boldface listing to a box to a color display ad, call your local phone book sales rep (look in the book itself for the number). Yellow Pages ads definitely work: consumers still let their fingers do the walking. But the question is, whether you can afford it. Ad rates vary from market to market, but reps often have specials you might want to take advantage of. Even so, is it truly worth it for *your* business? Or can you find lower-cost options that give you just as much (or almost as much) exposure to your target customers?

Calculating your costs: Most phone books offer attractive discounts for first-time advertisers and for those who increase their ad size from the previous year. Take advantage whenever you can—but understand that running the same ad will cost more next year because you won't get the first-timer or size-increase discount. Phone-book publishers may provide ad-design services at no cost, so you don't have to worry about production costs if you use the in-house ad department. Of course, you can hire a graphic designer or ad agency to create your ad, but if you do, make sure the designer or agency knows the book's ad specifications. Because phone books are printed at low resolution on low-quality paper, it's wise to work with an experienced designer (including the phone book's in-house team) who will know how to compensate for those factors to produce a crisp, clear ad that's easy to read and looks great.

✔ **Start-up Tip**

If you're in an area with more than one phone book publisher, you may want to run ads or at least listings in all of the books to make sure everyone in the area can find you.

Online listings Phone book publishers with Web sites (like BellSouth's realpages.com) typically provide free online listings in addition to the free White Pages and Yellow Pages basic listings they give their business-line customers. Online listings are usually posted soon after a new listing is received (i.e., when you arrange for your business telephone number). Most phone books with Web sites have special online-listing deals that give larger online ads to advertisers who run ads of a certain size in the phone book.

Co-op ads

Some manufacturers are willing to kick in funds from their own advertising or marketing budgets, called "co-op dollars," to help retailers run ads (newspaper, radio, etc.), provided their products are displayed prominently (and in some cases, exclusively) in the retailers' ads. They do this as a way to increase brand awareness and help retailers generate sales—which means more wholesale orders. Manufacturers usually calculate how much they'll contribute based on how much wholesale product the retailer orders during the year: the more product ordered, the more co-op dollars available.

You may not be able to take advantage of co-op dollars until you have a full year's orders under your belt. But each manufacturer has its own set of rules for co-op advertising, so it's possible some may work with you on a start-up contribution based on how much they can reasonably expect you to order in the next 12 months When you place your first order, ask for their co-op rules and keep them in your files. You may not be able to take advantage immediately, but when you *are* ready, you'll have the information.

Free ad materials
Your suppliers can also help you save money on advertising by supplying you with product

photos and even ad slicks (ads specially printed on treated paper with space for your store name, address, phone number, and some copy).

Co-op contributions can add up, so review your suppliers' offers thoroughly. If you're trying to decide between two suppliers with similar product prices but only one offers co-op dollars, it may be worth buying from that one. Keep in mind that to get your co-op dollars (usually in the form of a credit on your account), you first have to send copies of the ads (or a tape for a TV or radio spot) to the manufacturer for approval. If the ad doesn't follow their co-op ad rules, you won't get a credit, so know the rules before you run the ad.

Direct mail

Direct mail is any material sent to prospective and current customers. Most direct mail is unsolicited, but specialty retailers' direct mail is sometimes "solicited" or requested—their existing customers signed a mailing list—and is sent out periodically to promote upcoming sales or special events.

However, some specialty retailers also rent or buy mailing lists in order to reach new customers. Mailing lists are available from a variety of list brokers, and some lists are highly specialized or segmented. For example, you can rent or buy a list of individuals who are in a certain age group, have specific interests and live in a specified zip code, which can make for a fairly targeted advertising campaign. Generally speaking, the more closely these "selects"—age, gender, income level, interests, etc.—match your targeted customers, the better the results. Usually, you pay per thousand names, and the more selects you request, the higher the rate. List rentals are usually for one-time use only. You can find list brokers or "list houses" online and in the Yellow Pages under "Mailing Lists." Or ask other retailers and business associates how they got their mailing lists, and if they were happy with the list service and the results. Before you contract for a list, ask about that list's original source, how it was compiled, when it was first compiled, when it was last updated ("stale" names are worthless), what's their guarantee policy against "undeliverable" addresses, how many clients have used the list, and what the response rates have been.

Your own list Current customer mailing lists get better response rates than generic rented lists do. So the best mailing list—and the cheapest—is the list you compile yourself. It pays to start your own customer database as early as possible. From opening day on, have a sign-up sheet or guest book near your cash register. Actively encourage customers and browsers to sign up for your list so that you can notify them about sales or special events. For example, offer a monthly drawing for a $50 gift certificate for customers who sign up for your list. It's worth the $600 a year if you can collect more than 50 names a month (which would mean more than 600 new customer names a year).

Response rates Only a tiny percentage of recipients respond to unsolicited direct mail—for example, the credit-card industry sends out five billion direct mail pieces every year and gets a response rate of less than one percent. For most direct mail campaigns, a response rate of 2-3 percent is quite good.

Calculating your costs: The cost of renting mailing lists is on a per-thousand-name basis, anywhere from $5 to $100 per thousand or more, depending on the list. Usually there's a minimum order requirement, such as 3,000 or 5,000 names. As mentioned, the more specific the list, the more it costs. When you plan your direct-mail campaign, also factor in production costs and postage. How much it costs to produce a direct-mail piece plus the postage to mail it will depend on the piece itself. A 4"x 5" postcard, for example, might cost 40¢-50¢ each to print and mail; a multi-page, 8^1/$_2$"x11" catalog might cost $1 to $2 each to print and mail.

You may be able to take advantage of bulk postage rates instead of first-class rates if you meet the requirements (for size, quantity per zip code, etc.) *and* you have a bulk-mail permit. Apply for your annual permit and pick up the rules for bulk mail at your post office. Or a direct-mail house might help you save time and money by handling your mailing for you. Look under "Mailing Services" in your local phone book.

Pre-printed papers You can reduce printing costs by buying pre-printed postcards, fliers, brochures, certificates, newsletters, and the like. They come in hundreds of designs (often coordinated as sets) that give you the visual impact of color printing without the expense of a print shop printing a small multi-color job. Pre-printed papers have blank spaces for you to computer-print or photocopy your advertising message plus your business name, address, phone, etc. Office-supply stores carry a selection of pre-printed papers. Or shop around online: Idea Art (800.433.2287; ideaart.com) and PaperDirect (800.272.7377; paperdirect.com) are two of many companies that specialize in pre-printed papers.

e-mail

Every year, more retailers are recognizing the value of e-mail for interacting with customers quickly, efficiently and at little or no cost. However, more consumers are getting touchy about "junk" e-mail and invasions of privacy, so you need to strike a delicate balance. (See below for more about the "rules.") But If you have the capability, e-mailing customers may be a simple matter of setting up your address book and figuring out what you want to say.

Keep the message short, friendly and easy to read. No one likes long e-mails, especially when they're ads. If you have a Web site, be sure to include a link to it at the end of the message so readers can go to your site with one mouse click. Once you have your message nailed down, word the subject line effectively. Most e-mail systems are set up so that the recipient sees only the first few words, so you have to be succinct, and clear in that one little line. So if you're advertising a sale, put "Sale" plus the offer—percentage off, buy one/get one, or whatever the inducement—in the subject line.

The rules Know the rules of conduct (or "Netiquette") for online communications. The most important one is the opt-in/opt-out rule: Send e-mail only to customers who have "opted in"—signed up for or subscribed to—your e-mail list. And always give them a chance to "opt out": at the bottom of each e-mail you send, tell them how they can be taken off your e-mail list. For more on Netiquette and e-mail advertising, read one of the many guides on the Web (you can start with albion.com/netiquette).

Low-cost alternatives

Sometimes the hardest part of creating an effective ad or promotional campaign is coming to grips with what you *can't* afford to do, and finding cost-effective alternatives—like these.

Business cards and stationery

Business cards and stationery ("letterhead") are inexpensive and yet can greatly benefit your business. Even if you think you won't be sending many letters or handing out many cards, there's no good reason not to have these valuable tools. A set of 500 cards with matching letterhead and envelopes could cost little as $100; well worth it. Cheaper yet, order 1,000 cards (the price difference is usually minimal, and can cut the per-card price dramatically). That way, you can hand them out to as many people as possible your first year—your vendors, banker, prospective customers. You can even order "free" color business cards (you pay shipping) from online companies that print your cards in exchange for printing their business's name on the back. You get your cards free, and the printer gets to advertise. Search online for "free business cards" to find these companies.

 Start-up Tip

> *If you're a retailer who would benefit from having your product lines (collectibles, for example) listed on your card, you might want to print on both sides of the card, or use a double "fold-over" card.*

You may also want to consider using a business card that also serves as a frequent-buyer card. See p. 249 in this section for more frequent-buyer programs.

Brochures and catalogs

Brochures and catalogs can be image-enhancers as well as sales-generators. They give you more room than newspaper or Yellow Pages ads to explain the benefits of your products or the special services you provide. They're vehicles that can say "Here's why you should buy from us." You can even use brochures to spur sales: for example, make part of the brochure a coupon.

Brochures For low-cost, attractive brochures, use pre-printed brochure papers that have colorful designs to match your store's image and blank spaces for you to fill in your text. You can find pre-printed papers online (see "Direct Mail" on p. 241) or at some mass merchandisers and office suppliers. If you want a *completed* brochure instead of a fill-in-the-blank template, several online companies, such as Pro Brochure (probrochure.com), take care of the whole process for you. They'll take your notes, ideas and thoughts, and write the copy; they scan your photos or use your digital images; and they do the layout to create a brochure. And then they send you either a hard-copy proof or an electronic (pdf) file for you're approval. You can order quantities from 100 to 20,000, and although the final cost varies, these brochures cost about $1 each (plus shipping) for quantities of less than 600.

 Start-up Tip

> If you provide a coupon as part of your brochure or catalog, make sure the coupon is placed such that cutting it out won't also cut out pertinent information on another part of the catalog—especially your company name, address and phone number. If your brochure is a self-mailer (there's a space on it for the mailing address, rather than the brochure being placed in an envelope), put the coupon on the "back" of the mailing label so that when the coupon is redeemed, the customer's name and address will be on it.

Catalogs You don't have to produce a 24-page catalog to increase sales: sometimes four pages is enough to whet customers' appetites for a great new accessory or hot new toy. Your suppliers may be willing to help by giving you product photos or perhaps even complete, professional catalogs you can put your store name on and start accepting orders right away. Catalogs may not be able to reflect your complete line, but they can be an inexpensive way to get you started in mail-order sales.

Another option: You can sell a wider range of products than you offer at your location by joining a catalog group, which presents the products of various vendors in a catalog that has your name and, in some cases, custom pictures of your location or your staff. Your customers order from the catalog through you; you put your order into the group; and in many cases the products are shipped directly to your customers. Different catalog groups have different specialties (cosmetics, jewelry, gourmet foods, etc.). The easiest way to find a group that's right for you is to search online for "catalog group" plus whatever keywords are appropriate for your business.

Fliers and bag stuffers

You can use your computer to create and print your own fliers and bag stuffers (any printed material that you pop in a customer's bag) in-house at almost no cost. Or you can have them made at your local printer at low cost (shop around for the best prices). Place fliers that advertise upcoming events or special discounts at the cash register, and use them as bag stuffers. You can also post fliers on bulletin boards at local supermarkets, fitness centers, daycare centers and anywhere else your target customers are likely to congregate (ask the location managers' permission first).

 ### Start-up Tip

When you write the copy for fliers or bag stuffers, keep it short and simple. Use short sentences, bullet lists and lots of "white space" (no text or graphics) for quick and easy reading. A flier that's overloaded with words, pictures and designs isn't inviting or easy to read.

Gift certificates

Many consumers think gift certificates are "the perfect gift" because they let recipients pick out exactly what they want—plus, it takes some pressure off the gift-giver to know the right size, style, color, etc. Gift certificates are great for retailers, too: they generate income, don't take up inventory space, and practically eliminate the chance of a return. They're also a great way to advertise your business to new customers.

The cost of creating your own gift certificates is almost nothing—all you need is some nice paper and a decent printer. Even if you don't have that, your local printer can create gift certificates for you. You can also buy pre-printed color gift certificates with a professional look (see p. 242-243 for two sources) and fill in the details (your store name, dollar amount, giver and recipient's names, etc.). Also number each certificate and keep a log, so that no one can try to redeem a counterfeit certificate.

Newspaper classified ads

Many retailers feel that classified newspaper ads give them more bang for the buck than display ads do, because a classified is much cheaper, and because they allow the advertiser to put the ad in an appropriate classification. For example, an ad for a collectibles kiosk might get lost in the body of the newspaper, but the same ad in the "Collectibles" classification would be seen by readers who actively search for and read that classification because they're looking to buy collectibles.

Costs for classified ads are calculated on a per-word or per-line basis. Before you place an ad, familiarize yourself with the newspaper you plan to advertise in, so that you place the ad in the right classification. Write your own ad copy, rather than having the classified ad rep or department write it for you. That way, the copy will be fresh and won't look and sound the same as other ads they've written. But if your ad's getting too long (and pricey), ask the ad rep for ideas to shorten it—without weakening the message. (For more on writing ads, see "Writing great ad copy" on p. 250.)

 Start-up Tip

> *Use a headline in your classified ad, just as you would use a headline in a display ad. A powerful headline that says something special about you or your products will make your ad stand out from all the others.*

Retail packaging

Shopping bags, boxes, gift wrap and other packaging can be powerful communication tools that reinforce your image or theme. Your packaging can also "billboard" your business and spur additional sales when other consumers see your name on shopping bags in the hands of mall shoppers, or on gift boxes they receive.

Before you order any packaging, decide if the kind you're considering (for example, shopping bags with your color logo) will reinforce your retail identity, and if the cost is justified. You may be able to spend less than even the most reasonably priced custom pre-printed items by being creative. For example, you can turn a plain white bag into a custom one by using stamps, stickers or stencils. The same idea works for gift boxes, which you can finish with ribbons, bows or raffia to create an attractive, unique package, one that says something special about your store.

 ### Start-up Tip

Whether you want pre-printed items or plain vanilla, the easiest way to shop for packaging and prices is to go online. Search for "shopping bags," "gift wrap," and the like. Suppliers' Web sites offer a look at various packaging items, options and even design ideas.

Special-event cards

Special-event cards give you additional opportunities to send your marketing message to your target audience. Sending cards at Christmas, Valentine's, and every holiday on the calendar is a low-cost way to let your customers know they're important to you. You can also send cards for individual birthdays and special events such as graduations, anniversaries, and the like if you capture and track that information in your database. And you can invent your own "holidays"— The more your customers hear from you on a regular basis, the more likely they are to remember you when they're ready to shop. Always include an incentive, like a 10 percent "birthday discount" plus an expiration date in order to motivate the recipients to come in soon. (And don't forget to keep your mailing list updated, so that you won't waste money on undeliverable or returned mail.)

 Start-up Tip

> *To keep costs low and response rates high, buy pre-printed color cards from a company like Paper Direct or Idea Art (see p. 243). Choose designs that match your other marketing materials and reinforce your image.*

Frequent-buyer programs

Frequent-buyer or "loyalty" programs can be a great way to establish a relationship with your customers, reward them for their patronage, and increase your repeat-customer base. The easiest, lowest-cost way to start your own program is to create a frequent-buyer card. Most are the size of business cards, and fit easily in shoppers' wallets. You can order the cards from your local print shop. The cost will be the same as a business-card order with comparable elements (number of colors, type of paper, etc.). Or use business-card paper stock.

Most frequent-buyer cards give the "reward" after a certain number of purchases. To track customer visits (and prevent fraud), mark the card with a distinctive hole punch or rubber stamp (both are available at crafts and art-supply stores), or initial the card in an offbeat ink color. Or have a custom punch or stamp made—check with your printer or larger art-supply stores, or search online.

Public Relations: Free media coverage

Every business owner has a story. If you can find a way to present your story to the local newspaper in a way an editor or reporter will find interesting and informative, you may be able to score free press coverage. How? By determining the angle or slant you should take, writing a press release (or hiring a professional write it for you), sending it to the paper (with a few quality photos of you and your business), and following up your efforts a few days later (ostensibly to make sure the newspaper received your materials, but really to nudge the editor or writer).

The key to getting your story picked up is to give the editor a solid reason as to why the paper's readers would be interested in reading about you and your business. Is your story newsworthy? In what way? Is it inspirational, or does it have human-interest warmth? Have you overcome great obstacles to get to where you are? "Put yourself in the readers place" is the mantra of newspaper editors everywhere, so start there.

If you're not confident in your writing skills or don't have the budget to hire a professional writer, go online for help. You'll find hundreds of sites with advice on how to write press releases, when and how to send them, and how to follow-up so that you increase the chance of your story getting into print.

 Start-up Tip

When you deal with the press, don't exaggerate. Doing that will damage your credibility, make the editor or writer skeptical of you, and decrease (and very possibly destroy) your chances of the paper running your story.

Writing great ad copy

What do you want to advertise? What do you want to focus on? Do you want to promote your grand opening? If so, what message do you want to send—that you offer a new product or service for the area? Better prices than your competitors? First you need to determine how customers will benefit from shopping with you, and make those benefits clear.

Headlines An ad's headlines is where you spotlight a main benefit for the first time. Play up the benefits with one key word that can either stand alone or work in a phrase or short sentence. Powerful key words include:

Announcing	Enjoy	How-to	Protect	Stylish
At last!	Facts	Last-minute	Relax	Superior
Bargains	Finally!	Love	Reward!	Time
Best	Free	Luxury	Sale	Truth
Biggest	Fun	New	Save	Yes
Discover	Health	Now	Secret	You
Easy	Healthy	Only	Secure	Young

The words you choose depend on the nature of your business, your products or services, and your message. For example, if you plan to sell high-end home décor merchandise to upscale clientele, you may not want to use *bargain* because it won't set the right tone. But *save* is always safe.

Brainstorm at least 20 headlines and then test them on friends, family and business acquaintances before you commit. Which ones do they think work best, and why. What impressions did those headlines give? If those impressions aren't what you're aiming for, reject that headline.

Body copy This is the text of your ad. It's where you get to describe the benefits more fully. Give the reader as many reasons as possible to take action: i.e., calling or visiting your store. Ad copy should be brief, to the point, and easy to read. Use bullet lists when you can. You don't even have to use complete sentences. But you do have to check that spelling, grammar and punctuation are correct. And while exclamation points do generate interest, don't go crazy: only use one at a time: too many reduces your credibility.

Finally, include an action step. Create a sense of urgency by telling the reader to do something right away: "Call today!" "Call now!" or "Visit us today!" The action step should appear at the end of the body copy right above your store name, local and toll-free phone numbers, and other applicable information (e.g., your Web address). To create a stronger sense of urgency, set a deadline for your offer or sale, or give a gift to customers who take action immediately ("The first 20 customers who call/visit will receive . . . ").

When you've written copy that you think works, put it all together: headline, body copy, call to action and overall design, and review it against your goals for this ad and your overall marketing strategy. Does the ad reinforce the image you want to project? If not, see if tweaking the headline, the copy and the offer will help. If it doesn't, start over by brainstorming fresh ideas. There's no good reason to waste money on an ad that doesn't do what you need it to do.

Executing your advertising plan

Organization is the key to making sure your advertising plan works for you.

Insertion deadlines If you intend to advertise in newspapers, you have to get the ad to the ad department before their deadline (usually about a week before publication). Otherwise you could end up paying for an ad that does-n't run, especially if you're on a contract with the paper. If you miss the ad deadline for a newsletter, you may not be charged for the ad, but you will have missed an opportunity to reach that market, and there's no way of knowing how much you lost in sales.

Proof deadlines You have a very limited time to respond with corrections to or approval of proofs of your ad (whether on paper, e-mail or audio tape, depending on the medium). If you miss a proof deadline, you risk running an inaccurate or incomplete ad, which can cost you in any number of ways.

The easiest way to keep track of your ad deadlines is to put them on your calendar—not just the due date, but a lead-in date a few weeks in advance (especially helpful when insertion deadlines are at the start of the month— no surprises when you turn the calendar page). If you do a great deal of advertising, one option is to use a separate calendar so you can see all your ad deadlines at a glance. This gives you time to create a great ad as well as get it in on time.

After an ad runs, you'll automatically receive a copy. Newspapers usually send the whole page the ad is on; radio stations send a cassette. Check the ad again for accuracy, and if it's not the ad you approved, contact your ad rep to work out how you can be compensated (a free ad, a percentage off the rest of your contract, etc.).

Keep track of costs As you execute your advertising plan, track all of your ad costs as you go, so that your budget doesn't get out of hand. You don't want to be caught in Month 8 only to realize that you've already spent 11 months' worth of your ad budget. Track all production costs, including anyone you've paid for copywriting, design and layout, and printing. Also include any postage, courier costs or overnight-delivery charges.

Tracking results

The only way to really know if an ad is working for you (other than new customers showing up and telling you they saw your ad) is to put a tracking mechanism in the ad itself. The two most popular are coupons and codes (numbers or words). If you're advertising in a newspaper, for example, you can include a percent-off coupon that shoppers have to bring to the store to redeem. For a radio spot, you can give listeners a code phrase they have to mention in order to take advantage of the offer. If you're advertising in more than one paper, use a coupon and put a tracking code on it somewhere (it can be something as simple as a tiny A, B or C) to tell you which newspaper the redeemed coupon came from. Tracking codes also work if you're testing two different ads or coupons, especially if they appear much the same. Known as an A-B test, doing this helps you determine which ad was more effective.

If possible, track not only how many responses you received, but also how much money the ad generated in sales. Doing that will tell you if the ad was profitable. And it may also tell you if the readers of one paper spend more than the readers of the other papers you advertised in. This knowledge points you to the medium that generates the most *sales* for you, not just the most responses. So for every ad you run, tally the results and answer these questions:

- How many people responded to the ad?

- How many people were current customers?

- How many were new customers?

- How much did it cost to produce and run the ad?

- What is the total sales amount the ad generated directly?

If you find your efforts got little or no return, take another look at your ad *and* the medium you used. Perhaps that medium reaches the wrong audience after all. Or perhaps your ad copy didn't appeal to the audience you were trying to reach. The only way to fine-tune your advertising is to keep track of what worked in the past and what didn't as you go forward. As you review your less than stellar efforts, the ad rep is likely to suggest that your ad copy was the problem, not the medium itself. Could be, but maybe not. Be as objective as possible—especially if you wrote the ad yourself. If you ran the same ad in other similar publications, for example, and it worked well, you have a good indication that the same ad is fine and the outlet isn't right. On the other hand, if the ad didn't work in any medium, redo the ad (no matter how much you may love it).

To track direct mail results, you may want to track one additional factor: the source of your list names. For example, say you send a postcard to 1,500 names, 25 percent of which come from your in-store sign up sheet, and 75 percent come from a list you rented. In this case, tag either the rental-list names or the in-house names so you know which worked better when the responses come in. If you're going to create mailing labels on your computer, you'll find that most mailing list or database software has a code field for easy tracking, if you produce mailing labels in-house. If you use an outside source for putting labels or addresses on your direct-mail pieces, ask for suggestions for low-cost tracking methods you can use. Mailers usually have a system they offer small-business customers.

Teaming up with the mall

If you're going to operate in a mall, you may be paying a marketing-fund fee as part of your rent. The mall's marketing fund is designed to promote the mall in general (and sometimes specific tenants) through in-mall and outside advertising and marketing efforts. Ask your leasing manager to explain your mall's marketing and advertising program, and to suggest ways you can take advantage. For small retailers with limited budgets, the benefits of this unique type of co-op advertising can be tremendous, so get in on the action whenever you can.

Each mall has its own marketing/advertising program, but most include newspaper and radio advertising, on-site signage that's updated frequently, telephone or public-address system message repeaters, Yellow Pages ads and a Web site (both of which may list individual retailers). Some larger malls also produce a shoppers' newsletter with items about new retailers, money-savings offers, coupons and more. And just about every mall stages at least several special events a year to bring in traffic and promote its retail tenants. These events, which are heavily advertised by the mall itself, include promotions for holidays, seasons, and sometimes "theme" days.

Even if you can't get your store name/logo included on a newspaper ad for an upcoming special event, you can still highlight your products that correspond with these events at your location. To make it easy for your mall's leasing manager/marketing department to include you in a variety of promotions, provide them with the following items:

- Your logo (include graphics, taglines and your store name; if you use any unique fonts and you're providing these materials on disc, include the files for those fonts)

- Quality (professional) color photographs:

  - your headshot

  - you in front of your location

  - your location, with shoppers

  - your location, without shoppers

  - your best-selling or most unusual products

    ### Getting great photos:
    To get the best photos possible, hire a professional photographer. They know how to light the shot, get the best angle, and focus on the strongest elements. If you take the shots yourself or ask your cousin's nephew, you may end up with unusable photos and no time to have good ones made.

Good, clear, *usable* photos must have:

- A clean background. De-clutter and tidy your location. A messy background (such as boxes of products not yet unloaded) steals attention and clarity away from the intended subject (that is, whatever is in the foreground): you, your store, your products.

- Good, balanced lighting with no shadows. Too much or too little light dooms a photograph.

- Static shots *and* posed "candid" shots. Static shots are obviously posed: people are smiling at the camera. "Candid" posed shots are not obviously posed: people seem unaware of the camera.

If you take the photos yourself, it might help to get a book on how to set up and shoot these kinds of pictures—and buy plenty of film (or discs in the case of digital). Take at least three shots (five is better) of every subject, pose and angle you want, and dump all but the best ones. The pros always "bracket" their shots (making small adjustments in speed and f-stops) to ensure getting at least one really good photo out of every three shots. This way, you have a reasonable chance of ending up with several clear pictures you can be proud of.

No matter which route you choose for your advertising, it's crucial to stay focused on your message. At the end of every quarter (or if you're a seasonal retailer, at the end of every season), review *all* of your ads to make sure they convey a cohesive, targeted message. If, taken together, they don't create a clear idea of what your store offers and present a unified image of your business, it's time to revisit the marketing section of your business plan, brainstorm new ideas, and create a structured advertising campaign that will bring the bottom-line results you want.

□ □ □

Growing Your Business

O nce you're up and running, you can switch your focus from start-up planning and execution to fine-tuning. This includes examining everything from employee training to operating expenses, and then tweaking, cutting, shaving and fine-tuning accordingly at every opportunity. Why go to the trouble? Because every dollar you save by fine-tuning your operation is a dollar you add to your bottom-line profitability. This section covers some of the methods you can ensure that your new venture is running as efficiently and profitably as possible from opening day forward.

Fine-tuning your operations

There's more to running a profitable business than making sure sales increase from year to year. You also have to keep expenses under control, take advantage of new markets, and increase efficiency wherever and whenever possible. Here are just a few of the steps you can take to increase your profit potential—and your chances for creating a long-term, viable business.

Remove slow-selling products

Identifying and eliminating slow sellers can be difficult without the proper equipment, such as a cash register/POS system, that tracks inventory and generates detailed sales reports. If you don't have a POS system, you have to track manually what's selling and what's not—which means you have to do a pencil-and-paper inventory count at least once a week (for more about inventory counts and POS systems, see "Managing Your Inventory" starting on p. 207).

If you see that a particular product isn't selling as well as expected, or at levels that justify the shelf space it occupies, take immediate action. You can mark down the product to get it moving, or give it less shelf space, so you can use it for another product that does (or might) sell better. As you continue to identify slow-sellers, take into account seasonal sales patterns before you decide to ditch a product or product line. And re-analyze your space allocations every two months to be sure you're giving the right amount to each product/line.

Always offer something new

Once you open your doors, you may be tempted not to look for new products and focus on selling as much as you can of the merchandise you have on hand, and re-order more of the same. But don't do that. Successful retailers never stop looking for new products or services to add to their mix and/or replace slow-sellers. Take a look at your current product lines to see if there are there complementary products you could offer. Or perhaps there are completely different products that would add excitement or entertainment to your current mix. Is there a service you can offer that your competitors don't—personalization, for example? To get ideas (and motivation), visit your competitors once a month, or at least once a season, to see the new products or services they may have introduced. Check out non-competitor retailers, too. Maybe it will inspire you; maybe you can borrow some of their ideas.

Last, pay attention to products your customers ask for that you don't have, and consider the benefits of stocking those products. Better yet, ask your customers if there are products you don't carry that they might like. Even if you can't stock what they suggest (for whatever reason), customers will be pleased that you asked (one more notch in your customer-relations belt!). Here are a few more questions you can use to start a dialog with the very people who create your success:

- Did you come to us for a particular product? What is it?
- Did you find it?

- If yes: How long did it take you to find it?

- If no: Is it something you'd like us to carry? Are there other products you'd like us to carry?

- Why did you come to us for that product rather than shopping somewhere else?

- Did you plan to buy anything else while you were here? Did you buy anything else?

- What do you like about our cart/kiosk/store? What do you dislike?

- Did you have a pleasant shopping experience here? What's the best thing about shopping here? Was there anything unpleasant about shopping here?

- Do you have any suggestions for how we can improve?

Don't ask only paying customers—also ask the browsers. The point isn't to solicit praise from customers who already like you and your products: the point is to do a reality check by surveying customers to find out how your store looks through their eyes. One last thing: as they give you feedback, (particularly "negative" feedback), try not to react. You want honest, open answers, so try to stay neutral, even receptive, both verbally and visibly (e.g., your facial expression). If you grimace when customers tell you what they didn't like (which is something you really do want to know, no matter how painful), they might tone down or even change their responses. And that won't do you and your business much good.

Improve your supply chain

You can improve your supply chain in a number of ways. First and most obvious: decrease your cost of goods by negotiating better prices. Next, explore ways to keep shipping costs down by timing your orders differently. Also ask suppliers about minimum-order amounts that qualify for free shipping. You can also add to your supply chain by doing any of these:

- Finding additional suppliers who can give you a lower cost of goods or better seasonal discounts.

- Ordering online. Many suppliers offer online-order discounts, and some let you schedule an order for payment and delivery at a later date.

- Timing your orders to receive goods "just in time" instead of in advance.

"Just in time" means you order goods to be delivered when you need them, rather than in advance, where they sit around for a while taking up space and tying up money. Scheduling orders for just-in-time delivery can be tricky at first, so you might want to give yourself a little extra lead time in the beginning. That way, you're not caught off-guard with any empty shelves. Plus, with just-in-time ordering, you have to anticipate seasonal buying differences in advance. During your first season in business, you're likely to find it almost impossible to predict what customers will buy, and when. But when that season comes around again next year, you'll have sales figures and buying patterns from last year to guide you.

Decrease your overhead

It's much easier to decrease expenses than to increase sales. Tackle the big, recurring expenses first—your overhead. When and where it's logical to do so, consider renegotiating your rent rate (including miscellaneous fees and charges); phone rate (a calling plan may save you more than a low per-minute rate); and credit-card processing rate and/or fees (just be sure you're comparing "apples and apples"). You may also want to try some of these money-saving techniques:

- Switch to a business checking account that offers lower fees or a higher interest rate.

- Eliminate or lower the cost of hiring (search firms, etc.) by starting an employee-referral program with your employees and customers: anyone who refers a future employee gets a reward.

- Switch your insurance policies to another carrier at a better rate; or lower your existing coverages to levels that are still acceptable contractually (i.e., your lease requirements) and legally.

- If you need display fixtures, a cash register, a computer or other equipment for your store or office, consider buying used or reconditioned equipment. That can sometimes save you more than 50 percent.

- To save on postage, send faxes or e-mail.

- For direct mail (coupons, etc.), plan the mailings so that you qualify for the lowest possible bulk-mail postage rate.

- Comparison-shop for everything, on the street *and* on the Web. You'll often get the best deals online.

Comparison-shop online

Many Web sites specialize in letting visitors comparison-shop. Try some of these:

BottomDollar (bottomdollar.com)

Compare.com (compare.com)

DealTime (shopping.com)

MySimon (mysimon.com)

Pricewatch.com (pricewatch.com)

RoboShopper (roboshopper.com)

Wireless and Online Shopping Network (ecompare.com)

Yahoo ShopFind (shopfind.com)

Sell more

The fastest and easiest way to increase your sales is to get your current customers to buy more. There are three main ways to do this:

- Increase add-on sales ("upselling" and "cross-selling").

- Increase impulse sales.

- Persuade your customers to come to you again.

Add-on sales If you and your employees aren't trained in the art of add-on sales—selling a tie to a customer who's buying a dress shirt, for example—search online for some expert advice, or attend a sales-training seminar. Some seminars are inexpensive or even free (seminar speakers don't try to make money on seminars; their aim is to land future consulting clients). You can also increase add-on sales by creating a financial incentive for the customer: "Buy a dress shirt and get a tie at 25% off," for example.

You can increase your sales to current customers by keeping in touch with them. Send a postcard offering a special discount or announcing a special event for your "VICs"—very important customers. Or start a customer list of "preferred items" or "customer favorites" so you can notify your customers (by phone, e-mail or mail—give them the choice!) when their new favorites arrive. (For more ideas on staying in touch with customers, see "Advertising Your Business" on p. 231.)

Impulse buys Another approach to selling more is to generate impulse buys. The best way is to have effective, almost irresistible point-of-purchase (POP) displays. You know them: you see the most common ones at the check-out of every grocery store, convenience store, drugstore, bookstore and, most recently, department store (e.g., little boxes of upscale chocolates strategically placed at the jewelry cash wrap). POP displays are designed to provoke the quick "I need that!" grab as customers wait in line. The best POP displays are highly visible and:

- attract attention and create interest

- make products stand out

- communicate the product's benefits

- take up very little space

Some manufacturers and distributors provide POP displays at little or no cost. Some displays have pockets for product literature, and some even have custom lighting. Generic POP displays ready for stocking are available from major fixture suppliers. Or you can make your own POP display, especially for new merchandise.

Try fusion marketing

Fusion marketing means teaming up with other retailers to offer shoppers something special and at the same time create synergy among your business and others in the area. Think of it as a joint marketing venture, which can range from something very simple (e.g., you and another retailer include each other's brochures in mailings) to something more complicated (e.g., teaming up with several other retailers on a newspaper ad or a special event). If you pay attention to how the major brands advertise and market their products, you'll see quite a bit of fusion marketing going on. It's as if no one wants to go it alone, and for good reason: fusion marketing is a great way to generate new customers and sales, and keep customers coming back by giving them something they can't find anywhere else. The big-brand retailers know this, and now you do, too.

So look at your retail neighbors to see if they'd make good fusion partners, and how you might work with them to create some marketing synergy and increase your sales. A good fusion partner:

- is an exceptional retailer (interesting products, good merchandising, good customer rapport, etc.)

- has products or services that complement yours

- has a solid repeat-customer base and a good reputation

- can provide you with access to a large number of your target customers

For more about fusion marketing, search online for ideas, advice and general how-to guides.

Increase employee efficiency

Employees can be "efficient" in a lot of ways, few of which have anything to do with how fast your employees can tackle basic tasks like ringing up purchases and shelving merchandise. Of course, your employees have to be well trained in operating your cash register/POS system (and any other systems you have), so that they can complete their tasks quickly and easily. But knowing how to speak with customers, when and how to illustrate a product's features, and how to give customers a reason to buy—in other words, selling skills that contribute to the overall efficiency of your business (not to mention the bottom line)—are much more important than you might think. So it's worth it to pay attention to how well your sales staff sells. (If you're a member of your sales team, ask one of your sales staff to evaluate you.) Here's what you need to know about each of your sales people:

- Do they have a solid understanding of the products they're selling?

- Can they explain features and benefits simply and quickly? Can they suggest uses for a product that the customer may not have thought of?

- Do they know how to cross-sell: can they suggest the purchase of additional, related items to the customer?

- Do they know how to upsell: can they explain the benefits of a similar but higher-priced item to the customer?

If they're weak in any of these areas, train and re-train them. Also take advantage of sales-training programs for yourself and your employees whenever you can. Even if you're not on your selling team, learning what it takes to be an exceptional salesperson will help you run a more efficient business. Bottom line: If you give employees the ongoing training and knowledge they need, you give them the ability to work efficiently and sell effectively for you day after day.

Create a Web site

Once your retail business is open and operating, it's time to "think Net"—that is, consider the value of creating an online presence for your business: a Web site for your business. Many "brick-and-mortar" retailers flinch at the thought of creating and maintaining a Web site. While it's true that launching a Web site is more than registering a domain name, and slapping your logo and phone number on your page, it isn't necessarily difficult and doesn't have to be expensive (relative terms, admittedly). If you don't have the technical expertise (or the time!) to create and manage your own Web site, hire an individual or company to do it for you. Your options include hiring free-lancers (a writer, a designer and a Webmaster); contracting with an advertising, marketing or Web-design firm with experience in putting retail stores online; or buying an online-store "package" (combines site registration, design, programming, and hosting) from one of innumerable providers. The best place to find these companies and to learn more about online sales in general is, yes, online. Or you can start in print, with any of the hundreds of books on how a business with a physical presence (like yours) can sell and accept payment through multiple channels: store or RMU, direct mail, online and more.

Online credit-card sales

If you plan to sell online, you'll have to update your merchant accounts to allow for that. Contact all of your merchant-account reps for details. You'll probably pay a higher rate for online sales than for sales at your physical location. (For more on merchant accounts, see p. 175.)

Add locations

Once your retail business takes off, it's natural to consider expanding. Some owners build expansion into their initial business plan; others think about it for the first time later on. In either case, expanding requires developing "expansion strategies." For many owners that includes adding a second location, either in the same retail venue or a different one.

In the same retail venue Adding a location in the same mall or center—

sometimes even right next to your existing cart, kiosk or store—has several benefits. For starters, the leasing manager already knows you're a reliable, successful retail tenant, so you should have no trouble getting a second location. Another benefit is that you're there in the center every day as it is, so why not manage two locations there instead of one? That way, you have the potential to generate twice the sales without expending twice the energy. As for product, especially for side-by-side carts or kiosks, you can sell unrelated product lines. But if you find a product line for the second location that complements your current line in some way, even better. You've created synergy: your two locations working together to generate even more sales. Think of it as your ongoing fusion-marketing program, and all the fusion partners are you.

In a different retail venue   Or you may want to open a second location in a nearby mall or other retail venue. Because you already have a strong sales record for your first location, you can use those numbers in your pitch to the second venue's leasing manager. If you do open a second RMU or store, you have to project a retail image that's consistent or at least compatible with that of your first location. That's important, because you want to maintain your retail identity and project a clear, uniform image everywhere your business appears—you want customers to recognize your business, whether it's your first or fifth location. So even if your first location is an in-line store and your second is a kiosk, or vice versa, maintain image continuity by using the same name, logo/graphics and signage, incorporating the same visual merchandising elements or themes, and using the same design fixtures. Repeat the elements of your retail identity and image in *all* of your future locations.

Grow from RMU to in-line store

Many specialty retailers who start on RMUs move to in-lines once their concepts strike a chord with customers. How do you know if and when you're ready to move to an in-line store? You first have to determine if your product(s) can be strong sellers in an in-line. Demonstration products, for example, tend to sell far better on carts and kiosks in the common areas— where a product demonstration is too visible (and engaging) for strolling shoppers to miss. So if your product needs to be demonstrated in order to attract customers and make the sale, it may sell better from an RMU.

But if you decide an in-line *is* viable for you, the next step is to see if you can adequately stock it with your current product, or if you have to expand your lines or add new ones to accommodate and take advantage of the larger selling space. For each new product you're considering adding, objectively analyze its appeal to the target market, its cost, and its ultimate sales and profit potential. Market research will help, but in the end you may have to test-market several products before you can fine-tune your merchandise selection. The good news is that you can start test marketing before you go into an in-line by adding a few products here and there to your existing location and closely monitoring sales. In fact, a good strategy for testing not only new products but the idea of expanding is to test-market new products long before you make the decision to move into an in-line store.

Another decision: whether you need a more sophisticated cash register/POS system to manage an in-line. Tracking inventory can be much harder to do in an in-line than on a cart or kiosk. If all goes as planned, you're likely to have many more products—and sales—to track. Bar-coding your merchandise and linking those codes with a good POS system can help you control your inventory and track your sales. Clearly, then, the right equipment can make your life easier; not having it can put an additional burden on you. (For more about POS systems, see "Managing Your Inventory" on p. 207.)

Before you commit to expanding, do the math. At some point along the way, you have to decide if you can afford the rent plus all the other additional expenses of opening and running an in-line store—additional inventory, fixtures, payroll and more. The last thing you want is to take a thriving cart or kiosk enterprise and turn it into a struggling store, thanks to expenses you didn't anticipate. If you need help crunching the numbers, ask your accountant.

Grow from seasonal to year-round

Perhaps your thriving seasonal business, whether an RMU or an in-line, is a year-round business in disguise. How will you know? To see if you can make the leap from seasonal to year-round, ask yourself these questions:

- Am I emotionally prepared to run a business day in and day out year-round? And do I want to?

- Am I financially prepared to run a business year-round? Seasonal retailers sometimes don't anticipate the peaks and valleys that year-round retailers contend with. You need the financial resources to get you through the valleys so that you can cash in on the peaks.

- Can my products sell successfully year-round? If you're selling beachwear in a region that isn't hot and sunny all year, reconsider signing a 12-month lease or rotate your products.

- Can I depend on my suppliers to fill orders year-round?

If your answers are a resounding "Yes!" you may be a good candidate for going year-round, and can start looking for space and figuring out how much the space will cost you anytime. It's not unlike embarking on a true start-up, which, at this stage you've gone through at least once before—so you know to look beyond base-rent numbers to see what it's really going to cost to go year-round.

For every season

If you're successfully selling a seasonal product you're not sure you can sell year-round (beachwear in New England, for example), consider rotating your product lines as the seasons change. Some specialty retailers offer outdoor toys in the spring, beachwear in the summer, sports items in early fall, and Christmas merchandise in October through December. Talk with your leasing manager about which products you want to sell when, and make sure the "use clause" in your lease allows this before you sign it.

One expense that might not have occurred to you: a new cash register. If you're using a basic "ring it up" cash register for your seasonal business, consider investing in a feature-rich cash register or POS system to track inventory, generate sales reports—and track seasonal buying patterns. As a seasonal retailer, you probably don't have to worry about seasonal buying patterns—you're open for business only during the best season for your product. But as a year-round retailer, you need to know all you can about your customers' buying patterns, seasonal and otherwise. A POS system can help you stay on top of all of that.

Create your own turnkey program

Many specialty retailers have expanded their businesses by developing them into turnkey programs, and that may be an option for you. A "turnkey" program is a complete package that gives independent entrepreneurs an opportunity to "buy into" an existing retail business. Its most obvious advantage is that the new retailer can get into business without having to start a business from scratch.

If your specialty retail business is successful and you want to expand, it's worth exploring whether you can "package" it to offer to other entrepreneurs in the form of a franchise, business opportunity, owner-operator program or other turnkey structure. In addition, turning your business into a viable turnkey can be one of the best ways to create and expand your wholesale as well as your retail business because, as the owner of the offering company, you'll be supplying your turnkey operators with product. (For more on turnkeys and how they work, see "Buying a turnkey package" on p. 28.)

What do you need to turn your retail business into a turnkey venture? First, a complete package that, at the least, gives retailers the inventory they need for opening day and the ability to re-order as necessary. Beyond the minimum start-up inventory, your turnkey package might also include:

- signage and fixtures
- cash register/POS systems
- site-selection assistance
- visual merchandising assistance/advice/plans

- lease-negotiation assistance

- marketing assistance

- exclusive territories

- training (start-up/ongoing)

However, if you want to offer your turnkey as a franchise or business opportunity, both of which are legal structures that are tightly regulated by the Federal Trade Commission (FTC), you have to go well beyond that. For example, if you plan to offer a franchise, the FTC requires you to provide each franchisee with a "Uniform Franchise Offering Circular" (UFOC). Here's what it has to include:

- the history of your company

- background on the owners/officers of your company

- a breakdown of the investment you require of the buyer

- audited financial statements for your company for at least three years

- a written franchise agreement/contract

- a list of existing franchisees

- your litigation history, if any

- other pertinent information on your company and its operations

Before you offer anyone a franchise or business opportunity, become familiar with the rules and regulations. The FTC publishes a great deal of information online (ftc.gov). And as always—and perhaps this is more important now than ever—consult with your attorney and your accountant to make sure you're well within the law.

Expanding at the right pace

Despite the many examples of retail companies that expanded too fast for their own good, some retailers still think "the faster the better" when it comes to growth. And they sometimes learn costly lessons as a result. Lids Corp. (Westwood, MA), a specialty retailer of sports caps, started on a kiosk in 1992. Before long, the company had 400 locations in 47 states, with sales in excess of $120 million. Sound good? Not so fast. As the business publication *The Standard* observed, ". . . rapid expansion led the company to file for bankruptcy protection" in January 2001.

Businesses can and sometimes do grow too fast. How do you know if you're growing too quickly? Here are some clues:

- Customer service is suffering. You're too busy trying to handle the company's growth than trying to please your current customers.

- Your employees are *seriously* overworked.

- Your banker is calling. They're worried about your cash flow.

- You can't keep track of all of your locations and their sales. Losing track means losing control of your business—and that can spell the start of losing your company.

Plan for success

So before you commit to any expansion plan, map out your strategy in detail . . . be sure you have the funds you'll need to support your growth, and you have the people you need to make it happen . . . and have those contingency plans handy, in case your growth strategy doesn't play out as you thought it would. In short, when it's time to "pull back," don't hesitate. Better to delay your expansion plans than to stick with them against all odds, just to go down in defeat. Instead, keep your eye on your existing business. By doing everything you need to do to keep it alive and well, you'll be able to spot and seize the opportunity to expand when it swings around again.

□□□

Index

www.specialtyretail.com

✔ sample editorial

✔ order a subscription to *Specialty Retail Report*

✔ order the *Retail Resource Guide*

✔ order the *Ultimate Guide to Specialty Retail*

✔ entry form for Visual Victories (annual visual merchandising award program)

Visit today for this and other valuable information!